A REALIST
CONCEPTION
OF TRUTH

ALSO BY WILLIAM P. ALSTON

A REALIST CONCEPTION OF TRUTH

William P. Alston

Cornell University Press

ITHACA AND LONDON

First published 1996 by Cornell University Press
First printing, Cornell Paperbacks, 1996.
Printed in the United States of America.

Library of Congress Cataloging-in-Publication Data

Alston, William P.
    A realist conception of truth / William P. Alston.
        p.   cm.
    Includes bibliographical references and index.
    ISBN 0-8014-3187-5 (cloth : alk. paper).
    ISBN 0-8014-8410-3 (paper : alk paper).
    1. Truth.   2. Realism.   3. Knowledge, Theory of.   I. Title.
    BD171.A42   1995
    121—dc20   96-31251

⊗ The paper in this book meets the minimum requirements
of the American National Standard for Information Sciences—
Permanence of Paper for Printed Library Materials, ANSI Z39.48-1984.

For Hugh Fleetwood,
true friend

CONTENTS

PREFACE

Though I have been interested in issues concerning truth and realism from the beginning of my involvement in philosophy, I did not undertake to write anything substantial on the topic until my American Philosophical Association presidential address of 1979, entitled, against the advice of my wife, "Yes, Virginia, There Is a Real World". That piece was followed, after a long interval, by a paper entitled "Realism and the Tasks of Epistemology", presented at a conference on the implications of realism and antirealism for epistemology, held at Santa Clara University in 1992. (The proceedings of that conference are forthcoming in a book, *Realism/Antirealism and Epistemology*, edited by Christopher Kulp, to be published by Rowman & Littlefield.) These two papers were attempts, with different degrees of preliminariness, to formulate and defend a realist account of truth, an enterprise that has assumed much larger and, I hope, better-developed form in the present book.

Since the book is fairly narrowly concentrated on formulating and defending a realist conception of truth and does not stray from this path to meditate on wider implications, let me say here that I believe the question of how to think about truth is crucially important for intellectual issues generally. It is hard to overemphasize the amount of mischief, in this century especially, that has resulted from confusions, false assimilations, and sloppy thinking concerning truth. In particular, the conflation of truth value and epistemic status of one sort or another (justification, certainty, knowledge, rationality, general consensus . . .) has muddied the waters in religious thought, the social sciences, and literary studies, as well as in philosophy itself. (See my "Realism and the Christian Faith", *International Journal for Philosophy of Religion* [1995], for an exploration of one aspect of this.) The supposition that to call something true is simply to pay it some kind of compliment and the popular view that truth value is relative to a set of presuppositions, a conceptual scheme, a theory, or a "language game" have also wreaked a lot of damage in the learned world. I can't pretend in this book to have cleared up nearly all the confusions with which thought about truth is rife, but I hope to have made some contribution to that enterprise.

In thinking through these issues I have learned much from many people, not least from those with whom I disagree most. Many of them are discussed, at greater or lesser length, in this book. Among those whose ideas are, at most, touched on, and from whom I have learned much are G. E. Moore, Bertrand Russell, J. L. Austin, Peter Strawson, Crispin Wright, and Hartry Field. My thanks are due the participants in the already mentioned 1992 conference at Santa Clara University for many insights. Special thanks go to the members of a seminar I gave on realism at Syracuse University in the fall of 1992. That seminar was a kind of pilot project for this book, and much of the material underwent severe, and salutary, testing, in the fires of discussion there. In particular, Michael Lynch, Andrew Cortens, and Paul Bloomfield made many useful comments both in the seminar and in subsequent discussion. Two years later a manuscript of the book was discussed in a seminar given by Nicholas Wolterstorff at Yale University. I received weekly reports from Wolterstorff on successive chapters, and later in the fall I was privileged to meet with the seminar. Those comments have greatly improved the final result. Several other people have read the whole manuscript and have provided useful suggestions. They include Robert Audi, Mark Heller, Eleonore Stump, and especially Jonathan Bennett, who did his usual painstaking job of making detailed comments on each chapter. Linda Alcoff, Alvin Plantinga, and Steve Wagner gave me valuable reactions to particular chapters. Finally I received very helpful suggestions from two anonymous readers for Cornell University Press. Because of all these people the book is much better than it would have been otherwise. How good that is I leave it to the reader to judge.

Finally, my heartfelt thanks go to my wife, Valerie, for cheerfully putting up with an often baffled and frustrated philosopher.

WILLIAM P. ALSTON

Syracuse, New York

A REALIST
CONCEPTION
OF TRUTH

Introduction

The central aim of this work is the formulation and defense of what I call ALETHIC REALISM, that is, realism concerning TRUTH. We may think of alethic realism as comprising two theses.

1. The REALIST CONCEPTION OF TRUTH is the right way to think of truth in the sense of 'true' in which it applies to beliefs, statements, and propositions.
2. Truth is important. It is often a matter of considerable import whether a particular bearer of truth value is true or false.

Most of the book will be concerned with the first thesis. A consideration of the second thesis is reserved for Chapter 8. As this division of the book implies, what I call the realist conception of truth is at the heart of the enterprise. Most of the book is taken up with seeking the most adequate and perspicuous ways to formulate this conception, relating it to various other things, defending it against objections, and criticizing competing conceptions.

As an initial stab we can think of the realist conception of truth as follows. A statement, for example, is true if and only if what the statement is about is as the statement says it is. Alternatively in terms of propositions, the conception is such that the schema 'It is true that p if and only if p' yields a (necessarily, conceptually, analytically) true statement for any substitution instance. Chapter 1 is devoted to explicating the realist conception, exploring alternative formulations, relating it to other accounts of truth, and considering objections. A crucial part of the explication is deciding what we should regard as the primary bearers of truth value. The palm is awarded to PROPOSITIONS. It is argued that statements (assertions) and beliefs can be termed true or false only by virtue of their propositional contents. I argue that our concept of a proposition is, most basically, the concept of a *content* of a belief or an assertion—a concept of *what* is believed or asserted. There is also a critique of the currently fashionable practice of concentrating on *sentences* as bearers of truth value.

I discuss the relation of the realist conception to correspondence theories. They are closely connected, but correspondence theories try to bring out features of the *property* of truth on which the features embodied in our *concept* of truth supervene. My *minimalist* account of truth is distinguished from *deflationary* views that deny that there is any property of truth or falsity and seek to construe truth-value talk as not involving the attribution of any such property. The most prominent deflationary views are subjected to criticism.

In Chapter 2 I explore various forms of metaphysical realism, their interrelations and their relations to alethic realism. Much of the discussion is built around different forms of antirealism—particularly FLAT DENIALS and REDUCTIONS. I argue that alethic realism is largely neutral as between different metaphysically realist and antirealist positions, though alethic realism can be said to carry a very weak metaphysically realist commitment.

Chapter 3–7 are devoted to criticisms of the realist conceptions of truth—with detours into a number of associated issues. Chapter 3 deals with the argument that on a realist conception of truth it is impossible to determine what propositions (statements, beliefs) are true, since it is impossible to compare one of these with *facts*. The argument is shown to rest on indefensible conceptions of cognition, perceptual and otherwise, and to place unrealistic demands on the comparison in question. To this is added an argument in Chapter 7 that we are in a much better position to determine truth value on a realist conception of truth than on an epistemic conception—the chief alternative.

Chapter 4 takes up Michael Dummett's verificationist alternative to realism about truth. Dummett's verificationist semantics is laid out and subjected to criticism. I don't go into that matter as thoroughly as I might, since I also contend that this semantics does not have the implications for truth that Dummett supposes it to have. I argue, in fact, that his semantics is quite compatible with a realist conception of truth. I also throw cold water on the idea that Dummett's characterizations of realism cover a large stretch of the waterfront.

Chapters 5 and 6 are devoted to Hilary Putnam's assaults on what he calls "metaphysical realism", which contains a version of a realist conception of truth. Chapter 5 is mostly concerned with the much discussed "model-theoretic" argument that Putnam put forward in his presidential addresses to the American Philosophical Association and the Association for Symbolic Logic. I find that the attempt to come to grips with this argument is a salutary exercise that uncovers a number of fundamental issues. The model-theoretic argument is designed to refute the realist contention that it is possible for even an epistemically ideal theory to be false. My conclusions include the points (1) that the argument shows at most a logical possibility of an ideal theory's being true, something a metaphysical (alethic) realist could cheerfully accept, (2) that if the argument shows anything it shows that any theory we can construct is too indeterminate to be susceptible of a truth value, and (3) that Putnam's claim that *the realist cannot show that an interpretation on which the theory is true is not the "intended" interpretation* relies on an unworkable extensional construal of 'interpretation'. The chapter ends with briefer critical looks at arguments for indeterminacy of reference and against "brain in a vat" scepticism, arguments that are supposed to prove an embarrassment for the metaphysical realist.

Chapter 6 deals with Putnam's "conceptual relativity", one facet of which is that there is no unique true answer to the question of what objects there are in the world. Here I acknowledge that Putnam's case for this position is not without merit, though I don't make an all-out surrender. I explore various realist responses, including a number that are partly concessive. I suggest that all of these responses, even the most concessive, can preserve alethic realism. Indeed, I go further and argue that even Putnam's own position is compatible with a realist conception of truth, though Putnam himself does not avail himself of the possibility of combining them.

Chapter 7 is devoted to a mapping, and critical analysis, of epistemic conceptions of truth, the only significant alternatives to a realist conception that take truth to be a genuine property. Most of the discussion is focused on a version Putnam espoused (though he has since abandoned it), according to which the concept of truth is the concept of *being justified in ideal epistemic circumstances*. After an exploration of how to think of such circumstances, critical fire is directed at this position. Three objections are presented. (1) There are counterexamples—true propositions that are not ideally justifiable. (2) The account is circular; the concept of ideal justifiability presupposes the concept of truth. (3) The position is incompatible with the acceptance of the necessary truth of all instantiations of the T-schema, since, for any proposition p, that schema represents the fact that p as both necessary and sufficient for its being true that p. This would seem to leave no room for epistemic necessary and sufficient conditions. Two possible replies by the epistemic theorist are considered, but they are both found to be without significant merit.

Chapter 8 turns to the second component of alethic realism, that truth is important. The positive case for the importance of truth consists largely of a gaggle of truisms, typified by "We are more likely to succeed in our endeavors if they are guided by true beliefs than if they are guided by false beliefs". The most extensive discussion is accorded to the question whether a concern for truth value is crucial to various theoretical concerns, such as logic and epistemology. It is the latter that receives detailed treatment. The work of a number of epistemologists is examined to see what role truth plays in their accounts of knowledge and of epistemic justification. Truth is, by well nigh common consent, fundamental to the former, but the situation vis-à-vis justification is more diverse. Many epistemologists give truth a crucial role here, but some do not. I argue that the former are better positioned to deal with various fundamental problems than are the latter. The chapter ends with a critical examination of Stich's claims for the unimportance of truth.

CHAPTER 1

Alethic Realism

i Preliminary Formulation

This book is devoted to the exposition and defense of a particular brand of realism—one that I take to be especially fundamental. The core of the position is a certain doctrine about truth. Hence I shall call it "alethic realism".

At the heart of alethic realism is a conception of truth that I shall call the "realist conception". As a first approximation:

I. A statement (proposition, belief . . .) is true if and only if what the statement says to be the case actually is the case.

For example, the statement that gold is malleable is true if and only if gold is malleable. The "content" of a statement—what it states to be the case—gives us everything we need to specify what it takes for the statement to be true. In practice this means the "that" clause—the content-specifying clause—that tells us what statement we are referring to can also be used to make explicit what it takes for the statement to be true. Nothing more is required for the truth of the statement, and nothing less will suffice. In particular, and looking forward to the main alternative to this account of truth, there are no *epistemic* requirements for the truth of my statement. It is not required that any person or any social group, however defined, know that gold is malleable or be justified or rational in believing it. It is not required that science be destined, in that far-off divine event toward which inquiry moves, to arrive at the conclusion that gold is malleable. It is not required that it be accepted by a clear majority of the American Philosophical Association. It is not required that it have been rendered probable by some body of empirical evidence. So long as gold *is* malleable, then what I said is true, whatever the epistemic status of that proposition for any individual or community.

This way of thinking about truth has many distinguished antecedents, harkening back to Aristotle, who said in a famous passage of the *Metaphysics*, "To say of what is that it is and of what is not that it is not, is true" (IV, 6, 1001b, 28). In the course of the discussion I will be alluding to a number of more recent thinkers who have espoused similar views, as well as a number of opponents.

The realist conception is the one I claim to be expressed by the predicate 'true' only in some of its uses, namely, those involved in attributions of truth to propositions, statements, and beliefs. There are, of course, other uses of the term. It sometimes means something like 'genuine', as we speak of a "true friend", sometimes 'faithful', as in "true to the cause", sometimes 'legitimate', as "the true heir". I will not be concerned with these other senses in this book.

The formulation I just gave for the realist conception of truth as well as others I will give later, is put forward as constitutive of that concept. It is by virtue of the (a) meaning of 'true' that a statement is true if and only if what the statement says is the case actually is the case. This equivalence is put forward as conceptually or semantically true, and thus necessarily true in one of the ways a proposition can enjoy that status. This feature of the position will become important at later stages of the discussion.

Alethic realism is made up of two theses.

(1) The realist conception of truth is the correct one (for that use of 'true' in which statements, beliefs, and propositions are evaluated as true or false). This conception embodies what it is for a statement . . . to be true.

(2) It is important, for a variety of purposes, that statements, beliefs, and so on, be assessed for truth value. Truth is important.

As such, there will be two ways of deviating from it: (a) denying that the realist conception is expressed by 'true' in the relevant uses, and (b) denying that it is important whether statements . . . are true in this sense. The bulk of the book will be devoted to the first thesis, but the second will be treated in Chapter 8.

I have been presenting the realist conception of truth as if it were an important, exciting, and controversial philosophical position. But, you may suppose, it is nothing but a miserable truism that no one in his right mind would deny. What could be more obvious than that it is true that there are books in my study if and only if there are books in my study? What's all the fuss about? Well, it does seem to me to be an obvious truism that this is the way to think about truth. But nevertheless it has been frequently and enthusiastically denied, especially in recent times. I shall be much concerned in this book with philosophers who have taken contrary positions—what they say in defense of those positions and in criticism of alethic realism. And this reaction is by no means confined to academic philosophy. It is widespread in theology and religious studies, in literary theory, in the social sciences, and elsewhere.

As indicated above, the main alternatives to the realist conception construe truth in epistemic terms. At least these are the main alternatives that presuppose a property of truth and attempt to say what that property is. There is also a variety of "deflationary" accounts of truth talk that deny that there is any such property. I will explain why I regard them as defective in section xi of this chapter. As for epistemic accounts, they take the truth of a statement or belief to consist of some positive epistemic status of that statement or belief—its being justified (perhaps in conditions of some idealized sort), or being adequately supported by evidence, or being "warrantably assertable", or cohering with some system of beliefs. Traditional coherence and pragmatist theories of truth fall under this rubric, as well as some recent views. A large part of the book is taken up with criticism of epistemic accounts. Chapters 3–6 examine their objections to alethic realism, and Chapter 7 presents objections to them. I will also have to take account of the fact that epistemic theorists often take their position not to be incompatible with the realist conception, as I will be explaining it. Recognizing the obviousness of the point that it is necessary and sufficient for the truth of the statement that gold is malleable that gold be malleable, they seek to maintain that this point is neutral between different accounts of truth, and so perfectly compatible with their own. In Chapter 7 I seek to show that they can't get away with this.

Why do I call the position I defend in this book "alethic *realism*"? What is realist about it? The basic point is this. What it takes to make a statement true on the realist conception is the actual obtaining of what is claimed to obtain in making that statement. If what is stated is that grass is green then it is grass's *being* green that is both necessary and sufficient for the truth of the statement. Nothing else is relevant to its truth value. This is a *realist* way of thinking of truth in that the truth *maker* is something that is objective vis-à-vis the truth *bearer*. It has to do with what the truth bearer is about, rather than with some "internal" or "intrinsic" feature of the truth bearer, such as its epistemic status, its place in a system of propositions, or the confidence with which it is held. This is a fundamental sense in which truth has to do with the relation of a potential truth bearer to a REALITY beyond itself.[1]

Why do I consider alethic realism to be a particularly fundamental form of realism? It is because *everything* we believe can be assessed for truth value. Therefore our interpretation of truth affects the status of everything we believe, whatever the subject matter. And if our concept of truth is a realist one, then *all* our beliefs owe their truth value to the fact that they are related in a certain way to a reality beyond themselves. Thus alethic realism constitutes a global form of realism, one that is not restricted to any particular domain of reality, as is, for example, realism about properties or values or physical objects.[2]

But however plausible it may be that alethic realism is a genuine, and indeed basic, form of realism, there is no doubt but that 'realism' is more widely and more naturally used for a variety of positions that take something or other to really exist. In the middle ages—and beyond— "realism" was a view about the status of universals, roughly a Platonic position. There are various "realist" views about the status of perceptual objects and their relations to perception—"naive" realism, direct realism, neorealism, critical realism, etc. There is scientific realism— theoretical entities "really exist". There is moral realism. This is variously conceived, but the common core is the conviction of the objectivity of moral standards, properties, or truths. In the next chapter I will have something to say about some of these views and their relations to alethic realism. In this chapter I will be concerned with developing a more refined statement of alethic realism, mapping its relations to other views on truth, and answering preliminary objections.

That further refinement and elaboration is needed is easily seen. The initial formulation raises all sorts of questions. Can we provide something more explicit than metaphorical talk about a statement "saying" something to be the case? Can we give an explicit general formula for how a state of affairs (or whatever) has to be related to a statement in order that it make that statement true? How is our formulation related to the correspondence theory of truth, the idea that a statement is true if and only if it "corresponds" with the facts, or with a suitable particular

1. This has to be qualified to handle self-referential statements, some of which pose well advertised problems of their own. But since such statements are in a tiny minority, I will let the formulation in the text stand as a rationale for the use of the term 'realist'.

2. The foregoing is only a preliminary statement of the realist credentials of the realist conception of truth. In Chapter 2 I will carry out an extensive discussion of the relation of alethic realism to other realist positions—particularly various forms of metaphysical realism.

fact? Does the position have any implications for the metaphysical status of the facts (or whatever) that render statements true? We must go into all this. But first we must turn our attention to the choice of truth bearers. Are we to think of truth value as attaching to statements, beliefs, propositions, sentences, or what? I am convinced that my basic contentions are unaffected by how I answer that question. The issues between a realist conception of truth and its rivals take the same form whether we pose them in terms of statements, propositions, or whatever (provided we don't make too outrageous a selection). Nevertheless, the discussion will proceed more smoothly if we conduct it in terms of a particular choice, rather than in terms of a complicated disjunction. Hence I will survey the most prominent candidates sufficiently to explain and defend my preference.

ii Bearers of Truth Value: Sentences

Many readers will have been puzzled by the absence, in the above remarks, of any mention of what is currently the most popular candidate, in philosophical circles, for truth-value bearers: sentences. Since I feel that this preference is thoroughly misguided and hence decline to go along with it, I had better explain my determination to swim against the tide.

First here are what I take to be the main motivations for fastening on sentences for this purpose. (1) An aversion to "abstract entities", a category taken to include statements and propositions, and a corresponding preference for more "concrete" entities, such as sentences and other linguistic items. I shall have something to say about that at the end of this section. (2) Much of the philosophical discussion of truth is carried on in the context of a logical treatment of formalized possible "languages" that are not used for anything, either to perform speech acts or to express beliefs or otherwise articulate thought. Within that context only sentences are available to bear truth values. As for this second motivation, I will just say that my interest in this book is in the concepts of truth and falsity that are used in real life where we are subject to no such restrictions.

And now for my reasons for abstaining from attributing truth values to sentences. First, so far as I can tell, there is no ordinary, nontechnical practice of applying 'true' and 'false' to sentences, and no sense of these terms in ordinary use in which they apply to sentences. But it is easy to construct such a sense. If the statement that grass is green is true and if the English sentence, 'Grass is green' is standardly used to make that statement, that sentence can, derivatively, be termed true.

> (3) Sentence S is true $= df.$ S is standardly used to state that p, and it is true that p.[3]

But (3) does not provide a basis for ascribing a truth value to every sentence with a standard statement-making potential. At least, it does not guarantee a unique truth value for every such sentence because with respect to many sentences there is no unique statement they are fitted to make. Consider 'Harold Stassen is still running'. That sentence can be used to state that Stassen is still locomoting by moving his legs rapidly, and also to state that Stassen is still offering himself as a candidate for elective office. It may well be that at a certain moment one of these statements is true and the other false. So what are we to say of the sentence? Is it true or false? Both? But there are strong theoretical reasons for wanting bearers of truth value to be such that each one has a unique value. If my knowing that p requires that it be true that p, I would feel cheated if, after having been assured that it is true that p, one adds, "And it is false as well". Again, many logical relations turn on the truth values of the relata. Here it is crucial that each item have one and only one definite truth value.

The case just cited ran into this difficulty because of ambiguity, the fact that 'run' has at least two meanings, which ensures that the sentence in question has at least two readings. We could take care of that by modifying (3) to range over "sentences on a reading".

> (4) Sentence S, on reading R, is true $= df.$ S on R is standardly usable to state that p and it is true that p.

But more complications loom on the horizon. A sentence containing what are often called "indexicals" (but are better termed "token reflexives") can be used with one and the same meaning to make many different statements, depending on features of a particular utterance and/or its circumstances. Thus 'I'm hungry' can be used to make many different statements, with different truth values, depending on who is making the statement and when. Indeed, since tensed verbs and temporal ad-

---

3. Note that this does nothing to legitimate applying truth values to all sentences in natural languages. Many sentences cannot be used to make statements, e.g., "Is he coming?", "What a relief!", and "Please pass the salt". That poses a problem for the project of giving a general theory of the *meaning* of sentences in terms of their truth conditions for sentences, but that enterprise is outside the scope of this book.

verbs exhibit this feature, 'Harold Stassen is still running' lacks a unique statemental potential for this reason as well as because of the ambiguity of 'run'. At one time the sentence, on a given reading of 'run', will be used to make a true statement, and at another time a false statement.

There is more than one way for partisans of sentences to respond to these difficulties. One move is to shift from taking 'true' and 'false' as monadic properties of sentences to taking them as relational predicates, relating sentences and features of circumstances of utterance, just those features that help determine what statement is made by uttering the sentence on a particular occasion. Alternatively, one can switch from sentence types to sentence tokens as bearers of truth value. (A sentence *type* is what is ordinarily called a 'sentence', a unit of language that can be uttered, used, inscribed on many different occasions. A sentence token can be thought of as one of those utterances or inscriptions of the sentence type.) Clearly, a particular sentence token will not be liable to the variations we have seen to affect sentence types—at least provided the user of the sentence has made sure that it is being used to make just one definite statement.[4] In that case, if the sentence is ambiguous the speaker will be employing it in just one of its senses, and where aspects of the circumstances are required to interact with the relevant meaning of the sentence type to determine a particular statement they will have done so.

Thus the attribution of truth values to (statement-making) sentence tokens escapes all the objections thus far considered. But there are others lying in wait. First, note that there is no more an established practice of ascribing truth values to sentence tokens than there is with respect to sentence types. "Is that particular concatenation of chalk marks on the board true or false?" or "Is that sequence of sounds you just made with your vocal organs true or false?" has no natural interpretation, available to each fluent speaker of the language just by virtue of her linguistic competence. If we are motivated to talk that way, we have to provide a sense for such attributions. The obvious way to do so is as just laid out. We consider what statement is made by the production of the sentence token in question, and we take the latter to enjoy the truth value of the former. But this means that our understanding of the attribution of a

4. If one holds, as I would not, that a *written* token of 'It's raining here', being a physical object that can endure over a long period of time, is itself subject to change of truth value, then she can consider the ensuing discussion restricted to utterance tokens. I feel comfortable in setting aside the possibility of a variation in truth-value for sentence tokens, since, if that possibility is realized, the attribution of truth values to tokens is confronted with the same difficulties as the attribution of truth values to types. And so much the better for my critique.

truth value to the sentence token is based on our understanding of what it is for a statement to have a truth value. The latter is the groundwork for the former, not vice versa; nor do they each enjoy an independent standing. Thus, given that we must already have a grasp of what it is for statements to be true in order to make any sense of the truth of sentence tokens, why concentrate on the latter in our discussion of truth value?

In response the partisan of sentence tokens might invoke the possibility of kicking away the ladder on which we have climbed up. "In order to establish the practice of ascribing truth values to sentence tokens, we have initially to make use of ordinary talk of true and false statements. But once the former practice is in place, we can dispense with statements. It is not as if we have to refer explicitly to a statement each time we say of a token that it is true. We can move directly from what we would take to show the statement to be true to the ascription of truth to the token. Thus, confronted with a token of 'It's moving fast' we can determine what 'it' refers to in this utterance, take into account whatever is needed for determining relevant standards for rapidity of movement for that sort of thing, and determine the time of utterance. We then determine whether the referent is moving rapidly by those standards at that time. That will give us everything we need to determine whether the token is true. No statement or proposition need be brought into the deliberations."

But this fails to show that attribution of truth values to sentence tokens is not *conceptually* dependent on the attribution of truth values to statements. My opponent is surely right in saying that when assessing sentence tokens for truth I don't have to first determine, in each case, the truth value of a correlated statement. But the fact remains that my *understanding* of *what it is* for a sentence token to be true or false is derived from my understanding of what it is for a statement to be true or false. That means that we still have statements as truth-value bearers in our conceptual-ontological repertoire. And we had better not kick that ladder away, or our posterity will not be able to acquire the ability to play the sentence token truth-value game.[5]

Another difficulty with taking sentences as basic, independent bearers of truth value has to do with the rationale for giving some sentences

5. Nicholas Wolterstorff has pointed out to me that I have done nothing to rule out the possibility that a new generation might be introduced to the practice of ascribing truth values to sentence tokens directly, not by derivation from the practice of ascribing them to statements. And so I haven't. But I am concerned here to understand our actual practice of truth-value attribution, not what alternative practices are possible. My concern in sections ii–iv is to make the choice of truth-value bearer(s) that best reflects that actual practice.

rather than others this status. It is clear that only indicative sentences could qualify; " 'go to bed' is true" or " 'what time is it' is false" make no sense. And for that matter, not all indicatives are clearly qualified. J. L. Austin contended that "performative" sentences like 'I promise to pay it back tomorrow' are not properly regarded as true or false; and evaluative sentences are excluded by some thinkers.[6] So we are faced with the question why some sentences and not others are bearers of truth value.[7] The natural, and perhaps the only satisfactory, answer is that a sentence is a bearer of truth value if and only if it has a statement-making potential. So here too it seems that the concept of the truth value of a statement is prior to that of the truth value of a sentence.

In the light of this discussion let's go back to the point that sentences are preferable to statements or propositions as truth bearers because they are "concrete" rather than "abstract", and there are metaphysical reasons for avoiding commitment to abstract objects. Since I am un-moved by such reasons, this is not a live issue for me, but I should say something about how this sort of nominalism influences the choice of truth bearers. First, an aversion to abstract objects provides no basis for a preference for sentence *types* over statements because sentence types are also abstract; they are not spatiotemporally locatable, for example. But we have, in any case, been driven to sentence tokens as the most plausible linguistic bearers of truth values, and it cannot be denied that a sentence token is a concrete entity by the usual standards for that category. Hence if we could restrict truth value attributions to sentence tokens, we would avoid positing abstract entities for this purpose. But we still have to explain the notion of the truth value of a sentence token in terms of the notion of the truth value of a statement made by produc-ing that token; and so we have to recognize statements after all. Hence, taking sentence tokens as bearers of truth value does not enable us to avoid abstract objects.

I don't claim to have decisively put the quietus on the claim that sen-tences are the most fundamental bearers of truth value. But I fancy that I have cast enough doubt on the claim to warrant me in picking some nonlinguistic candidate as the truth bearer of choice.

iii Bearers of Truth Value: Statements and Beliefs

With sentences out of the way, the main candidates in twentieth-cen-tury English speaking philosophy have been beliefs (judgments), state-

---

6. This latter problem comes up in another connection in section xii.

7. For a penetrating discussion of this problem see Price 1988, esp. Chap. 3.

ments (assertions), and propositions. I am going to fasten on propositions as the favored candidate. Here is why.

Let's begin with the attribution of truth values to statements (assertions) and beliefs (judgments). All these terms exhibit a familiar act-object ambiguity. An "assertion" can either be an act of asserting or what is asserted. A belief can either be a certain psychological state one is in—perhaps a certain neural disposition or pattern of activity—or what that state is "directed onto", what is believed. Though in many attributions of truth value it is not made explicit which side of this distinction is the operative one, it is clear to me that truth values attach primarily to what is believed (asserted), and only secondarily, if at all, to the state of belief or the act of asserting. Suppose I assert that the tree is dying, and you reply "That's very true". What is the antecedent of your 'that'—my act of asserting that the tree is dying, or what I asserted, namely, that the tree is dying? Clearly the latter. A natural way of spelling out "That's very true" is "What you said is quite true" or "Yes, it's true that the tree is dying". While "Your act of asserting that the tree is dying is true" doesn't have any ready interpretation. Note that the availability of "Your assertion is quite true" doesn't help to make the choice, just because of the ambiguity noted above; "your assertion" could be either your act of asserting or what you asserted. Similar points can be made about belief. You indicate to me that you believe that Sanders will be promoted. Perhaps the most natural way to agree with you is to say "That's right" or "You're quite right about that". But if we insist on an answer containing 'true' or a cognate, the most natural choice, again, would be "That's very true". And we will have the same reasons for taking 'that' to refer to what you believe rather than to your believing it. "Your believing that Sanders will be promoted is true" has no better claim to be standard English, or to have a natural interpretation, than "Your asserting that the tree is dying is true".[8]

To be sure, we could introduce a sense of 'true' and 'false' in which they are applicable to psychological states of belief and acts of asserting. Since we already understand these terms as they apply to what is believed or stated, a simple procedure is ready to hand.

(1) Your act of asserting that p is true $= df.$ What you asserted, namely, *that p*, is true.

---

8. I can supplement this description of my linguistic phenomenology with a report of an exchange with my chief subject among native (nonphilosophical) speakers—my wife. In the course of a quasi-Socratic dialogue with her on these matters, I was quite unable to elicit from her any predication of 'true' or 'false' of beliefs (as psychological states) or of acts of asserting. She was, indeed, bewildered by the suggestion of any such predications.

(2) Your belief that *p* is true = *df.* What you believe, namely, *that p*, is true.

But, obviously, as with the construction of senses of 'true' and 'false' for sentence tokens, this innovation trades on our prior mastery of the application of 'true' and 'false' to the *contents* of beliefs and statements. It is those applications that are conceptually prior for us. Hence it is on them that I shall concentrate.

iv Bearers of Truth Value: Propositions

Our concentration on beliefs in the sense of *what is believed*, and assertions in the sense of *what is asserted*, as bearers of truth value has already brought us to *propositions* as the primary bearers. For *what* is asserted or *what* is believed, the *content* of an assertion or a belief, *is* a proposition. Let me be explicit as to the intended import of this statement. It is not as if I had searched through some list of candidates for the position and finally discovered that propositions best fill the bill. If that were the way it went, I would have had some independent way of identifying propositions such that it could be a *discovery* that this is what the content of a belief or assertion is. But although, as we shall see, there are various suggestions as to the nature of propositions, it seems that the concept of a proposition—at least in the sense of the term in which it figures prominently in logic, metaphysics, philosophy of language, and philosophy of mind—stems primarily from this root. That is, our most basic notion of a proposition is of what forms the content of assertions and other illocutionary acts, and what forms the content of beliefs and other (aptly named) "propositional attitudes". So far as I can see, any other statements about the nature, individuation, metaphysical status, or entanglements of propositions are responsible to this primary context. For those to whom this claim is not evident on the face of it, here are some considerations in its support.

(1) The "propositional" phrases that we use to make explicit the content of illocutionary acts like assertions and "propositional" psychological attitudes like beliefs, most prominently phrases of the form 'that *p*', are just the phrases that we use to specify what proposition we are talking about. I can make explicit what proposition I have in mind by saying 'the proposition *that lemons are sour*', just as I can make explicit the assertion I have in mind by saying 'the assertion *that lemons are sour*', and make

explicit the belief I have in mind by saying 'the belief *that lemons are sour*'.

To be sure, propositional content does not always wear a 'that'. It doesn't with many illocutionary acts other than assertion. What did I promise? *To take him to the meeting.* I *could* say that I promised *that I would take him to the meeting*, but the former locution is the more natural. Again what I requested him to do was *to give me a hand with this box*, rather than *that he should give me a hand with this box*. With psychological propositional attitudes, the 'that' form is more constant. One can hope that p, doubt that p, suspect that p, be inclined to suppose that p, and be surprised that p, as well as believe that p. But here too there are variations. One questions *whether p*, and one intends *to* go to the store. But throughout these variations one can see propositions just below the surface. The proposition *that he gives me a hand with this box* is clearly involved in requesting him to give me a hand with this box. And the proposition *that I go to the store* is clearly involved in intending to go to the store. This implicit involvement of the proposition can be made explicit in various ways. We can regiment reports of requests, suggestions, orders, etc., in terms of "making true" a certain proposition. Thus the above request could (unnaturally) be reported as my requesting him to make it true *that he gives me a hand with this box*. And the intention could be specified as intending to make it true *that I go to the store*. Thus what are paradigmatically propositions can be seen to provide the content for all sorts of illocutionary acts and psychological attitudes.

(2) The familiar logical relations of propositions can be seen to carry over to the logic of illocutionary acts and propositional attitudes. If I believe that *all dogs have fleas,* then I believe something that entails that if *Fido is a dog* then *Fido has fleas.* This is by virtue of the modus ponens structure in which the three propositions stand. If I hope that *Susie will come* and that *Susie will not be late*, then I hope that *Susie will not be late*, again because of the simplification structure into which these propositions fit.

(3) Illocutionary acts and psychological attitudes can be related by sharing propositional contents, as well as by the logical and other relations in which these contents stand. You can believe what I doubt, namely, *that Robinson will be elected mayor.* I can order you to do what you intend not to do, namely, (in canonical notation) *that you get off my property.* Again, it seems clear that it is the involvement of propositions that brings about these relationships.

We can also approach this issue by considering how we would introduce a novice to the philosophical concept of a proposition, other than in terms of what is asserted or believed or the like. Sometimes propositions are introduced as the meanings of sentences. But, leaving aside questions about the metaphysical status of meanings, we have seen in section ii that this will not do. There we saw that the meaning of a sentence is not, in general, sufficient to determine a unique assertion (i.e., what is asserted, i.e., a proposition). For this reason, whatever else may be said about the proposal, the meaning of 'I am hungry' cannot be thought to *be* a proposition, for it does not determine any particular proposition, but rather an indefinitely large class of propositions with certain features in common.

If one tries to explain 'proposition' by saying that propositions are bearers of truth values, that doesn't suffice to locate the concept uniquely until more guidance is provided as to what it is of which truth values are predicated. At most it puts a constraint on the concept. Nothing can be a proposition unless it has a unique determinate truth value.

A perfectly reasonable way of explaining 'proposition' to someone is to say that it is what is designated by a clause beginning with 'that' and followed by a declarative sentence that could be used to make an assertion. But this is not a real alternative to the explanation in terms of the content of assertions and psychological attitudes. For this is just the way in which we specify those contents. Thus there is no real alternative to taking proposition to be, most basically, the contents of illocutionary acts and psychological "propositional" attitudes.

"But if what is asserted when I assert that sugar is sweet is *the proposition that sugar is sweet,* and if what is believed when I believe that Sam is strong is *the proposition that Sam is strong,* then why is it awkward, at best, to report the assertion as *asserting the proposition that sugar is sweet* and to report the belief as *believing the proposition that Sam is strong?* After all, 'the proposition that sugar is sweet' refers to the proposition that sugar is sweet if anything does." I don't think that this is a serious difficulty. I would surmise that we tend to reserve the explicit denomination of a proposition *as* a proposition (with a phrase like 'the proposition that p') when we take the proposition "out by itself" and consider it in abstraction from its involvement in illocutionary acts or propositional attitudes. This would account for the awkwardness in question.

v The Nature of Propositions

But what are propositions? What is their nature, their ontological status? What sort of thing is it the involvement of which in an illocutionary act or propositional attitude provides that act or attitude with its content? And do things of this sort live a life of their own when not so involved?

There are many answers to these questions on the market today. These may be divided into ONTOLOGICALLY SERIOUS and DEFLATIONARY answers.[9] Let's begin with the former and first attend to views that take propositions to have a mode of being independent of the content-bearing function we have been discussing.

(1) Propositions are STATES OF AFFAIRS that may or may not "obtain". Let's say that states of affairs are designated by gerundial phrases like the following.

> Nixon's living in California
> Sam's hitting Harry
> 2 + 2's being 4
> John's being stout
> Gold's being malleable
> All dogs' having fleas
> There being some horned owls left
> Some Mormons' being such that if offered a cup of coffee they would accept it
> All gases' being such that they will increase in temperature if compressed

A state of affairs that obtains can be called a FACT.[10]

(2) Propositions are complex abstract objects, where the constituents vary with the content of the particular propositions, and where the structure into which these constituents fit varies with the form of the proposition. In practice, thinkers have modelled both the contents and the structure of propositions on the sentences in natural language that are used to assert or express them. Since the canonical way of designating a proposition is by a phrase of the form 'the proposition that p', where what replaces p in a particular case is a declarative sentence that can be used for asserting just that proposition, one does not have to look beyond our standard proposition-specifying expressions to find the model for propositional structure. Thus the proposition that gold is malleable, modelled on the sentence 'gold is malleable', will consist of the referent of 'gold', namely, gold, and the property of malleability, glued together

---

9. I'm not suggesting that deflationists about propositions are not serious about ontology, only that they are not ontologically serious about propositions.
10. See Chisholm 1976, 1981.

by the relation of property possession. This view may or may not differ from (1), depending on just how states of affairs are constituted.

(3) Various difficulties with (1) and (2) have led some thinkers to take a proposition to be a set of possible worlds, or alternatively, a function from possible worlds to truth values.[11] The intuitive idea is that a proposition can be identified with the set of those possible worlds in which the proposition is true. This construal will relieve us of worries about structure—and with a vengeance! A particular proposition will be so devoid of structure that all propositions necessarily equivalent to each other will be identical. This has, inter alia, the consequence that all necessarily true propositions are identical. There is only one true proposition of pure mathematics, which is the same as the one true proposition of deductive logic. On a humbler level, the proposition 'that either Jones is married or Susie isn't' turns out to be the same proposition as the proposition 'that it is not both the case that Jim is not married and Susie is.'

(4) Let's move now to views that do not take propositions to have a mode of being independent of their content-bearing involvements—construals that are Aristotelian rather than Platonic. The most metaphysically realist of such views would, following Aristotle, think of them as really existing but only as aspects of propositional attitudes and illocutionary acts. If a tiresomely persistent ontologist were to insist on an answer to the question as to just *what* those aspects are, the answer would be that they are specified by the clauses we use for content specification. *That* is what those aspects are. If we can understand, for example, what it is to insist *that Susie is not here* or to be thankful *that the parade is over*, we have all the understanding of what a proposition is that we need.

(5) There are variations of the *only in the context of illocutionary acts and propositional attitudes* move that are less realist, and less ontologically serious, more *deflationary* about propositions. There can be an analogue of the reduction of properties to similarity relations between particulars. The proposition *that gold is malleable* simply *is* a respect in which certain assertions, expressions of opinion, beliefs, and doubts are similar to each other and different from other such items. And more draconian reductions have been suggested. For example, it has been suggested that the proposition that gold is malleable can be identified with the class of sentences that could be used to assert that gold is malleable. It should be noted that on any of these reductive accounts one can, in a way, countenance a reification of propositions, speaking of them as if they

11. See Stalnaker 1984.

are independent entities in their own right about which we can say various things—their logical and other interrelations, their truth values, their involvement in propositional attitudes, and so on. That is, a reductionist can go along with this in a "fictionalist" or "instrumentalist" spirit, acknowledging that it is useful to speak of propositions as if they were entities without supposing this to be the sober truth. This would parallel the way in which an instrumentalist in science countenances apparent references to quarks and positrons for the sake of the empirical pay off of such talk, while metaphysically taking it to be an "as if" kind of discourse.

The above list is *not* a prelude to an exposition and defense of my metaphysical theory of propositions. I do have views on the subject. My preference is for the "Aristotelian" position (4). It is more economical than (1)–(3), while giving propositions a foothold in reality, but saying as little as possible about their nature. If one wonders how, on this view, we are to interpret talk about propositions that have no realization in (actual) illocutionary acts or propositional attitudes, the answer is that we are thinking of contents of *possible* acts and attitudes.[12] Moreover, I do not consider all the views on the list to be live options. If, as I hold, our basic grip on propositions is by way of their furnishing content for illocutionary acts and propositional attitudes, then they must be individuated so that items that have different contents must involve different propositions. And (3) radically fails to satisfy that condition just because it makes all necessarily true propositions to be identical. Surely the assertion *that* $2 + 2 = 4$ is a different assertion, with a different content, from the assertion *that* $695 \times 2 = 1,390$. Moreover that view makes two propositions that are necessarily equivalent to be the same. And yet the belief *that either Jim is married or Susie isn't* is not the same as the belief *that it is not both the case that Jim is not married and Susie is.* One who didn't realize the necessary equivalence might believe one and disbelieve the other.[13] As for (1), whether it satisfies this requirement on individuation depends on how the notion of a state of affairs is developed. To take a case close to the concerns of this book, is the state of affairs *sugar's being*

12. That does not necessarily involve taking possible acts and attitudes to *exist* or have some kind of *being*. Whatever construal is given to talk of possibilities (and we can't do without such talk) can be deployed here.

13. No doubt, the partisans of this view would have various things to say in response to these criticisms. The issue may largely hang on what one takes to be most fundamental in our pretheoretical notion of a proposition. I have indicated deficiencies of the "sets of possible worlds" view if we take propositions to be, most basically, contents of psychological "propositional attitudes" and illocutionary acts. In any event, I am far from aspiring to a proper discussion of these issues in this book, as I now go on to make explicit.

sweet the same state of affairs as *its being true that sugar is sweet*? If it is, then (1) runs into the same difficulty. For it is clear, or so it seems to me, that an assertion *that sugar is sweet* is not the same assertion, with the same content, as the assertion *that it is true that sugar is sweet*. The latter involves conceptual content absent from the former.[14]

This is a beginning of what I would say if I were to embark on the metaphysics of propositions. But I will not do so. I would like to refrain because to do a proper job would require a long and tortuous discussion that would distract me from the main issues of the book. And the abstention is possible because it is not necessary for my purposes here to adopt a particular position. My central concern here is the articulation and defense of a realist conception of truth, in opposition to epistemic conceptions. For that purpose it doesn't matter what metaphysical status we take propositions to have. So long as they can serve as subjects for truth-value attributions, the metaphysical chips can fall where they may. For that matter, propositions don't even have to "be there" in any robustly metaphysically realist sense. It would be enough to exhibit them as subjects of truth values in a "fictional" or "instrumental" spirit. My project is even tolerant of reductive accounts of propositions.

Lest you think that my choice of propositions as truth bearers is so permissive as to be vacuous, I will specify what is nonnegotiable in the position. The position is most deeply committed to the primacy of locutions in which 'true' and 'false' are predicated of what is specified by 'that' clauses and other proposition-specifying clauses. These attributions don't have to have the surface grammar of *proposition-specifying phrase + truth-value predicate*. They range over 'It is true that p' as well as 'The proposition that p is true'. And they also include 'The assertion that p is true' and 'The belief that p is true', since, as pointed out above, I take those predications to be of *what is asserted (believed)* rather than of the act of assertion or the state of belief. So long as we recognize these to be the truth-value attributions on which all others are built, then that amounts to what I have been understanding by "taking propositions to be the basic truth-value bearers".[15]

I will refrain not only from advancing an ontology of propositions, but also from giving an account of how illocutionary acts and propositional attitudes have to be related to a proposition for the latter to be the content of the former. There are, again, many such accounts in the field (not all of which take propositions seriously). Many, though not all, are

14. See section xi for discussion of this last point.
15. Cf. Mackie 1973, 21.

developed under the aegis of some general metaphysical orientation, such as "physicalism" or "naturalism", and seek to show that the possession of content can be understood in a physicalist or naturalist fashion.[16] I have no sympathy for such programs, but my present point is that the aims of this book do not require me to go into these issues. So long as we can understand illocutionary act reports and propositional attitude reports which contain 'that' clauses or other content-specifying clauses, we have all that is needed for a working grasp of the notion of an illocutionary act or propositional attitude "involving" a propositional content. And that is sufficient for us to extract the notion of a proposition as a truth-value bearer.

Thus my choice of truth-value bearers is completely neutral with respect to the view we adopt on the nature of propositions and of propositional content. In fact, I can be even more permissive than this. So far as I can see, the issues with which I will be dealing assume the same shape whatever we take the bearers of truth values to be, provided our choice is not untenable on other grounds. If it is defensible to take sentence tokens to be the primary bearers of truth value, then everything in the rest of the book could be restated in those terms.

vi General Formulations of a Realist Conception of Truth

We can now return to the task of developing a more explicit statement of the realist conception of truth. Let's recall the initial formulation.

I. A STATEMENT IS TRUE IF AND ONLY IF WHAT THE STATEMENT SAYS TO BE THE CASE ACTUALLY IS THE CASE.

The first point to make about this, in the light of sections ii–v, is that, since 'statement' here has to mean 'what is stated' rather than 'the act of stating', and since we have seen good and sufficient reason for identifying that with a proposition, I. really tells us what it is for a proposition to be true. But this claim requires qualification. What is stated when a statement is made is to be identified *ontologically* with a proposition; but when a proposition is referred to as a *statement*, we are thinking of it as figuring in that context, as *being what is stated*, rather than as existing on its own as something that may or may not play that role. This is significant because if we were to think of a proposition in abstraction from any

16. See, e.g., Davidson 1984; Carnap 1947, chap. 1; Stich 1983; Fodor 1975.

such context, it would be unnatural to think of it as "saying" anything. To be sure, we are also speaking figuratively when we speak of a statement's "saying" something. It is speakers who literally *say something* in the course of making a statement. But we are obviously closer to a literal use of 'say' when we predicate it of a proposition as the content of a statement than when we predicate it of a proposition in abstraction from any such involvement.

Something analogous can be said about an account of truth for beliefs. A principle for beliefs parallel to I might run:

II. A BELIEF IS TRUE IF AND ONLY IF WHAT THE BELIEF TAKES TO BE THE CASE ACTUALLY IS THE CASE.

Again, beliefs don't literally take anything to be so-and-so. It is believers who do so. But, again, propositions are, so to say, closer to this literal substratum when they figure as belief content than when they are in splendid isolation.

We can avoid figures of speech by explicitly linking statements and beliefs to what staters and believers do, and then, at a second remove, link propositions to statements and beliefs. Thus:

III. A STATEMENT IS TRUE IF AND ONLY IF WHAT A MAKER OF THE STATEMENT IS SAYING TO BE THE CASE IN MAKING THAT STATEMENT, ACTUALLY IS THE CASE.[17]

IV. A BELIEF IS TRUE IF AND ONLY IF WHAT ONE WHO HOLDS THAT BELIEF TAKES TO BE THE CASE IN HOLDING THAT BELIEF, ACTUALLY IS THE CASE.

Then the extension to propositions as such would go as follows.

V. A PROPOSITION IS TRUE IF AND ONLY IF WHAT A MAKER OF A STATEMENT WITH THAT PROPOSITION AS CONTENT IS SAYING TO BE THE CASE IN MAKING THAT STATEMENT, ACTUALLY IS THE CASE.

VI. A PROPOSITION IS TRUE IF AND ONLY IF WHAT ONE WHO HOLDS A BELIEF WITH THAT PROPOSITION AS CONTENT TAKES TO BE THE CASE IN HOLDING THAT BELIEF, ACTUALLY IS THE CASE.[18]

17. Cf. Mackie 1973 , 50. "To say that a statement is true is to say that whatever in the making of the statement is stated to obtain does obtain."

18. It may be objected that something about statements *and* something about beliefs cannot each be both *necessary* and *sufficient* for the truth of propositions. For since either of these conditions is sufficient, the other one can't be necessary; and since each is necessary the other one can't be sufficient. Perhaps the objector overlooks the point that what is said to be both neces-

At a considerable cost of pedantry, this spells out how we can think of the truth of statements, beliefs, and propositions as determined by whether the content of the proposition (statement, belief) is actually realized. A bonus of these transformations is that they permit us to oscillate freely and in good conscience between speaking of statements, beliefs, and propositions as bearers of truth value.

At this point I should say something in defense of my limiting these formulations to BELIEFS and STATEMENTS, in addition to propositions, given that, as pointed out above, propositions furnish content to illocutionary acts and propositional psychological attitudes of all sorts— requests and promises as well as statements, and doubtings and wonderings as well as beliefs. The basic reason has to do with the fact that we speak of statements (assertions) as true or false but that we do not ascribe truth values to requests, promises, appointings, expressions of gratitude, hopes, doubts, or wonderings. Nor is this selectivity arbitrary. The reason for it is that in making statements and holding beliefs we commit ourselves to the propositional content's being true. Whereas to request someone to bring it about that p or to wonder whether that p is to make no such commitment. If I assert that p, there is something wrong with what I did if not-p,[19] but there is nothing analogously wrong with my performance if I ask you to close the door when the door is not already closed. Quite the contrary! And a similar contrast holds between beliefs and other propositional attitudes. A false belief has thereby failed to achieve the aim of believing, but if I hope for something that will not eventuate, I have not thereby failed to attain the fundamental goal of hoping. (Hoping is not designed to bring about what is hoped for.) No doubt, the truth value of the propositional content is relevant to these other illocutionary acts and propositional attitudes, but since they don't essentially involve a commitment to truth, we don't ascribe truth values to them. Hence they are not considered truth-value bearers, even though the embedded propositions are.

Another notable feature of I–VI is that they assume, in effect, that every statement (belief, proposition) can be construed as being of the

sary and sufficient in each case is what *would* be the case *if* the proposition were the content of a statement (belief), not something that actually happens. But that doesn't suffice to clear up the difficulty. For if the consequent of V really is sufficient for the truth of the proposition, how can the consequent of VI also be necessary, whether these consequents are categorical or hypothetical? The answer has to be that the consequent of VI, for example, is necessary, though the consequent of V is sufficient, because the former is necessary for the latter and vice versa. A propositional content can make III true of a statement only if it makes IV true of a belief, and vice versa.

19. To be sure, even if I assert what is not the case, I might not be rightfully taken to task if there are sufficient extenuating circumstances.

form 'It is the case that . . . '. It seems clear that any statement could be so reformulated, though most are not ordinarily in that form. This reflects a general point of some importance. One obvious way of being explicit, in some general fashion, about what it takes, on a realist conception, to make a statement (belief, proposition) true, is to use some account of the structure of statements. A general formulation of what sort of fact must obtain in order that a given statement be true will be a recipe for picking out that fact. And that recipe will be in terms of what a statement states.[20] I–VI provides one example of that strategy. If no unrestrictedly general account can be given of "what statements state", we will have to settle for separate principles for statements of different forms—singular subject-predicate statements, singular relational statements, universal quantifications of singular subject-predicate statements, conditionals, etc.[21]

Although I–VI identifies a general form into which all statements could be cast, it would be good to find a more natural characterization, one that, arguably, applies to statements as they are actually made, not just as they might be transformed. A promising candidate would construe all statements as being about something(s), and asserting something of that (those) something(s)—claiming that a certain property applies to it (them). If we can make good the claim that that there is such a referential component to every statement, there will be no difficulty in construing the rest as what is being asserted of that referent (those referents). Singular statements obviously fit this model. As for quantified statements, on a classical understanding of quantification, they can be understood as saying something about all values of the variables.[22] Conditional and other complex statemental forms can be taken to complicate the predicate that is being asserted of one or more individuals or of the entities that are the values of variables. Thus the statement that *If Jim is healthy, he will come to the meeting,* could be construed as asserting *will come to the meeting if healthy* of Jim. And the statement that *all dogs have fleas* can be construed as attributing the property of *having fleas if a dog* to all the entities in the domain of the quantifier. There will, of course, be the usual questions as to what to do about truth

20. This point would apply even more obviously to a general account of the truth of sentences.

21. We would have to do that anyway if we were to embark on the Tarskian project of giving a formal theory of truth conditions for sentences; but that is no part of my agenda here. For more on this, see section viii.

22. If we allow substitutional quantification, as I will suggest we can do for explaining truth, this characterization can no longer claim universal coverage.

evaluation in cases of referential failure; but those questions have to be faced in any case. This suggests the following formulation.

> VII. A STATEMENT IS TRUE IF AND ONLY IF WHAT THE MAKER OF THE STATEMENT IS ATTRIBUTING TO WHAT THE STATEMENT IS ABOUT, IN MAKING THAT STATEMENT, DOES ACTUALLY QUALIFY WHAT THE STATEMENT IS ABOUT.

This can be seen as an extension of the familiar formulation of a truth condition for singular statements of the form [s is P], namely, that *what is referred to by 's' have the property connoted by 'P'*.

Taking I–VI as our guide, it will be a simple mechanical exercise to construct accounts of the truth of beliefs and propositions analogous to VII. For example:

> VIII. A PROPOSITION IS TRUE IF AND ONLY IF WHAT THE MAKER OF A STATEMENT WITH THAT PROPOSITION AS CONTENT IS ATTRIBUTING TO WHAT THE STATEMENT IS ABOUT, IN MAKING THAT STATEMENT, DOES ACTUALLY QUALIFY WHAT THE STATEMENT IS ABOUT.

> IX. A BELIEF IS TRUE IF AND ONLY IF WHAT ONE WHO HOLDS THE BELIEF SUPPOSES TO CHARACTERIZE WHAT THE BELIEF IS ABOUT, IN HOLDING THAT BELIEF, REALLY DOES CHARACTERIZE WHAT THE BELIEF IS ABOUT.

And so on.

vii Propositional Truth and the T-Schema

The above formulations deal with the truth of propositions via their involvement in illocutionary acts and propositional attitudes. Can we find a way to get at propositional truth more directly, a way that would bring out what it takes for a proposition to be true, apart from its figuring as the content of an actual or possible statement or belief?

As noted above, we can't simply ape I and II with propositions taking the place of statements or beliefs. For no sense can be attached to propositions "*saying* something to be the case" or "*taking* something to be the case". Some classical forms of the correspondence theory of truth sought to treat propositions directly by developing a theory of the structure of propositions and taking a proposition to be true when there is a fact that "matches" or "corresponds to" that structure. But this requires an account of the nature of propositions, and I have already eschewed that for this book.

There is, however, a very simple way of sidestepping this enterprise. Instead of digging into the structure of propositions in order to say, in general, what it takes to render them true, we can take the proposition as an unanalyzed whole and generalize over that. Consider the following analogue for propositions of Tarski's famous form (T) for sentences.[23]

X. The proposition that *p* is true *iff p*.

I will call X. the T-schema ('T' for 'truth', *not* for 'Tarski'). The T-schema can be turned into a statement by substituting the same declarative sentence for both occurrences of '*p*', restricting substitutends, of course, to sentences that can be used to make statements. Thus:

XI. The proposition that grass is green is true if and only if grass is green.
XII. The proposition that Joe is hungry is true if and only if Joe is hungry.[24]

Call any statement of the form specified by the T-schema, such as XI and XII, a T-statement. The suggestion is that if we understand that any T-statement is *conceptually, analytically* true, true by virtue of the meanings of the terms involved, in particular the term 'true', then we thereby understand what it is for a proposition to be true. Understanding that amounts to recognizing how it is that the content of a proposition, what it is "a proposition *that*", determines a (necessarily) necessary and sufficient condition for the truth of that proposition. And once we see that, we grasp what it is for a proposition to be true in a realist sense. This gives us the realist CONCEPT of propositional truth.

To be sure, this does not amount to an explicit general statement of what it is for a proposition to be true. The T-schema is not a statement but a statement schema, a form of statement. And each instantiation thereof, each T-statement, provides a condition for the truth of a particular proposition, not a general statement of what it is for a proposition

23. That form is 'X is true if, and only if, *p*'. We get a particular sentence of this form by replacing '*p*' with a declarative sentence and 'X' with an expression referring to that sentence. See section viii for more on Tarski.
24. Where necessary, the substitution for '*p*' is assumed to come with contextual indications of reference and whatever else is necessary to determine a particular proposition.

to be true. Nevertheless, there are two ways of turning this suggestion into a general account of propositional truth.

First, and most obviously, we can universally generalize the T-schema.

XIII. (p) The proposition that p is true *iff p*.

This certainly seems to be an unrestrictedly general statement of the conditions under which a proposition is true. The only reason for denying that would be a dissatisfaction with the sort of quantification involved. It cannot be standard objectual quantification, in which a substitution instance of a quantified proposition is achieved by replacing variables with singular expressions that refer to entities in the domain of the variable. An objectually universally quantified statement is true if and only if the open statement quantified is true of every object (or n-tuples of objects) in the relevant domain. An objectually existentially quantified statement is true if and only if the open statement quantified is true of some object, or n-tuple of objects, in the relevant domain. XIII is not a quantified statement of that sort, because what replaces 'p' in a particular T-sentence does not refer to any entity. That is not because propositions do not deserve the honorific title of 'entity'. Even assuming they do, declarative sentences, which are what replace 'p' to yield instantiations of the schema, are not referring expressions. They don't refer to anything, abstract or concrete. Thus if we have an objectual quantification model of what a general statement is, XIII will not qualify. What we need to interpret XIII is substitutional quantification. Such quantification is not to be understood in terms of whether the relevant open statement is true of certain *objects*, but whether singular statements that result from appropriate substitutions for the variables are true. Call such a singular statement a SUBSTITUTION INSTANCE of the quantified statement in question. Then a universally quantified statement is true if and only if all substitution instances are true, and an "existentially"[25] quantified statement is true if some substitution instance is true. Substitutional quantification puts no restriction on what sort of expressions can replace variables. Of course, any particular variable will range over some kinds of expressions rather than others. But the range of expressions that can replace variables in one or another quantified statement is unlimited. This makes it possible to employ sentential variables as in XIII, and so makes it possible to say in general what the conditions are under which a proposition is true on a realist conception of truth.

25. This term is inappropriate for substitutional quantification, since the existence of objects is not the main point at issue; but I will retain it because of its familiarity.

Many philosophers have doubts about the viability of substitutional quantification. Its logic certainly has not been developed to nearly the extent of objectual quantification. But the formal logic of the matter is not my concern here. I am concerned with formulating and defending a certain view as to the conception of truth we use in application to propositions, statements, and beliefs. That conception might be felicitously, informally, expressed in substitutional quantification, even if there are thus far unresolved difficulties in working out its logic in a comprehensive manner. Thus I shall take it that XIII is an acceptable way of saying what it takes, on a realist conception, for a proposition to be true.[26]

There is a specific objection to the use of substitutional quantification in this connection that is worth special attention. The natural way to explain substitutional quantification is the one we used above, in terms of the truth of substitution instances. But doesn't that introduce a circularity in the use of a substitutionally quantified formula to explain the realist conception of truth?

There are three points that make this objection less serious than it seems at first sight. First, the explanation of substitutional quantification in terms of truth does not occur in the account given by XIII. Substitutional quantification is *used* but not *mentioned*, much less explicated. Nor is it clear that truth must be mentioned to give someone an understanding of a formula like XIII. The neophyte could catch on just by being shown how to derive instances from the universal statement. Second, and more fundamentally, XIII is not a *definition* of 'true'. We'll have more to say later on what its status is, but it is not a definition of the classical type, in which a synonymous, and more fully analyzed, expression is equated with the definiendum. Hence there is no danger of a definition's being invalidated by circularity. Third, and equally important, even as a kind of explanation of a meaning of 'true', it does not aim to be reductive, to reduce 'true' to terms at a more fundamental level. (Again, more on this later.)

But for those who are motivated to shun substitutional quantification here, there is another way of deriving a general account of propositional truth from the T-schema—going metalinguistic. Remember that the basic idea of this approach to the explanation of realist truth is that any T-statement is conceptually, analytically true. Why not just say that? This suggests the following formulation.

26. For vigorous defenses of the viability of substitutional quantification see Prior 1971, chaps. 2, 3; Mackie 1973, chap. 2, sec. 5; C. J. F. Williams 1976, chap. 3.

XIV. TO DETERMINE A (NECESSARILY) NECESSARY AND SUFFICIENT CONDITION FOR A GIVEN PROPOSITION, R, USE THE FOLLOWING RECIPE. FORM A T-STATEMENT BY SUBSTITUTING A SENTENCE THAT EXPRESSES R FOR p IN THE T-SCHEMA. THIS T-STATEMENT WILL BE CONCEPTUALLY, ANALYTICALLY TRUE, AND WILL THEREFORE GIVE US A (NECESSARILY) NECESSARY AND SUFFICIENT CONDITION FOR THE TRUTH OF R.

Though XIV is not a universal statement that says in general what it takes for a proposition to be true, it does succeed in explaining how to specify, for any proposition, what it takes for it to be true. It therefore constitutes another spelling out of the basic intuition of the realist conception of truth—that a proposition is true when its "content" is "realized" in the way things are, that by asserting the proposition we have thereby specified (whether we realize it or not) what would make the proposition true.

viii Relation to Tarski

I have learned by bitter experience that it is extremely difficult to prevent people from assimilating X—the T-schema—to formulations of Tarski. Therefore, before continuing with the exposition of the realist conception of truth I will pause to set the record straight on the relation of my enterprise to Tarski's. I have already pointed out that my T-schema is reminiscent of Tarski's "form T", which he formulates as:

XV. X is true *iff p.*

We get a particular instance of this form by replacing 'p' with a declarative sentence and 'X' with an expression referring to that sentence.

Nevertheless there are large differences between Tarski's development of a "semantic conception of truth" and my development of a realist conception of truth. Tarski's project is to define 'true' for each of a number of formalized artificial languages. The semantics of these languages is such that my earlier objections to attributing truth values to sentence types do not hold. There is no ambiguity. Each meaningful unit has one and only one meaning. There are no token reflexives or other expressions the contribution of which to a statement is, in part, determined by features of the context. Unlike the case of natural languages, each proper name is assigned a referent as part of the semantics. The languages are purely extensional. Working within these limits, Tarski can treat sentence types as bearers of truth value. He is not concerned with the attribution of propositional content to propositions, psychological attitudes, or speech acts. His aim is to provide an explicit definition of truth for one or another formalized language, using only extensional notions, subject to the constraint that all sentences of form T that are formulable in the language should be entailed by the definition. Each distinguishable language will require a different definition. There is no aspiration to explain TRUTH *überhaupt*.

This project looks to be worlds away from my project of developing an informal, discursive understanding of what it is for a proposition (statement, belief) to be true or false, and so it is. The notion of truth on which I concentrate has no special connection with any particular language or, indeed, with language in general, though my primary truth bearers, propositions, do provide content for speech acts.[27] My account is something quite different from any formalized logical affair. Moreover, Tarski's equivalences of form T are material equivalences, in keeping with his restriction to extensional languages, whereas my T-statements are presented as analytically, and hence necessarily, true.

Nevertheless, there is more than an accidental similarity between my T-statements and Tarski's equivalences of form T. Although Tarski does not allow himself to say so, I think it is reasonable to surmise that he takes equivalences of form T to be a "material condition of adequacy" for a definition of truth just because he is sensitive to the point I have been making—namely, that the content of a truth bearer contains everything we need to specify what it takes to make that bearer true. Hence the obvious parallelism between:

XV. X (the sentence 'p') is true *iff p*.

and

X. The proposition that p is true *iff p*.

27. Contrary to recent practice, I do not treat truth as primarily or essentially a "semantic" notion. This point is closely connected with the fact that I do not take sentences to be the primary bearers of truth values. This does not mean that I rule out the possibility that truth should play some role in semantics. Many notions come into the semantic description of a language. Even when we recognize that truth cannot be attributed to sentence types, we might try to think of sentence meaning in terms of its contribution to the truth conditions of statements for the making of which the sentence is fitted by its semantics. In saying that I do not take truth to be primarily or essentially a semantic notion, I mean that in bringing out what truth is we need not advert to any semantic considerations concerning the meaning of linguistic items.

I will look further into the putative semantic entanglements of truth in my discussion of Dummett in Chapter 4.

Apart from the insight that what is required for a sentence (proposition, statement, belief) to be true is that its content be also the content of an actual fact, I don't see any rationale for Tarski's dictum that it is a "material criterion of adequacy" for a definition of truth that the definition entail all equivalences of form T.

ix Minimalism about Truth

Borrowing a term from Horwich (1990), XIII and XIV may be said to be formulations of a MINIMALIST account of truth. There are several respects in which they are minimal by comparison with a more full-blooded theory of truth, like the correspondence theories in Russell (1912) and Wittgenstein (1922). I don't mean to suggest that my account contrasts in this way only with correspondence theories. It is also stripped down relative to coherence and pragmatist theories, and to epistemic theories of truth generally. But just because it is more nearly akin to correspondence theories than to other "robust" theories of truth, its minimalism is best highlighted by a comparison with rich correspondence theories.

(1) I have already stressed the point that XIII and XIV generalize over propositions as unanalyzed units, rather than being put in terms of some view as to their internal structure, whereas a full-dress correspondence theory must include some account of the structure of propositions (statements . . .) in order to be in a position to say something significant about what would constitute *correspondence* with a fact. Whatever the details of the correspondence that is supposed to constitute truth, it must involve some structural "matching" or "fitting" of proposition and fact to each other. And so any serious elaboration of this idea will have to be in terms of an account of the structure of propositions. My minimalist realism deliberately steers clear of that.

(2) A deeper difference is this. XIII naturally leads into the idea that a true proposition is made true by a fact. Mind you, the term 'fact' does not appear on the right hand side of the equivalence; that is one aspect of the minimality. But in saying that the proposition that lemons are sour is true *if and only if* lemons *are* sour, we are, in effect, committing ourselves to the thesis that this proposition is *made true* by lemons being sour. And that could just as well be put as saying that it is made true by *the fact that* lemons are sour. This nicely brings out the kinship of my minimal-realist conception of truth with the correspondence theory, for the latter could be seen as taking off from this point. If a true proposi-

tion is made true by a fact, there must be something about the relationship between *that* proposition and *that* fact that is responsible for its being *that* fact that does the truth making here, rather than one of the innumerable other facts that obtain. And the correspondence theory sets out specifically to say what that relationship is. It seeks, we might say, to delineate the fact-proposition relationship on which the truth making supervenes. The proposition that lemons are sour is made true by the fact that lemons are sour, rather than by the fact that water is wet, because the proposition *corresponds* with the former fact and not with the latter; it "fits" or "matches" the former and not the latter. And the correspondence theory shoulders the responsibility of delineating that correspondence.

Having come this far, we can bring out another facet of the relationship between the minimal-realist theory and the correspondence theory. The answer to the question, "By virtue of what does one fact, rather than any other, make the proposition that lemons are sour true?" is, so to say, already implicit in the T-schema. For when one looks at a particular T-statement it leaps to the eye that there is an identity of content between proposition and fact. But we would naturally like to spell out more explicitly just what this "identity in content" amounts to. And that is what the more ambitious correspondence theory seeks to do. Shortly I shall have more to say about the way in which a minimalist realism could be looked on as an inchoate correspondence theory.

(3) It follows from the difference just mentioned that a robust correspondence theory must develop an explicit account of propositions (statements . . .) and facts so as to be in a position to spell out what correspondence amounts to. And classical correspondence theories, such as those of Russell and Wittgenstein, have sought to do just that, whereas a minimalist realism, not aspiring to say just what correspondence amounts to, can shirk that ontological task.

(4) Neither XIII nor XIV can lay serious claim to being a *definition* of truth, whereas a correspondence theory, in purporting to lay bare the proposition-fact relationship on which truth supervenes, does typically claim to provide a definition, at least a contextual definition, one that unpacks what is being said when truth is ascribed to a proposition or other truth bearer.[28] The statement that there is a fact with which the proposition that R corresponds (imagine this formulation elaborated by an account of what that correspondence consists in) is claimed to be

---

28. A correspondence theory may or may not aspire to provide an *explicit* definition, in the sense of providing a synonym that can be substituted for 'true' wherever the latter occurs.

synonymous with the statement that the proposition that R is true, the former differing from the latter only in making explicit what is implicit in the latter. But the equivalence in the T-schema, universally generalized in XIII, cannot seriously be claimed to be synonymy. The *meaning* of 'The proposition that *lemons are sour* is true' cannot be the same as that of 'Lemons are sour'. The former has conceptual content absent from the latter. One could understand 'lemons are sour' perfectly well without having any concept of truth whatever. I make this point as though it were obvious, and so it seems to me. But I must admit that it is widely denied. "Redundancy" theorists, for example, hold that to assert 'It is true that lemons are sour' is merely to assert 'Lemons are sour'. I will shortly be distinguishing such views from my own and explaining why I find them unacceptable.

These are the most salient respects in which the account of truth embodied in XIII and XIV is MINIMAL in contrast to more robust theories.[29] But what about my earlier formulations, I–IX. Are they properly regarded as "minimalist"?

To answer this question I will have to recognize that minimalism is a matter of degree. A theory can be more or less ambitious, more or less modest, more or less rich, more or less sparse. Of the ways just brought out in which the T-schema based formulations are minimal, some apply to the other formulations and others do not. (1) and (4) do not. As for (1), XIII and XIV were explicitly distinguished from their predecessors by the fact that they eschew any account of the internal structure of propositions and statements, while those predecessors all proceed on one or another suggestion as to a universal form for propositions. As for (4), note that I–IX all make *reference* to the truth-value bearer on the right-hand side of the equivalence as well as on the left-hand side, and attribute a property to it that could seriously lay claim to being an explicitly spelled out formulation of the property of truth; whereas XIII has only the propositional content of the truth-value bearer on the right-hand side and attributes no property to it on that side. Thus I–IX are at least in the right form to constitute a contextual definition of 'S is true'. They can be taken to provide a more analyzed synonym of the truth attribution.

But as for (2) and (3), I–IX contrast with correspondence theory in pretty much the way that XIII and XIV do. The former as well as the latter make no attempt to spell out the proposition-fact relationship on which truth making supervenes, and by the same token they make no

29. Cf. the "simple" theory of truth in Mackie 1973. See especially p. 57.

pretense of being based on an ontology of propositions and facts. So are they "minimalist"? Yes, in comparison with classical theories of truth like the correspondence theory, but not as minimal as the T-schema based formulations.

If XIII and XIV are not definitions, not even contextual definitions, then what are they? What status do they have? What is being claimed for them? Here is the way I see it. These formulations convey the *concept* of realist truth in that anyone who realizes that XIII and/or any T-statement is analytically, conceptually true, thereby possesses the realist concept of truth. Such a person is thereby in a position to employ the concept and to understand talk in which it figures. In this respect these formulations are like other nondefinitional devices for identifying, delimiting, or inculcating a concept. Think of applying a term to paradigm cases, of bringing out salient features of items to which the term applies, and of putting the term through its paces in a theory. We have become familiar in this century with many such ways of conveying a concept other than definition. I take XIII and XIV to belong to this category. More specifically, the species of that genus which is exemplified here could be put as follows: *providing particularly illuminating necessary and sufficient conditions for the application of a term without thereby providing a synonym for such an application.* In any event, it is, I maintain, clear on inspection that one who appreciates the conceptual truth of XIII or of any T-statement thereby understands propositional truth in the realist sense.

The time has come for me to say something more about the relation between my various formulations, particularly between the two groups, I–IX, and XIII–XIV. I take it to be unproblematic that inside each group there is substantial equivalence. But we have already seen significant differences between the groups, particularly with respect to whether a contextual definition of 'true' is being proposed and whether a commitment is made to a universal form for propositions. Given differences of this magnitude, how can I put them all forward as specifying the realist concept of truth? Isn't this mere shilly-shallying? Shouldn't I buckle down and decide which of them "tells it like it is" with respect to that concept of truth? How can they all be doing an acceptable job of identifying the concept?

In response to this I can only say that I will continue to shilly-shally. My apologia for this is that I believe all these formulations bring out the central realist conception of propositional truth in one way or another. I have sought to make a case for the intuitive plausibility of taking them to be formulating the same basic conception of what it is for a proposition to be true, but doing so in slightly different ways. "But", you may say, "how can a statement's being true both be a matter of what the statement's saying to be the case actually *being the case*, and also a matter of the right side of an appropriate T-statement's obtaining?" Well, why not? It seems clear to me that when I say that the statement that water is wet is true if and only if water is wet, I *am* saying, in a more concrete, more first-level, less formal way what I say when I say that this statement is true if and only if what it says to be the case *is* the case. I am just putting the point differently. The T-statement version is all in the object language, while I–IX move up to a metalevel and talk about what statements say and whether what they say "obtains" or "is real". I throw this multiplicity of versions at the reader rather than picking one version and suppressing the others, just because here as elsewhere, I believe, the underlying idea can be more more fully, more richly, grasped if it is displayed in several ways, from several perspectives, rather than in a single portrayal.

Although I took the term 'minimalism' from Horwich (1990), and although our accounts are in much the same spirit, they also differ in more than one respect. For one thing, he relies exclusively on the T-schema. In fact, what he calls his theory of truth is said to *consist* of all the instantiations of that schema. He eschews substitutional quantification, thus depriving himself of my XIII, nor does he present analogues of my other formulations. I will note other differences below. A closer antecedent of the present account is Mackie (1973). In chapter 2 he presents an account of what he calls "simple truth" that is very much in the same vein as mine, though the details are different. My attention was called to this book only after I had substantially completed this one, or else the parallels might have been still closer.

Having said what I did about the multiple-formulation character of my account, I am committed to allowing the reader to think of the realist conception of truth in terms of any of my versions—I–IX, or XIII–XIV. It will make no difference to the issues discussed, and to my arguments for alethic realism and against its opponents, which choice you make. Even the most minimal formulation, XIII, contains everything that we need to determine a distinctively realist conception of truth, although it doesn't make explicit everything that is involved. Still, it would be helpful if I were to pick a single canonical version that I can be taken to be referring to whenever I mention "the realist conception of truth" without further qualification. For this purpose I pick the initial formulations in terms of what is being said or believed to be the case actually being the case. This means III for statements, IV for beliefs, and

V or VI for propositions. These formulations give a more explicit account of what is being said in truth attributions without getting into the problems raised by VII–IX concerning the assumption made there about a universal form for propositions. Nevertheless, much of the subsequent discussion will be in terms of the T-schema and its generalization, XIII.

x Minimalist Realism and the Correspondence Theory

Now I want to "locate" my realist conception of truth vis-à-vis other approaches to truth in the literature. This will serve several purposes. It will enable me to define more sharply the contours of my account by specifying what it does and doesn't imply, what it is and isn't consistent with. It should help the reader by relating the present account to others in the literature with which she is familiar. And it should place the present enterprise in the larger context of the ongoing discussion of truth, currently a very lively affair.

I can (almost) ignore at this point the relation of my account of truth to epistemic accounts, since the entire book is structured around this opposition, and a large proportion is devoted to criticizing epistemic theories and responding to their criticisms. Suffice it to say here that the realist and the epistemic accounts propound incompatible answers to the question: "What is it for a truth-value bearer to be true?". As I noted earlier, many philosophers think that epistemic theories of truth are compatible with a minimalist realism about truth, especially in its T-schema based versions. But in Chapter 7 I will seek to show that this is not the case.

I have already had a fair amount to say about the relation of my account and correspondence theory. I have just two additions to make. First, I have already suggested that my minimalist realism might be thought of as an inchoate correspondence theory. I can put more flesh on that skeleton by alluding to the distinction between *concept* and *property*. It is familiar point nowadays, thanks to the work of Putnam and Kripke, that a property (or a kind) may have features, may have a constitution, that is not reflected in our concept that picks out that property. What heat really *is* is mean kinetic energy, though our (ordinary) concept of heat is not in those terms at all. The essential nature of water is to be H_2O, though our ordinary concept of water is in terms of its observable properties. And so on. In the same way, the *property* of truth may have various features that are not reflected in our *concept* of truth. In terms of this distinction, my realist account of truth is an account of our ordinary concept of truth. It holds, to deploy one of my versions, that in saying that a statement is true we are saying that what the statement is about is as the statement says it (them) to be. But the property of statements, etc., thus identified and delimited may have features that go beyond our conceptual access to it. In particular, it may have the features embodied in the correspondence theory, features on which the aspect embodied in our concept supervenes. Thus we can think of the correspondence theory of truth (or rather a successful correspondence theory) as related to my minimalist account in the way an analysis of the ordinary concept of anger is related to a successful psychophysiological theory of the nature of anger. This helps us to see that there is room for both.

Second, my minimalist account could be a rather less inchoate correspondence theory without going beyond the concept to the property. In laying out the second way in which my account is minimal, I pointed out that the T-statement 'The proposition that lemons are sour is true if and only if lemons are sour' naturally suggests that lemons *being* sour is what makes that proposition true, which in turn could just as well be put by saying that it is the *fact* that lemons are sour that makes the proposition true. To be sure, this talk of facts *making* propositions true is not on the surface in the T-statement, but it is not difficult to see it just below the surface. So we might formulate a minimalist correspondence account as follows:

> XVI. (*p*) If the proposition that *p* is true it is made true by the fact that *p*.

Or still more minimally:

> XVII. (*p*) The proposition that *p* is true *iff* it is a fact that *p*.

That this marks out the right sort of correspondence between proposition and fact is guaranteed by the requirement for instantiations of the schema, that the same substitution be made for '*p*' in its two occurrences. This guarantees that the proposition and the fact that makes it true share the same propositional content. What the fact is a fact *that*, is the same as what the proposition is a proposition *that*. My suggestion, one of startling simplicity (and hence minimal), is that this feature of the T-schema ensures that any instantiation will imply the right kind of correspondence between truth bearer and truth maker. How more intimately could a proposition and fact be related than by virtue of sharing the same content?

This "correspondence theory" is minimalist in that it does nothing to spell out what the relation is between the proposition that p and the fact that p by virtue of which the fact makes the proposition true. In true minimalist spirit, it *displays* that relationship by the identity of content, by the fact that the same sentence is used to specify the content of both the proposition and the fact. Whatever the best story is on the details of the correspondence relation, we can know in advance that it will satisfy the constraints laid down by XVII. The right kind of correspondence will obtain if and only if the same declarative sentence can be used to specify the contents of proposition and fact. And though this is not all we would like to know about correspondence, it is enough to assure us that truth and correspondence are tightly connected.[30]

Lest it be thought that this minimalist correspondence has been purchased at the price of trivializing the concept of a fact—making facts mere shadows of propositions—let me hasten to point out that this is not so. Though XVII makes no commitments as to the nature or the ontological status of facts, it is quite compatible with taking facts to be genuine denizens of the extralinguistic, extraintentional world. And I do so regard them and think of my minimalist correspondence theory in those terms. But the role of XVII is only to place a crucial constraint on how the correspondence relation is to be construed. It has no precise implications for the ontological character of the relata.

But if we do take facts to be full-blooded constituents of reality, that will expose us to attack on another flank. Some philosophers regard facts as mere shadows of our practice of making statements—mere pseudo entities that have no standing independent of our linguistic activity. Hence the supposition that the statement that grass is green is made true by the fact that grass is green is not so much false as vacuous. It no more throws light on the nature of truth than saying "Dancing is good when you dance a good dance" brings out what makes a case of dancing good. A fact no more has resources of its own that are usable to confer truth on a statement than a "dance" has any status independent of the dancing that constitutes dancing that dance. Here are some remarks along this line from P. F. Strawson's contribution to his famous Aristotelian Society symposium on truth with J. L. Austin (Strawson 1950a).

---

30. Cf. the minimalist statement of correspondence in Wright 1992, 25, and in Horwich 1990, Chap. 7.

'Fact', like 'true', 'states' and 'statement' is wedded to 'that'-clauses; and there is nothing unholy about this union. Facts are known, stated, learnt, forgotten, overlooked, commented, communicated or noticed. (136)

[W]hat could fit more perfectly the fact that it is raining than the statement that it is raining? Of course, statements and facts fit. They were made for each other. If you prise the statements off the world you prise the facts off it too; but the world would be none the poorer. (137)[31]

In opposition to this position, it can be pointed out that it is a fact, for example, that the earth was previously much hotter; and this fact obtained long before any human beings busied themselves with making statements. How then, can facts be dependent on language? Strawson would, no doubt, reply that when we talk about the early condition of the earth in fact language, rather than just making a statement about the earth at that time, we are talking about these states of the earth (which themselves are, obviously, not dependent on our linguistic activities) in a way that reflects our present statemental ways of encoding this subject matter. I don't think that this is an adequate reply, but rather than get into an argument about that, I prefer to rest my case on a consideration that can scarcely be denied to be crucial. Strawson's position rests on the claim that there is an intimate *conceptual* dependence of fact talk on statement talk. We couldn't have the concept of a fact unless we had the concept of a statement or assertion or other fact-related linguistic activity or cognitive state. But it seems to me quite possible that there should be a language community that had developed the capacity to use 'fact that ____' (and 'proposition that ____') locutions, but had not yet attained the kind of reflective self-consciousness required for developing concepts of, and capacities to talk about, their own speech acts. They *engage* in speech acts, of course; but they have not yet developed higher level speech in which to speak of those speech acts. Until it is shown that this is not a human possibility (I won't insist

---

31. I omit mention of Strawson's repeatedly pointing out that facts are different in fundamental ways from things or happenings. ("Facts are not broken or overturned, interrupted or prolonged, kicked, destroyed, mended, or noisy" (136).) This is all clear enough but of doubtful relevance. Strawson takes it to be relevant because he thinks that "the whole charm of talking of situations, states of affairs or facts as included in , or parts of, the world, consists in thinking of them as things, and groups of things" (139). By contrast, as I go on to say in the text, I believe a convincing case can be made for taking facts to have an objective reality independent of our linguistic and cognitive activities, while resolutely eschewing the conflations and assimilations Strawson rightly deplores.

on a demonstration that it is not a logical possibility), I see no reason to suppose that facts are not objectively real, and as such capable of rendering true propositions true in a nontrivial sense. Their mode of reality is, no doubt, quite different from that of substances, states, properties of substances, and events, as Strawson and others have been at pains to point out. But that should not, and does not, prevent them from playing a truth-conferring role.[32]

xi Minimalist Realism and "Deflationary" Accounts of Truth

I am mostly concerned to relate my minimalism to "deflationary" accounts of truth, since it is widely believed that the latter constitute the only alternative to a far from minimal, "robust" theory of truth, such as we have in traditional correspondence, coherence, and pragmatist theories.[33] It is important for my project to insist that my minimalist realism is fundamentally different both from deflationary views and from classical theories that present an explicit ontology of truth.

First we have to decide how to use the term 'deflationary'. As the name implies, any view properly so called will be concerned to oppose various attempts to construct richer accounts of truth. It declares attempts to do so to be misguided, thus seeking to "deflate" them. Thus what counts as "deflationary" will vary with the "inflated" target to which it is directed. For present purposes I am particularly interested in the claim that it is mistake to suppose that there is a *property* of truth (falsity) that one attributes to propositions, statements, beliefs, and/or sentences. The view is not that people just never have occasion to make such attributions. It is rather that truth talk that appears on the surface to involve property attribution is properly understood in some different way. Deflationary accounts differ primarily in the alternative construals they offer.

My minimalism (along with the minimalism in Horwich (1990)) is firmly committed to there being a property of truth, and to apparent attributions of truth values being just what they seem. My formulations are designed to identify that property by way of identifying the concept by which we grasp it. As I brought out in discussing the relation of minimalism to the correspondence theory, minimalism does not answer all the questions one might be interested in asking about the property, but

---

32. For a penetrating recent account of facts, and their differences from other "entities", see Bennett 1988.

33. See, e.g., M. Williams 1986, 223; C. J. F. Williams 1976.

it does not foreclose attempts to answer them. It leaves room for answers like those proffered by one or another version of the correspondence theory.

I will now survey the most prominent forms of deflationism and indicate briefly in each case why I take the position to be inadequate. I will not undertake to provide detailed expositions and criticism of each form. As I pointed out, the main concern of the book is the opposition between realist and epistemic accounts of truth. But since this is an opposition over how to think of the property of truth, I must give some attention to accounts that deny the common presupposition of those rivals—that apparent attribution of truth values is just that. I must at least indicate why I find the denials of this presupposition to lack force. Moreover, deflationists rely heavily on the T-schema (or allied schemata like Tarski's), something that is central to my account as well. Hence it is important for me to show that my claim that generalizations of the T-schema, XIII and XIV, convey the realist conception of truth does not play into the hands of deflationists, rendering my view deflationary after all.

As just indicated, deflationists typically employ the T-schema to argue that since 'The proposition that p is true' is equivalent to 'p', in saying the former one is asserting only that p. Hence it is a mistake to suppose that the former involves the predication of a property of truth to a proposition or to anything else. The locus classicus for this contention is the dictum of F. P. Ramsey. " 'It is true that Caesar was murdered' means no more than that Caesar was murdered. . . ."[34] This has come to be called the "redundancy theory", since it holds that 'true' is redundant in that it makes no contribution to what is asserted. Ramsey, of course, realized that not all uses of 'true' involve an apparent attribution to a specified proposition; and he realized that other uses have to be explicated in other ways. (See Ramsey 1978, 45.) All the prominent deflationary accounts start from Ramsey's redundancy claim and provide different accounts of what we are doing with the term 'true' in apparent attributions of truth to propositions, etc., as well as seeking to deal with the whole range of uses of the term.

First let's look at what is often called the "speech act theory". This is an infelicitous way of referring to it. It is so called because it holds that what we are doing when we make an apparent attribution of truth to the proposition that p, other than asserting that p, is not to make some

---

34. Ramsey 1978, 44. The essay in question was written in 1927. In this discussion I will call equivalences of the form 'It is true that p iff p' "Ramsey equivalences".

further assertion but to perform some other kind of speech act, such as agreeing with a speaker that *p*, confirming the claim that *p*, or conceding the point that *p*. (The term 'speech act theory' is infelicitous here because assertion has just as much right to be called a "speech act" as these alternatives.) The standard exposition of this view is an essay of Strawson's, "Truth", published in *Analysis* in 1949 and republished in Macdonald (1954). In that essay Strawson roundly affirms that "The phrase 'is true' *never* has a statement-making role" (1954, 271). " 'That's true' makes no statement in its own right. It makes no meta-statement" (273). "The phrase 'is true' is not *applied* to sentences; for it is not *applied* to anything." And hence "Truth is not a property of symbols; for it is not a property" (262).

Strawson has since abandoned this theory,[35] and with good reason. There are three crucial objections. First, although utterances like 'That's true' do often have concessive force, and often express agreement, and so with the other uses Strawson mentions, there are many cases in which making an assertion about a proposition is the only thing in sight. For example, I am initially incredulous when it is claimed that Jim can jump 14 feet, but then when I see him do it, I am moved to say 'It really is true that he can jump 14 feet', thereby registering my realization that the proposition in question is true. Second, the view is powerless to deal with many other contexts in which 'true' is used, particularly its use in conditionals and in generalizations. "If it's true that he put arsenic in the soup, he must be the murderer." "A belief counts as knowledge only if it is true." What analogue of agreeing or conceding is involved in these cases? Third, and most fundamental, even if when the locution is used to concede a point or to express agreement, or do one of the other things mentioned by Strawson, this is by no means incompatible with its also being used to do what on the surface it seems to be used to do, namely, attribute the property of truth to a proposition. When I express my agreement with you by saying "What you've just said is very true", I do so *by* attributing truth to the proposition you asserted. At least, the fact that I was expressing agreement has no tendency to show that I wasn't asserting that the proposition is true. And so the "speech act theory" is useless as a device for deflation.

With Strawson's apostasy it is difficult to find an adherent of his 1949 account. The closest thing to it on the current scene is found in Price (1988), in which the author presents the view that apparent truth and falsity ascriptions have the function of rewarding (punishing) speakers

35. See Strawson 1964, 68.

for saying things we agree (disagree) with, thereby providing them "with an incentive to justify their utterances to others". Price arrives at this "explanatory" account of the function of truth talk after having argued for the impossibility of a satisfactory theory of the nature of truth.[36] The idea is that since such a theory is impossible, the reasonable approach to take to the topic is to explain why we find it useful to employ 'true' and 'false' as normative terms. But once again, even if truth-value ascriptions have the functions Price emphasizes (and I find this quite implausible), that is quite compatible with their being used to attribute properties to propositions and, indeed, could well be based on their use to make such attributions.

The other leading forms of deflationism do not stick as closely to Ramsey's redundancy suggestion. They recognize that 'true' is often used to make assertions that are not simply assertions of some proposition that has been called true. But they seek to construe those assertions in such a way that no property of truth is in the picture. They take it that the surface structure of these utterances is misleading, and that when their deep structure is revealed it turns out that the apparent property of truth has disappeared. I will discuss two versions of this kind of deflationism, in C. F. J. Williams (1976) and Grover (1992).[37]

Williams's book, strangely enough, deals only with sentences in which 'true' is predicated of a definite description like 'What Percy said', though it is readily apparent how his account would be applied to quantified statements generally. What is not clear is how he would handle apparent ascription of truth to a specified proposition—"The proposition that sugar is sweet is true". I will take him as buying the redundancy account for those cases, and seeking to supplement this with a treatment

36. His basis for this is what I take to be arbitrary requirements for a satisfactory theory of truth. See a brief discussion of these in section xii.

37. One approach that I will not treat in this rather sketchy discussion is "disquotationalism". The term stems from Quine's suggestion that the truth predicate is a "device for disquotation". The idea behind this characterization seems to be that in the Tarski formula, " 'Snow is white' is true if and only if snow is white", by applying the truth predicate to the quoted sentence, we are enabled to pass, via the equivalence, to the unquoted sentence. So far this sounds like the Ramseyan redundancy suggestion; the equivalence cancels out any assertive force of the predication of 'true'. But Quine, in fact, holds that truth attribution is required for certain kinds of generalization like principles of entailment. If you want to generalize over all cases like 'She is slim and she is wealthy; therefore she is wealthy', we have no alternative, short of substitutional quantification, to saying "Whenever something of the form 'p and q' is true, something of the correlated form 'p' is true". So it is not clear that this is really deflationism at all. (For an elaborate development of a kind of "disquotationalism" that claims to be deflationist, along with some acute criticism of the view, see David 1994.) My basic excuse for ignoring this approach is that it necessarily involves treating sentences as truth-value-bearers; otherwise there is nothing to "disquote". And I have already set this choice of truth bearers aside for purposes of this book.

of quantified statements. His treatment is rather complex, and I will give a simplified version. The initial analysis of 'What Percy said is true' is 'For some p, both Percy says that p and p'. At a later stage Russell's theory of definite descriptions is employed to guarantee uniqueness, and the analysis is complicated to 'There is some p such that, for all q, q is identical to p if and only if Percy says that q, and p'. Or more simply put, 'There is exactly one p such that Percy says that p, and p'. A universal generalization like 'A belief counts as knowledge only if it is true' comes out as 'For every p, if there is a q such that q believes that p, then q knows that p only if p'. (Clearly these formulations use substitutional quantification.) The point of all this is that there is not only no predicate in the analysans that can be substituted for 'true' in the analysandum; in addition, the analysans contains no predicate that can be applied to what 'true' is (apparently) applied to—statements, propositions, and the like. Thus these analyses, Williams claims, make it clear that 'is true' is not a predicate and truth is not a property of propositions or of anything else (1976, xii, 28, 84–85).

The "prosentential" account of truth developed by Grover, Camp, and Belnap,[38] takes a different and ingenious route to the same goal. The authors point out that there are expressions other than pronouns that have an anaphoric function, that is, substitute for a previous primary expression of the same syntactical form. There are *pro*verbs ('Mary ran quickly, so Bill *did* too'), *pro*adjectives ('To make men happy and to keep them *so*'), and even *pro*sentences ('I don't believe Rachel is sick, but if *so*, she should stay home'. (Grover 1992, 83–85) Their suggestion is that 'It's true' and 'That's true' can be treated as prosentences. Thus "It's true that gold is malleable" can be construed as "Gold is malleable. That's true".

Moreover, pronouns and other pro-forms can be used as variables for quantifications, as well as used to substitute for an "antecedent" (82–83). "If any car overheats, don't buy *it*." "Whatever Mary *did*, Bill *did*." And so with prosentences. 'Whatever John says is true' is construed as 'For each proposition, if John said that it is true, then it is true.' 'John's last assertion is true' becomes 'There is a proposition such that John asserted it last, and it is true'. (Again the quantification involved will have to be substitutional.)

It is crucial for the deflationary force of this account that prosen-

---

38. My references are to Grover 1992, a book that contains essays written and coauthored by Grover. The central essay, "A Prosentential Theory of Truth," by Grover, Camp and Belnap, *Philosophical Studies* 27 (1975) appears as Chap. 3 of the book.

tences be treated as semantically unanalyzed units. And since all occurrences of 'true' (as applied to propositions) are, in their analyzed form, in prosentences, and since 'true' there is a but a fragment of the prosentence that has no separate meaning (80), 'true' is not a genuine predicate (108ff.).

Thus we have different accounts that are taken by their protagonists to show that we can take all our sentences that apparently use 'true' as a predicate applied to propositions and as expressing a property of propositions, and analyze them (reveal their deep structure) so as to show that no such truth predicate is involved. Furthermore, in arguing this Williams, at least, relies heavily on the T-schema. It is the equivalence of 'It is true that p' and 'p' that enables him to do the rewriting of apparent truth ascriptions in which that ascription disappears. Just as that equivalence is supposed to enable us to replace 'It is true that gold is malleable' with 'Gold is malleable', so it permits us to replace 'what Percy said is true' with (in simplified form) 'If what Percy said is that p, then p'. The T-schema does not figure as obviously in the prosentential theory, but it is behind the scenes nonetheless. It is because of the equivalence of 'It is true that p' and 'p' that 'that is true' in 'If John said that p, then that is true' can be construed as a prosentence. That construal implies that 'that is true' in the last conditional functions as an anaphorically related substitute for the sentence John used to say what he said. And whatever plausibility that has rests on the principle that 'it is true that p' is necessarily equivalent to 'p'.

Thus if I am both to defend the assumption that what appear to be attributions of truth to propositions really have that status, and to show that a principle like XIII. is a formulation of a realist account of the concept of truth, rather than a deflationary account of the function of 'true', then I must indicate what is wrong with the way in which these deflationists exploit the T-schema.

A variety of questions can be raised about the claim of these theories to provide analyses for all the contexts in which 'true' occurs, but in line with my policy of eschewing detailed criticism of the positions, I will not go into that here.[39] I will restrict myself to two fundamental points. First, the deflationary force of these views depends on the analysans in each case having the same propositional content as the analysandum. If, for example, (1) 'For all p, if S asserts that p, then p' does not capture all the content of (2) 'Everything S asserts is true', then trotting out the

---

39. For a number of such criticisms see Kirkham 1992 and the articles cited there, and David 1994.

former will not suffice to show that we can *say what is said* by the latter without predicating 'true' of anything.[40] And in some cases, I contend, it is clear that the propositional content is not the same. This disability can be found at the basis of the whole enterprise in Ramsey's initial redundancy claim. (3) 'Caesar was murdered' clearly does not contain all the propositional content of (4) 'The proposition that Caesar was murdered is true', for the latter includes in its content the concept of a proposition, which it uses to set up a subject of predication; and the concept of truth is used in that predication. While (3) is about Caesar, (4) is about a proposition.[41] Moreover, it is clear to me that prosentential analyses do not capture the content of ordinary putative truth-value attributions. The idea that 'it is true' and 'That's true' are semantically unanalyzable prosentences, the constituents of which have no specifiable meanings, will come as a great shock to any ordinary speaker of a natural language in which expressions like that occur. I realize, of course, that naive speakers are often mistaken in their suppositions about the linguistic status and structure of various expressions in their languages. But the prosentential claim would seem to be concerned with a point on which it is highly implausible that the naive speaker could be so far wrong. Surely, fluency in a language carries with a knowledge of which components of complex expressions possess meanings that they contribute to the meaning of the whole. And even if a fluent speaker could be mistaken at certain points about this, how could millions of speakers be mistaken in supposing that 'true' and 'false' have meanings that they carry around from one context to another in which they occur? If this is right, the prosentential theory cannot be accepted as an account of the semantics of truth talk as that is ordinarily understood. At best, it is an interesting proposal as to how that talk might be replaced by something different.

One is led to assume an identity of content in these cases because of the analytic, conceptual equivalence that obtains. I have no objection to a claim for such equivalences. Indeed, such an equivalence is guaranteed for Ramsey cases by the conceptual necessity of XIII. It is easy to

40. In that case one could still *propose* that we restrict ourselves to sentences like (1) and abstain from using sentences like (2). But that would be a different ball game, and a different set of considerations would be required to support such a proposal.

41. Don't suppose that this is just a rerun of that old saw, the "paradox of analysis". That arises from the fact that an analysans explicitly spells out content that is not explicit in the analysandum. But here, it is the "analysandum" that contains the extra content. Furthermore, in cases that give rise to the paradox of analysis it seems clear that there is an identity of meaning. That is what is supposed to be paradoxical about the apparent differences between the two sides.

suppose that such equivalences are always equivalences of meaning or content. But such is not the case. There are innumerable conceptual equivalences that do not exhibit an identity of propositional content.

(5) The tie is red *iff* the tie exemplifies the property of redness.

(6) Columbus is north of Cincinnati *iff* the relation of *being* north of holds between Columbus and Cincinnati, in that order.

And to take a case that is closer to our central topic:

(7) An omniscient being would know that sugar is sweet *iff* sugar is sweet.

In both (5) and (6) it is clear that the right hand side involves conceptual material absent from the left-hand side. In (5) that includes the concepts of exemplification and of a property, while in (6) we have the concept of a relation and of a relation *holding* between relata. The lack of identity of content is particularly clear in (7). Surely 'sugar is sweet' is completely innocent of any involvement with the concept of an omniscient being! And in each case a speaker might understand one side of the equivalence while lacking some of the concepts employed by the other side—the concepts of exemplification, a property, an omniscient being, and so on. Similarly, with Ramsey equivalences. One might perfectly understand 'Caesar was murdered' and yet lack the concept of truth that is needed to understand (4). Thus analytic, conceptual equivalence is by no means a guarantee of identity of content.

If the above is right, the prosentential translations and the Ramsey translations cannot claim to be identical in content with the sentences they purport to translate. And hence those translations cannot support a claim that apparent truth-value attributions are not what they seem.

My second criticism runs as follows. I am not prepared to contest a claim of identity of content for all the translations undertaken in a deflationary spirit. In particular, I am prepared to recognize that the 'true'-free reformulations Williams gives of generalizations involving 'true' do capture the meaning of the latter. It seems intuitively right to me that when I say 'There is exactly one p such that Percy said that p, and p' what I say is the same, though differently put, as what I say when I utter 'What Percy said is true'. And, be that as it may, I want to consider whether, if and when the translations proffered by a deflationist do involve an identity of content, this has the intended deflationary force of showing that apparent truth attributions are nothing of the sort. For this purpose I

will even accept, for the sake of argument, that the prosentential translations attain identity of content, though I balk at the Ramsey equivalences. In any event, take such translations as do have this status, and
consider whether they show what deflationists claim they show—that the
originals do not, after all, amount to attributing a truth value to, for
example, propositions.

Well, why suppose that they do show that? The deflationist says they
do because they show that we can say what we were saying with a truth
predicate without using any such predicate, or any other predicate that
applies to what we were allegedly applying that truth predicate to. But
perhaps that only shows that there are different ways of saying the same
thing. Perhaps it doesn't show anything about *what* we are saying, what
that "same thing" is. Here there is a head-on confrontation between the
deflationist and the minimalist, Both Williams and I acknowledge that
(8) "What Percy said is true *iff* (9) There is exactly one p such that Percy
said that p, and p" is analytically, conceptually true. Moreover, we agree
that there is an identity of content between the left-hand (8) and right-
hand (9) sides of the equivalence. But Williams takes this to show that
on neither side are we really attributing truth to what Percy said, whereas
I take it show what attributing truth to a statement amounts to. How can
we tell who is in the right here? Why should we suppose that the right-
hand side is to be given priority when we try to characterize the content
they have in common? Equivalence is a symmetrical relation, so (9) is
just as much equivalent to (8) as (8) is to (9). Why shouldn't we say that
the equivalence shows that when we assert (9) we are really, contrary to
surface appearances, attributing the property of truth to a proposition,
rather than saying that the equivalence shows that when we assert (8)
we are really, contrary to appearances, doing something other than that,
something that is perspicuously represented by (9)? One who denies
that the synonymy tells against the "attribution of a truth property"
reading of (8) doesn't have to take the position that (9) does nothing
to illuminate the content of (8). On the contrary, my position is that it
brings out a way in which truth is a *realist* affair, having to do with things
being as they are stated to be. But it can make explicit certain features
of the common content without militating against supposing that this
content involves the attribution of a truth property to a statement.

There are, of course, various reasons for giving the deflationist reading of the situation.[42] Considerations of ontological economy dictate

42. Kirkham 1992, sec. 10.7, stresses the need for extra assumptions if a philosopher is to
draw deflationist conclusions from analyses of the sort we have been considering.

that if we can get along without committing ourselves to a property of truth we should do so. Disillusionment with traditional theories of truth motivate the disillusioned to eschew the object of such a theory. Suppositions that truth is somehow "mysterious", "obscure", "nonphysical", "non-naturalistic", or suffers from some equally disabling defect, plays a role. I can't get into all that here, though I will say that I find these considerations much less than compelling. My basic point, however, is that it is far from clear on the face of it that even if there is an identity of content in the equivalences we have been considering, we should give the situation a deflationist rather than a minimalist reading. In this connection we would do well to think about a similar issue with respect to "reductions" like the reduction of beliefs to various disposition, the issue as to whether the reduction should be taken as showing that there are no beliefs but only dispositions, or taken as showing what sort of thing a belief is. (This issue is touched on in chapter 2, section iv.) Absent compelling reasons to give the deflationist reading, I would contend that where there is an identity of content in the equivalences, it is just as reasonable to say that the equivalences show something about what kind of property truth is as to say that they show that there is no property of truth.

It will also illuminate the matter to contrast this situation with one in which there is much a stronger case for the nonexistence of a property. Consider the standard twentieth-century arguments against taking 'exist' to be a property. As in the truth case (on the synonymy assumption), we can translate 'Crows exist' into a formulation in which neither 'exist' nor any other grammatical predicate is asserted of crows: 'There is at least one X such that X is a crow'. So far the two cases are on a par. But in the existence case there are additional considerations that support a deflationist reading. Quite apart from this reformulation, 'Crows exist' lacks some of the paradigmatic features of subject-predicate statements. Most crucially, in an ordinary subject-predicate statement we presuppose that the subject exists and then go on to predicate something of it. But if we try to treat 'exists' as a predicate, we find that the existence of the subject of predication is something we are *already* committed to before we get around to the predication. A predicate of existence comes onto the scene too late, as we might say. This basic point is reflected in various ways 'exists' differs from undoubted predicates. It makes sense to say 'Some crows are not black' but not 'Some crows do not exist'.[43] There are important differences between 'All crows are

---

43. Of course, we can say that some crows do not *really* exist (fictional or mythical ones), but we can't deny existence totally of some crows.

black', 'Most crows are black', and 'Some crows are black', but if we substitute 'exist' for 'are black' in these sentences, the resulting sentences are either meaningless, or they all come to the same thing. There are no analogues for these points with respect to using 'true' as a predicate. For example, the statements 'All propositions are true', 'Most propositions are true' and 'Some propositions are true' are all different and are all perfectly in order. Thus the translations don't give us anything like the case for denying that there is a property of truth that the analogous translations give us for denying that existence is a property.

Before leaving the question of whether there really is a property of truth, I should mention that some thinkers, while not denying that truth is a property, deny that it is a property of a certain type: *substantial, theoretically important (interesting, explanatory)*, that it is a *natural kind*, or that it *possesses an underlying nature*. Horwich, for example, denies that that truth is "an ordinary sort of property—a characteristic whose underlying nature will account for its relations to other ingredients of reality. Therefore, unlike most other ·predicates, 'is true' should not be expected to participate in some deep theory of that to which it refers—a theory that goes beyond a specification of what the word means" (1990, 2). As his discussion indicates, Horwich is here contrasting 'true' with theoretical terms in science. And there certainly are differences. But I fail to see that this prevents us from developing a "deep theory" (how deep remains to be seen) of *what truth is*, a theory that goes beyond saying what the word 'true' means. As I have pointed out, the project of developing a correspondence theory of the nature of truth, a project that goes beyond the minimalist account of the meaning of 'true', is a reasonable project to undertake, though I do not undertake it in this book.[44] Again, it seems clear to me that truth enters into various explanations. (Here Horwich is on my side.) When I am successful in reaching a goal, part of the explanation is often that my efforts were guided by true rather than by false beliefs. Thus, though I agree that truth differs markedly from theoretically important concepts in science, that merely contributes to showing what kind of property it is, and this difference in no way prevents the property of truth from enjoying other sorts of importance, some of which will be detailed in Chapter 8.

---

44. Moreover, Horwich is clearly misguided in supposing that it is only theoretically important properties or natural kinds that deserve the title of "ordinary". We attribute countless properties that are not "characteristics whose underlying nature accounts for their relations to other ingredients of reality". There are the properties of congeniality, high fat content, being a table or a chair, being a sophomore, being unchurched, etc., etc. We would search in vain for an "underlying nature" for these and innumerable other familiar properties, nor do they have any significant theoretical or explanatory importance.

xii Objections to the Minimal-Realist Account of Truth

My claims for the account of truth presented above will undoubtedly elicit various objections. In this section I will respond to the most important of those I have encountered, whether from others or from my own reflections.

(1) As a confidence builder, I begin with an objection that can be easily answered. One might feel that the account is completely trivial and unilluminating. This reaction takes different forms for different formulations. I have already responded in section x to such an objection to my minimalist-correspondence account—the objection that facts are but "shadows" of statements. A triviality reaction to I–VI might run as follows. "In explaining 'is true' in terms of 'is the case that' we have not moved beyond alternative locutions for the same thing, or near enough the same thing. There is no important difference between saying 'It is true that lemons are sour' and 'It is the case that lemons are sour'. The display of such verbal equivalents provides no real advance in understanding."

But 'is true' and 'is the case that' are importantly different. 'Is true' applies to the likes of propositions, statements, and beliefs, items on the *thought* side of the thought–world relationship, whereas 'is the case that' belongs to the other side. A proposition is *true* when it is related in the right kind of way (identity of content) to something that *is the case*. A state of affairs' being the case is the worldly realization that renders the proposition *true*. What is the case is the *truth maker*. What is true is the *truth bearer*. And this is precisely the the realist conception of truth. To bring this out *is* to bring out the content of that concept.

As for the T-schema and its progeny, a charge of triviality might runs as follows. "In saying that the proposition that sugar is sweet is true *iff* sugar is sweet, aren't we, in effect, saying that what is asserted by asserting that sugar is sweet constitutes a necessary and sufficient condition for the truth of the proposition? But that condition just amounts to the *truth* of the assertion that sugar is sweet. And that, in turn just amounts to the truth of the proposition asserted, namely, the proposition that sugar is sweet. And so in the end, the T-statement just comes down to saying that the proposition that sugar is sweet is true if and only if the proposition that sugar is sweet is true. And that is a miserable tautology."

I don't think we should be worried by this. The crucial point is that the T-statement doesn't explicitly present the truth of the proposition that *p* as equivalent to the truth of the proposition that *p*. The above account shows that we can provide a chain of entailments from the condition that *is* given to what it is a condition of. But that just shows that the condition works, that it is (necessarily) equivalent to what it is a condition for. And that is what the account is supposed to do.

(2) I have maintained that the T-schema suffices to uniquely locate the concept of propositional truth. If we realize that it is conceptually true that for any *p*, the proposition that *p* is true if and only if *p*, we thereby have grasped the realist conception of propositional truth. But that assumes that 'true' is the only predicate that makes propositions of the form 'The proposition that *p* is ＿＿ *iff p*' analytically true. And this is not the case. 'Is known by God' is another.[45] Or, in order to avoid problems about the reference of 'God', and to sidestep doubts about whether 'The proposition that *p* is known by God *iff p*' is *analytically*, *conceptually* true even if necessarily true in some way, let's change the example to 'would be known by an omniscient being'. Surely the proposition 'The proposition that *p* would be known by an omniscient being *iff p*' has as much claim to being analytically true as 'The proposition that *p* is true *iff p*'. Hence the T-schema does not uniquely pick out the concept of truth.

One response to this would be to moderate the claim against which the objection is directed. The objection does show that 'true' is not the only predicate that fits into the slot 'The proposition that *p* is ＿＿ *iff p*' in such a way as to make the statement conceptually true. But it does not show that the T-schema fails to provide a recipe for constructing a (necessarily) necessary and sufficient condition for the truth of any proposition. Even if that schema can do a similar job for other predicates, that doesn't nullify the fact that it works for 'true'. However, to be warranted in claiming that XIII is one way of presenting the realist conception of truth, I need more than this. I need to claim that one who has no prior understanding of 'true' at all could, in accepting the conceptual truth of XIII, come into possession of the realist conception of truth, just by seeing how it fits into that context. But that is possible (or guaranteed) only if the concept of truth is the only one that is identified by this schema. And the above counterexample seems to disprove that claim.

What I need to find, then, is some further feature that is unique to the way in which 'true' functions in this context, or that is distinctive of the relation of the schema to the realist conception of truth when it is 'true' that fills the slot in question. In thinking about this, we should be struck by the fact that in the omniscience case, there is additional

---

45. I am indebted to José Benardete for calling this difficulty to my attention.

conceptual content that could not possibly be acquired just by recognizing the analytic truth of the omniscience analogue to XIII. Imagine someone with no prior understanding of 'would be known by an omniscient being' being confronted with 'For any *p*, the proposition that *p* would be known by an omniscient being *iff p*'. Suppose this person understands all the rest of the sentence and takes my word for it that the statement is conceptually true, understanding what that amounts to. Would she thereby come into possession of the concept, *would be known by an omniscient being*? Not except by a miracle. The specific content of 'known' and 'omniscient' could not possibly be imparted by this means. To grasp the concept of knowledge one has to understand many things—what it is to be a cognitive subject, a potential knower; what is the difference between knowledge and (mere) belief; how knowledge is restricted to what is true or what is the case; and so on. This content goes far beyond what is constituted by the term in question fitting into this particular context so as to make the whole conceptually true. Hence just seeing that the term does that is radically insufficient to convey that content. It seems plausible, however, that the concept of propositional truth can be conveyed in this way. That is not to say that the T-schema or XIII is a *definition* of 'true'. I have already made it sufficiently clear that it is not. Formulations I–VI. bring out aspects of the meaning of 'true' that are not made explicit in the T-schema. Nevertheless, as I have argued, these aspects are latent in that schema, in such a way that the concept can be conveyed by pointing out the conceptual truth of any T-statement; whereas the concept of knowledge, and much more the more complex concept expressed by 'would be known by an omniscient being', cannot be so conveyed. Hence even though 'true' is not the only predicate that, when inserted into the slot in 'For any *p*, p is _____ *iff p*', renders the whole statement conceptually true, it *is* the only predicate such that, when one appreciates that the statement generated by that insertion is conceptually true, one is thereby in possession of the concept expressed by that predicate. And that is the claim that is of central importance to me.

Though I believe that the considerations just proffered suffice to defuse the objection, there is another aspect to the matter that deserves notice. We can also discern the following difference between the ways the two predicates function in the schema. We can explain why 'would be known by an omniscient being' turns the schema into a conceptually true statement. It is because the concept of omniscience is such that an omniscient being would know all *true propositions*. Thus the feature this predicate shares with 'true' has a complex explanation that turns on the relation of concepts expressed by this predicate with other concepts, particularly the concept of a *true* proposition. Whereas there is no such explanation in other terms of the fact that 'For any *p*, the proposition that *p* is true *iff p*'. Here we can only say "That's just the way truth is; that's what it *is* for a proposition to be true."[46] Indeed, the explanation for the functioning of 'would be known by an omniscient being' crucially involved the concept of propositional truth! What I take all this to indicate is that 'true' is the only predicate that functions *fundamentally* in this way in the schema, and that any other concept that functions in this way does so because it bears a certain kind of relation to the concept of truth.

(3) Here is a difficulty with the T-schema and its offspring in particular. Consider an "emotivist" theory of evaluative discourse, according to which evaluative utterances are not to be construed as assertions that are intended to correspond to objective facts, but rather as *expressions* of the speaker's attitudes or emotions.[47] An emotivist is not prepared to "seriously" assess such utterances for truth value. But wouldn't XIII legitimate the application of the realist concept of truth to them? Isn't 'The proposition that stealing is wrong is true *iff* stealing is wrong' just as respectable (and just as necessarily true) a T-statement as 'The proposition that sugar is sweet is true *iff* sugar is sweet'? So it looks as if this version of the realist account of truth makes it impossible for the emotivist to say what he wants to say—that ethical utterances do not express propositions with truth values. The same point holds for other views according to which one or another kind of declarative sentence cannot be used to make true-or-false statements—counterfactual conditionals, probability assignments, and "performative" utterances like "I promise to pay you 5 percent interest".

One emotivist response to this problem is an "If you can't lick 'em, join 'em" move. Why can't the emotivist avail himself of the equivalence schema, while continuing to hold the position he takes on the status of evaluative discourse? Suppose he were to say, as I have heard Charles Stevenson say, "I don't object to speaking of ethical utterances (statements) as having a truth value. That is just to say that it is true that stealing is wrong if and only if stealing is wrong. And there can be no

46. Of course, one can say: "It is because a true proposition is one concerning what is the case", or "because a true proposition is one that corresponds to a fact". But that is just to display the connection between 'true', 'the case', and 'fact', to revolve in a small circle. Whereas the other explanation got us out of the circle of close equivalents to 'know' and made contact with, e.g., 'true proposition'.

47. The locus classicus for this view is Stevenson 1944.

objection to saying that." But to let our emotivist into the club in this way has the effect that the minimalist theory becomes indistinguishable from a "redundancy" theory, according to which 'It is true that p' has no "assertive", "cognitive", or "propositional" content over and above that of 'p'. Insofar as there is a point in using the truth attribution, it is for emphasis, lending one's authority to the statement that p, or doing something else that does not constitute asserting a proposition other than p. But this is to subvert the realist position, which, as I pointed out in section xi, is firmly committed to truth as a genuine property of propositions, statements, and beliefs. Hence I will not avail myself of this "permissive" option.

If we are to prevent the T-schema and the realist conception of truth it identifies from being hospitable to items that are not candidates for realist truth, we must place some restrictions on what can replace 'p' in that schema. But before looking at candidates for a principle of restriction I need to define the problem better. We don't want a principle that would exclude all evaluative sentences. That would freeze out the moral realist (objectivist) just as surely as the lack of restrictions prevents the emotivist from formulating his position. What we need is a principle that would prevent a person from forming T-statements with a declarative sentence that person doesn't take to be usable to specify a subject of realist truth value.

So what principle will do this job? The most obvious suggestion is to use the formulation just proffered. *A person, P, is not entitled to use sentence S as a substitute for 'p' in a T-sentence if P does not regard S as usable to formulate the subject of an attribution of realist truth value.* But the trouble with this is that it makes use of the notion of realist truth, thereby raising the spectre of circularity. Of course, the points made earlier about the charge of circularity leveled at the use of substitutional quantification apply here as well. XIII is not put forward as a definition. Moreover, the restriction on permissible substitution is no part of what is explicitly stated in XIII. And the present account makes no pretension of being a *reductive* account of truth. An explication of the concept by relating it to other concepts would satisfy the aims of the endeavor. Nevertheless, and with all that noted, the account would be more illuminating if we could avoid utilizing the realist concept of truth in formulating our restriction, especially avoid utilizing it so centrally and so early. How else might we do the job?

Since XIII deals with *propositions*, a natural suggestion is that the permissible substitutions are those that express propositions. And that is obviously a necessary condition. But there are various problems with the suggestion that it is sufficient. There are different ways of expressing propositions. Clearly, 'Lemons are sour' expresses a proposition in such a way as to be a suitable substitution for *p*. But it is often said that interrogative, imperative, and optative sentences express propositions as well. 'Is it raining?' expresses the proposition that it is raining, though in a different way from 'It is raining'. 'Please close the door' expresses the proposition that the door is closed, though in a different way from 'The door is closed'. To be sure, interrogative and imperative sentences are regularly excluded on syntactical grounds. It is always taken for granted, but rarely mentioned, that only declarative sentences may be used. No one, to my knowledge, has objected to the minimalist theory that it would imply that questions and orders have truth values, since we may as well instantiate the schema by saying 'The proposition that *is it raining?* is true *iff* is it raining?', or 'The proposition that *leave the room!* is true *iff* leave the room!'. But limiting substitutions to declarative sentences is not our present problem anyway. We are concerned to make discriminations within that class. We are concerned to lay down conditions under which it is permissible for a person to substitute a certain declarative sentence for '*p*'.

Getting back to the "express a proposition" requirement, it may be that an emotivist, or anyone else who takes a certain declarative sentence not to be usable to formulate a subject of realist truth value, would likewise not be prepared to regard that sentence as expressing a proposition. But even if we could secure an extensional equivalence here, it would leave the situation shrouded in mystery. Just what is it to "express a proposition" in a way that it is reasonable to require as a condition for a permissible substitute? And how does that differ from other ways of expressing a proposition?

At this point we might do well to remember that realist truth value is ascribed to statements and beliefs as well as to propositions, that is, to propositions as stated and as believed, as well as to propositions in isolation. Perhaps that holds a clue to the mystery. Emotivists typically hold that evaluative utterances are not (full-blooded) statements, not "statements of fact", not claims as to what objective facts obtain, not claims as to "what is the case" objectively. This last locution is reminiscent of my initial formulation of the realist conception of truth in terms of "what is said to be the case actually being the case". Perhaps the key to the substitutivity requirement lies here. Might it not be that what should inhibit the emotivist from inserting 'killing is wrong' in the T-schema is that she does not regard that sentence as usable to make a statement of fact, a claim as to "what is the case". So the restriction is to sentences that have (are taken to have) a statement-making potential.

Again a threat of circularity looms on the horizon. If the only way of distinguishing statements (assertions) from other illocutionary acts is in terms of their susceptibility to realist truth and falsity, that notion has entered into the explanation, albeit not so quickly as the last time. But the panoply of terms just exhibited in characterizing "genuine" statements shows that we need not rely on the terms 'true' and 'false'. No doubt these other terms are closely related to 'true' and 'false'. The conviction that 'is the case' is closely related is what lies behind my initial formulations. And the close connection of 'is a fact' lies behind my minimalist correspondence formulation (XVII). But if we were to forbid the use of terms that are themselves usable to define 'true', we would truly be hamstrung. So let us think of a statement as an illocutionary act that is most basically assessed in terms of whether what it says to be the case is the case, or in terms of whether there is a fact to which it corresponds. Alternatively, we could put this in terms of what the issuer of a statement that p thereby commits herself to—that it is the case that p or that it is a fact that p. With this background we can say that P is entitled to form a T-statement by substituting S for 'p' in the T-schema provided P regards S as usable to make a statement.

Since we have put this restriction in terms of what a person takes to be the case, there is always the possibility that the person is mistaken. The emotivist may be mistaken in supposing that evaluative sentences can't be used to make genuine statements of fact, and the objectivist may be mistaken in supposing that they can. If there is such a mistake, some T-statements will be ill-formed, or some chances to form T-statements will have been missed, but the person will have proceeded correctly according to his lights. Of course, we can formulate an objective restriction as well. "S is a permissible substitute for 'p' in the T-schema provided it *is* usable to make a genuine statement." We got off on the more subjective foot because our approach to this problem was by way of whether the reliance on the T-schema left room for the emotivist's convictions. But we could have focused on the more objective principle of substitutivity, and then portrayed the emotivist as believing that the principle does not allow the substitution of evaluative sentences.

Finally, turning to the other kind of bearer of realist truth values, we could distinguish statements from other illocutionary acts by the fact that they express *beliefs* rather than other propositional attitudes. Again, if we wanted to avoid bringing truth into the account, we would assume, or show, that the concept of belief can be explicated in other terms, for example, in terms of the functional role beliefs play in the psychic economy. In so doing, we would not have to deny that beliefs are assessable as true or false. We would only maintain that it is not necessary to say this in explaining what distinguishes beliefs from other kinds of psychological states. And we could appeal to belief more directly by thinking of sentences as expressing beliefs and allowing those sentences to substitute for 'p' that do so.[48]

(4) There is another complaint about a minimalist account like mine that might be considered a *triviality* charge, but of a different sort from those considered under (1).[49] This objection consists of the allegation that the account is not a *substantial* theory of truth. This term, and allied terms like 'serious', 'philosophically (theoretically) interesting (important)', is used somewhat differently by different writers. But the suggestion is always that a minimalist account fails to do a job or to have implications or uses with which the. writer is particularly concerned. Since the jobs emphasized are often *explanatory*, the charge tends to be that the minimalist theory does not suffice to explain one thing or another. Among the explananda that are most often said to be neglected by the minimalist theory are *linguistic meaning* and *assertion* or *fact-stating discourse*. A *substantial* theory of truth would provide the basis for a theory of linguistic meaning and/or provide the basis for bringing out what is distinctive about assertion among the total range of illocutionary acts. An account of truth that fails to throw sufficient light on the particular philosopher's favorite explanandum is deemed not to be "substantial" or "philosophically interesting", not what a theory of truth should be.[50]

The need to undergird a theory of meaning, along with related matters such as (radical) translation and linguistic understanding, is stressed, for example, by Davidson (1984 and 1990), by Dummett

48. Price 1988 is an extended discussion of how to distinguish genuine statements of fact from expressions of attitude, and beliefs from attitudes, in connection with the problem of understanding truth. Though I have no sympathy at all with Price's deflationary approach to truth, it is a great merit of his argument to emphasize the importance of these questions for an understanding of truth.

49. I did not introduce it at that earlier stage because in one prominent version (that of Price) it is closely connected with the demarcation problem of how to distinguish suitable from unsuitable substitutes for 'p' in the T-schema, the problem just discussed.

50. Although I present these claims as a call to develop a substantial theory of truth and, as a spin off from this, a negative evaluation of accounts that are not directed to this end, at least one of the authors I cite in this section, Huw Price, is concerned rather to show no such theory is possible. He uses this conclusion as a way of rejecting what he calls "analytic" theories of truth, attempts to say "what truth is". But he shares with those who endorse the attempt to develop such a theory the conviction that an attempt to say what truth is lives up to its billing only if it is a "substantial" theory. The negative assessment of nonsubstantial theories is what is common to all these thinkers.

(1973) and by Wiggins (1980). Wiggins enumerates a number of marks of truth, marks it must have if it is to furnish the basis for a theory of meaning of the Davidsonian sort that incorporates a theory of radical interpretation of a language; and he insists that a "substantial" theory of truth develop a conception of truth that will embody those marks. A concern with distinguishing assertion from nonassertive uses of language is pre-eminent in Price (1988), as I pointed out earlier. With respect to this aim he lays down certain desiderata for a *substantial* theory of truth. He points out that the account of truth cannot be in terms of the notion of assertion or of anything else *it* is designed to explicate, which for Price includes bringing out what distinguishes *beliefs* from other propositional attitudes (23–25). Nor can the theory just assume that, for example, only indicative sentences can replace 'p' in the T-schema, for that is one thing on which the theory of truth should throw light. For this last reason accounts like the versions of mine that are based on the T-schema are not "substantial".[51]

It would be a long and tortuous affair to determine whether my account of truth can make an important contribution to theories of the sorts these writers stress, and my primary concerns here are such as to leave me insufficient space for that enterprise. I am convinced that my minimalist account of truth explains various facts about truth, for example, the fact that it is important for the guidance of behavior that we have true rather false beliefs. For since it is obviously important that where our success in a certain enterprise depends on whether it is the case that p, that enterprise will be more likely to succeed if we believe that p only if p. And, on my account, that will be the case if and only if the belief is true.[52] But I need not establish an explanatory role for my account to make the point I am chiefly concerned to make here, namely, that it is arbitrary to evaluate accounts of truth on the basis of whether they make important contributions to the explanation of, explication of, or theory of one or another phenomenon in which the philosopher in question happens to be particularly interested. The most basic aim of a philosophical account of truth is to explain what we are saying when we attribute truth to one or another truth bearer, and, more generally, how we are to understand discourse containing the term 'true'; that is, we want to spell out the concept(s) expressed by the

51. See similar allegations in Davidson 1990; Putnam 1978; Wiggins 1980, 190; and B. Williams 1973, 202–3.

52. Horwich 1990, an account of truth which is more minimal than mine, provides a spirited defense of the claim that the view of truth presented there can explain a variety of things that people often try to use a theory of truth to explain. See chap. 3.

term. If, in the course of so doing, we elaborate material that is useful for a theory of meaning, or the assertive use of language, or whatever, so much the better. But it is misguided to make any such explanatory usefulness a basic requirement for the interest, importance, seriousness, or "substantiality" of an account of truth. And since there are a number of different explanatory projects in the course of which truth has been appealed to, to pick out one or two of these as *the* basic requirement for the interest or adequacy of a theory of truth tells us more about the interests of the writer in question than about truth.[53] If my account of truth is not "substantial" as judged by such criteria, this leaves me wholly untroubled.

(5) The next item on the agenda is not so much an objection as a problem. So far all my formulations have concerned truth. How is falsity to be handled? The simplest way is to take it to be the contradictory of truth. Any truth-value bearer is false if and only if it is not true. This would be a commitment to bivalence for propositions, but I am not prepared to accept that. In Chapter 4 I will consider, and criticize, Dummett's verificationist reasons for rejecting bivalence. But there are other reasons available. I will concentrate here on reference failures that have been taken, notably by Strawson,[54] to generate propositions that are neither true nor false.

As a change of pace from the present king of France, let's consider my youngest sister. (I have no siblings at all.) Suppose that in a deranged state I am convinced that I had several sisters all of whom died before reaching maturity. While in that state I say to a friend, "My youngest sister had great musical talent". Clearly I haven't said something true, but have I thereby said something false? This question was the occasion of a notable debate between Russell and Strawson. According to Russell's theory of descriptions, the sentence I used is to be construed as equivalent to "There exists exactly one person who is my sister and younger than any other sister I have; and whoever satisfies that description had great musical talent."[55] This statement is obviously false, since the initial existentially quantified conjunct is false. But Strawson maintained that this analysis is incorrect. Whereas the Russellian analysis represents me as *asserting* that there exists a person who is my youngest sister, that is *presupposed* rather than asserted. I operate on a background

53. In Chapter 4, section iii, I point out the parochial character of Dummett's claim that "philosophical theories of truth have usually been intended as contributions to delineating the outlines of some theory of meaning . . ."

54. See Strawson 1950b.

55. Russell 1919, chap. 16.

assumption that I have a sister younger than any other sister of mine, and on that basis I go on to assert something of the person in question. The existential presupposition is false, but my statement is neither true or false. In order for it to be false there would have to exist someone to whom I attributed musical talent. And since there isn't, my statement does not get so far as to be false. There must be a subject for a singular subject-predicate statement to be about in order that it possess a truth value.

I have no intention here of deciding between Russell and Strawson. My own view is that Strawson has the better of the argument, but that is not my present concern. My only point is that if, here or elsewhere, there are propositions that lack truth value, the present account can accommodate them. This will require a more complicated account of falsity than merely taking it to consist in the failure of a sufficient condition for truth. The account will need to spell out separately the conditions under which a proposition is false. And it would also be useful to make some general remarks concerning situations in which neither conditions of truth nor conditions for falsity obtain. But I will not enter onto that project in this book.

(6) One category of live candidates for a neither-true-nor-false status is worth separate consideration, namely, propositions formulated by the use of vague terms. It may be thought that all my formulations of a realist conception of truth run into trouble over the fact that our language is pervasively infected with vagueness. How can it be a determinate objective matter whether the statement that Ithaca, N.Y., is a *city* (in the ordinary, nontechnical sense of 'city') is true, given that 'city' suffers from degree vagueness? Its meaning doesn't "lay down" any precise number of inhabitants that a community must have in order to count as a "city", rather than as a "town" or a "village". (For that matter, 'inhabitant' is interestingly vague also. Is a person who owns a house in Albany that he occupies, on the average, four months of the year an inhabitant or not?) It is determinate that, for example, Paris is a city and that a tiny English village like Lower Slaughter is not; but there are many cases in between for which there is no objectively correct answer to the question. For those cases there is no fact of the matter as to whether or not the community is a city. And so XIII and our other formulations fail to provide determinate truth conditions for all statements of the form 'X is a city'. And so for many terms in our language, including those that exhibit other forms of vagueness, not just degree vagueness.[56]

---

56. Consider, for example, terms like 'religion' that exhibit what I call "combination of con-

Does this problem affect attributions of truth value to propositions and beliefs as well? It must, since, as we have seen, when a truth value is attributed to a statement it is attributed to *what is stated*, and that is a proposition. Thus if a statement is neither true nor false because of vagueness, it is the proposition that is stated that suffers this disability. And the same disability will attach to the proposition when it is what is believed, when someone believes, for example, that Ithaca is a city. On many accounts of propositions they cannot be indeterminate; any indeterminacy attaches to our attempts to linguistically express them. But on my way of getting at the concept of a proposition, a proposition is the sort of thing that provides the content of a statement or a belief, and so if statements or beliefs can be indeterminate, it follows that propositions can as well.

At one time I thought that this was a serious difficulty for a realist conception of truth. I was even tempted to take the position that such a conception applies only to idealized, perfectly precise languages, and that with respect to (at least many) statements, made by our far from completely precise natural languages, the best we can do is to suppose the realist conception to apply *approximately*. But after some illuminating conversation with Jonathan Bennett I see that this was a mistake. The only way in which the vagueness of language affects the situation is by preventing us from formulating a *precise* set of conditions for the truth of many statements and propositions. If, to go back to the minimalist version, what is necessary and sufficient for the truth of a proposition of the form *X is bald* is that *X is bald*, then, since there is sometimes no objectively determinate answer as to whether X is bald, we have failed to provide a condition of truth that will always settle the question of whether a proposition or statement is true. But that just means that we can no more always talk (think) about truth with absolute precision, than we can about cities, baldness, religion, and countless other matters. And just as the vagueness of 'city' does not prevent us from engaging in much useful thought and talk about cities, so it is with truth. To think or talk with less with perfect precision is not to think and talk with no intelligible content. To give less than perfectly precise conditions for X's being P is not to say nothing useful (and even true) about what it takes for X to be P. Why should this situation be more fatal when 'P' is 'true' than when it is 'city' or 'religion'? Indeed, the vagueness that infects our

---

ditions" vagueness. Just what combination of typical features of religion is both necessary and sufficient for a form of social organization to be a religion? Again, there seems to be no determinate answer to this question. See my article, "Religion", in *The Encyclopedia of Philosophy*, ed. P. Edwards 1967.

talk of truth is wholly traceable to the vagueness of the terms we use to pick out the truth bearer and the conditions of its truth. V and XIII fail to yield a completely precise condition for the truth of the proposition that Ithaca is a city *just because* of the fact that we fail, for the same reason, to pick out a perfectly precise proposition by the phrase 'the proposition that Ithaca is a city'. The vagueness of the truth condition exactly matches the vagueness of the the truth bearer. We have the strongest guarantee of such a match, since we use the same linguistic resources to do both jobs. Thus, even though we are unable to speak and think about truth with perfect precision, we are not thereby prevented from saying useful and true things about it.[57]

It is also worth mentioning that insofar as vagueness does present a problem for the realist conception of truth, it is not a problem that attaches specifically or uniquely to that conception. Since the problem, if any, stems from pervasive features of the languages we use to say anything about anything, it will affect all our talk about truth, whatever views we have on the subject.[58]

57. I certainly don't mean to deny that there are important problems concerning vagueness, problems concerning its implications for logic, for the formulation of criteria of the application of terms, and so on. Here I am only concerned with the question whether the phenomenon of vagueness makes special problems for a realist conception of truth.

58. In conversation Bernard Katz has urged the thesis that a "true realist" would not allow that a proposition lacks determinate truth value and determinate truth conditions. He thinks the proper realist position is to make a distinction between a proposition and our cognitive grasp thereof. The latter can be indeterminate, but not the former. No doubt, this is a realist position, more realist, perhaps, than my own. But my concern is not to be as realist as possible, but to delineate things as they are, in so far as in me lies. And, as I see it, truth-value bearers do suffer, more or less, from vagueness, and this affects the extent to which they can be determinately true or false.

CHAPTER 2

Alethic Realism and Metaphysical Realism

i Metaphysical Antirealism: Flat Denials

I now turn to a survey of various forms of what we may properly call "metaphysical realism" and to a consideration of the relations of these forms to each other and to alethic realism.

As a perfunctory gesture at penitence for my use of the term 'alethic realism', let me repeat that 'realism' is most felicitously used for views that items of certain kinds are "real", "really exist", "have an independent status in reality", and the like. Such views differ both as to what kinds they have to do with and as to what being "real" or "really existing" is thought to be. As for the former, the field is wide open. One can be a realist or not about physical objects, events, universals, facts, propositions, intentional psychological states, space, time, meaning, God, and so on. As for the latter, I believe we can best bring out what it is to be realist about Xs by considering what that excludes, by considering what would be involved in being nonrealist about them. It will be convenient to begin with a distinction, among ways of rejecting realism about Xs, between (1) a flat *denial* that Xs exist and (2) a *reduction* of Xs to Ys. We shall see that the line between these two is not always clear, and we shall also see various complications on both sides of the realism–nonrealism divide.

To begin with what is apparently the simpler case, we find many philosophers forthrightly denying the existence of propositions, meanings, theoretical entities, moral properties, or God. There are no such things. The category is empty. In other times there were such bold thinkers as Parmenides, Zeno, and Bradley who denied the existence of multiplicity, motion, time, and relations. Surely, if someone is committed to the proposition that there are no such things as Xs, that counts as being nonrealist about Xs in the strongest possible way.

But though it may seem perfectly clear what it is to deny the existence of Xs, that appearance can be deceiving. Sometimes the denial is not clear just because it is not clear what it is to assert the real existence of the entity. Consider disputes over the existence of "abstract entities" like properties, propositions, and facts. When someone takes an antirealist position here, just what is he denying? If I deny that "there are any such things" as properties or facts, am I denying that, for example, it is a *fact* that Paris is the capital of France or that science has developed many ways of measuring physical *properties?* If so, I am in a peck of trouble. Antirealists about properties or facts try a variety of moves to get out of this uncomfortable situation.

(1) "We aren't denying commonsense or, more broadly, nonphilosophical statements that seem to be about properties or facts. We are only opposing *metaphysical* commitments to the ULTIMATE REALITY of such entities. We are denying that they belong to the 'ultimate furniture of the universe'." But this doesn't help much unless something is done to explain the difference between recognizing such facts as the fact that Paris is the capital of France, and the commitment to facts as something "ultimate", something "out there" in a metaphysical sense. There are, to be sure, distinctions between more and less basic entities. If mental facts, properties, states, and processes are wholly determined by physical facts, events . . ., then there is a real sense in which the mental is less basic in the scheme of things than the physical. But to hold that mental phenomena are not part of the "ultimate furniture of the universe" in this sense could not possibly be construed as denying their existence. This understanding of ultimacy does not help to pin down what a person is denying when he denies the existence of facts.

(2) A more promising approach is that taken by Quine. We make the linguistic turn, and instead of trying to clarify in ontological terms what it is to regard Xs as "metaphysically real", we make the distinction in terms of the place reference to Xs has in our discourse. It becomes a question of what we are ineliminably committed to by what we say. If putative references to facts or to properties cannot be replaced by something that does not make such references, then we are "ontologically committed" to facts or properties. On the other hand, if we can say everything we wish to say without any such apparent references, we are not ontologically committed to them. For example, I might replace 'It is a fact that Paris is the capital of France' with 'Paris is the capital of France' and be satisfied with the latter as formulating everything I was

concerned to assert with the former. Or, in Quine's quantificational version of this, I am ontologically committed to facts if and only if the truth of all the assertions I am prepared to make requires that facts be among the values of my variables. I am ontologically committed to facts if and only if the variables of my quantified statements have to include facts in the domain over which they range in order that those statements all be true. In Quine's famous slogan, "to be is to be the value of a variable".

This approach does seem to substitute a clear issue for a muddy one.[1] But the question remains as to whether being ontologically committed to Xs *in this sense* captures what people were after in disputes over whether Xs really exist. Suppose I acknowledge that I could say everything I want to say without referring to facts, but still insist that I take facts to be real when I say things like "The facts of the matter tell against your hypothesis", take them to be real in any way in which people do take facts to be real. In that case the locus of the problem will have shifted to the question whether Quine's criterion of ontological commitment succeeds in capturing what it is to be committed to the thesis that entities of a certain type really exist.[2]

It is far from my intention to try to settle this issue here, or any other issue concerning metaphysical realism. I am surveying forms of metaphysical realism (antirealism) only as a foil for my central concern in this book, *alethic* realism. Hence I can confine myself here to pointing out that there are problems as to what many cases of philosophical denial of the existence of Xs come to. This is by no means always the case. No obscurity attaches to denials of the real existence of theoretical entities like quarks and positrons, or of God. We must scrutinize each case to determine whether it is puzzling in these ways or not.

However we seek to clarify the distinction between asserting and denying the real existence of Xs, it is worthy of note that those on the antirealist side of the divide often seek to find some place for discourse that is superficially about Xs, while stoutly denying that Xs really exist. There are several ways of doing this.

(a) One way is illustrated by "instrumentalist" or "conventionalist" or "fictionalist" views about the status of theoretical entities in science. One who has scruples about recognizing the existence of unobservables, or who for some other reason is averse to supposing that unobservable entities in terms of which scientific theories are constructed are really

1. But not one that is totally unproblematic. There are still nagging questions as to the criterion of "what I wanted to say", when we consider whether a second formulation preserves everything I wanted to say in using the first.

2. See Alston 1958 for more on this.

"out there" independently of our theorizing, may still acknowledge that talking in these terms has scientific utility. Theories that deal in positrons, quarks, and wave functions give us mathematically elegant formulas which can be used to generate empirically testable predictions and to guide our attempts to control the course of events. Talking and thinking as if there were such things can be useful because it gives us a manageably simple way of getting from observations to observations; whereas if we tried to do it all in terms of observables, the complexity of the route would overload our psyches. Similar suggestions are made by those who deny properties or propositions. In Chapter 1 I provided an example of this by suggesting that one who balked at the real existence of propositions could follow the discussion in the rest of the book by treating propositions as convenient fictions.

(b) An older tradition invokes a reality–appearance distinction. Though space and time are not truly real, they constitute a form under which things appear to us, just as perceptual objects appear to us as variously colored, even if colors do not attach to them as they are in themselves.[3] Though thoughts, experiences, and desires are really neurophysiological states and activities, they do not present themselves to our awareness as such, but rather as items of a nonphysical sort. The fact that we talk of them as nonphysical is explained, and justified in a way, by the fact that we naturally tend to think of them as they appear to our experience.

(c) One who denies the real existence of Xs may seek to preserve X-talk by construing it as nonstatemental, as not saying anything that is to be evaluated as true or false. On this approach X-talk that looks to be statemental will be construed as "expressive", "directive", or nonassertive in some other way. This move has been made most often with respect to the moral and, more generally, the evaluative. Imputations of obligation, moral rightness or wrongness, goodness, and value that look for all the world like statements that are designed to be objectively true, are really to be construed as expressions of attitudes toward what is being evaluated. Indeed, we could well count *taking X-talk to be merely expressive* as a third major way of denying the real existence of Xs, along with *flat denial of existence* and *reduction*.[4]

(d) Finally we might try to reconcile the denial of the metaphysical reality of facts with the preservation of ordinary fact talk by holding the

3. This is, of course, highly controversial. I mention it only as an example of something that is often claimed.

4. For suggestions of expressivist approaches to matters other than the evaluative, see Blackburn 1984, chaps. 5 and 6.

latter to be neutral as between opposing metaphysical positions on facts. Though it looks as if one who says "It is a fact that Paris is the capital of France" is committing herself to the real existence of facts, an adequate account of the way this sentence is used in ordinary discourse will show this to be a mistake. Such a statement does the job it is supposed to do and can be true as intended, even if there really are no such things as facts. For further development of this line of thought see van Inwagen (1990, chapters 10 and 11).

ii Metaphysical Antirealism: Reductions

Rather than say more about the "flat denial" version of antirealism at this point, I will bring in the next category of antirealism—REDUCTION; for it will turn out that we can best appreciate what flat denial does and does not amount to, as well as the difficulty of drawing boundaries around it, by looking at its relations with reduction. As I am using the term, to "reduce" a type of entity is to show that entities of that type are really so-and-sos, where this differs from what they are commonly thought to be or taken unreflectively to be. The account of what Φ's "really are" must come as a surprise to the neophyte, or it would not deserve the label "reduction". It would hardly count as a "reduction" to point out that mammals are animals that suckle their young or that races are events in which there is competition with respect to speed of movement. Moreover, although I just now followed the ordinary semantics of 'reduce' as a "success term" by saying that to reduce an entity is to *show* it to be so-and-so, I will use 'reduce' in a more relaxed fashion, so that any *attempt* to show this will be placed under the REDUCTION category.

Familiar examples of reduction in this sense are the (attempted) reductions of:

(a) Physical objects to patterns of actual and possible sense data. (Phenomenalism)

(b) Mathematical entities to logical constructions.

(c) Linguistic meanings to synonymy relations.

(d) Social entities (communities, organizations, nations . . .) to patterns of relationships between individual persons.

(e) Space to patterns of spatial relations.

(f) Mental states to complexes of behavioral dispositions.

   (g) Mental states to neurophysiological states.

   (h) Properties to classes of individuals that are similar in a certain re-
        spect.

For convenience, let's use the dummy term 'X' for an entity (or type of
entity) to be reduced, and 'Y' for the entity to which it is reduced.

There are two important distinctions to be made between types of
reductions. First, when philosophers advocate such reductions, they
often make the claim that it is a conceptual, semantic, or analytic truth
that Xs are Ys. The claim is that we can recognize Xs to be Ys if we reflect
carefully enough on what we mean by 'X' and 'Y' or on our concepts of
Xs and Ys. Examples (a)–(c) are typically understood in this way. But
the fact that I include both (f) and (g) on the list shows that I am not
restricting myself to conceptual reductions. Although (f) has usually
been put forward as a thesis of "logical behaviorism" to the effect that
our concept of an intention, for example, is a concept of certain dispositions to behavior, (g) is almost never held in this form. Practically no
one thinks that our concept of believing that it will rain tomorrow is the
concept of a certain kind of neural activity or state. The claim rather is
that the relevant facts of the matter are such that this belief is best
thought of as a neurophysiological state or activity of a certain sort. Here
we have what is sometimes called a "theoretical" identification.[5] Examples (d) and (e) are often thought of in the same way. It strikes me that
we are much less likely to regard the second kind of reduction as a form
of antirealism than we are the former. "Central state materialists" who
take mental states to *be* neurophysiological states of the brain are not
typically regarded as antirealists about the mental as logical behaviorists
have been. It is not clear to me just what is responsible for this. But
because of it I shall henceforth ignore the nonconceptual forms of reduction in this quick survey.

The second major distinction is between a straighforwardly metaphysical reduction and a more linguistically conceived version. The oldest
forms of phenomenalism were cast in the form of a thesis about the
constitution of physical objects. A given physical object is a certain complex of actual or possible sense data. Difficulties with this gave rise to a

5. There is also the distinction between type and token physicalism about the mental. The
former holds that each type of mental state can be identified with a certain type of neurophysiological state. The latter does not claim any such type–type identity, but holds that each particular
mental state is identical with some particular neurophysiological state. If I were concerned with
metaphysical realism and antirealism for its own sake, I would have to get into this distinction;
but I can ignore it for present purposes.

linguistic version in which there was no attempt to identify each physical object with some particular set of sense data. Instead the view was that each *statement* in which terms for physical objects occur can be "translated" into statements the only singular referring terms of which refer to sense data.[6]

Reductive theories are embraced for various reasons. (1) There may be background metaphysical commitments that conflict with recognizing Xs in an unreduced form. A materialist or physicalist ontology may seem incompatible with recognizing the existence of "abstract entities" like properties, propositions, or relations as entities in their own right; whereas if propositions can be identified with sets of sentences that bear a certain kind of equivalence to each other, or properties to sets of physical particulars that would ordinarily be said to have the property, those scruples will be satisfied. The same metaphysical prepossessions may encourage the reduction of psychological states to complexes of behavioral dispositions.

(2) Epistemological considerations often play a role in sparking reductive enterprises. Suppose that one is impressed with the idea that if physical objects are taken to have an existence independent of our experience, they are forever hidden from us behind a "veil of perception". That will provide an impetus for showing that physical objects are not impenetrable to our experience after all, since they are nothing but patterns or complexes of such experiences. To know about the physical world through experience is, at bottom, nothing but a matter of knowing about experience through experience. Again, it may seem mysterious that one should know anything about meanings, construed as independently existing abstract objects that are related in certain ways to linguistic expressions. But if to ascribe a meaning to a word is just to talk about the semantic relations of that word to other words, it may seem to fall more clearly within human cognitive powers to find out what words mean.

(3) A powerful motive for reductions in this century has been the sense that entities of a certain kind, left unreduced, are "obscure", "puzzling", or even "unintelligible". Many philosophers have reacted in this way to "abstract objects" of all kinds, particularly propositions. What is it, one asks, for there to be a complex consisting of Napoleon

---

6. There is a further distinction between the linguistic version just adumbrated and a more holistic view in which there is no claim to produce a sense-datum equivalent for each physical object sentence, but where the claim is that physical discourse as a whole can be replaced by discourse in which there are terms referring to sense data but no terms referring to physical objects.

and the property of timidity, related by the relationship of exemplification, just sitting out in logical space somewhere, forever unrealized. Even if we can understand what an actual fact that Napoleon is timid would be, how can we grasp what it would be for the corresponding proposition to be a constituent of reality, given that there is no such fact? Identifying propositions with sets of sentences brings them "down to earth". Possibilities, especially their inflation into possible worlds, have elicited similar reactions. What is it for there to *be* states of affairs, and even *worlds*—maximal consistent states of affairs—that do not exist? Possible individuals have especially drawn fire. How can we understand the "existence" of an individual that doesn't exist? If possible worlds can be reduced to sets of propositions (with, perhaps, further reductions being performed on the propositions), things look more manageable.

(4) There are also more purely linguistic grounds for reduction. The most familiar of these concern attachment to languages of certain restricted sorts. This often stems from the fact that logic has been more fully and satisfactorily developed for some languages than for others. Better for extensional than for intensional languages. Better for first-order quantification than for higher-order quantification. Better for truth-functional complex sentences than for those involving propositional attitudes. This can lead to an attempt to get rid of modal contexts or opaque contexts or propositional-attitude contexts by showing that such talk can be replaced with other talk that does not exhibit these undesirable logical features. Another linguistic motivation for reduction involves a desire to save a certain account of linguistic meaning. A famous historical example is Russell's theory of definite descriptions. Since Russell did not recognize any distinction between meaning and reference, he felt that if we left the sentence 'The present king of France is bald' (spoken at a time at which France has no king) in that form, the sentence would be meaningless, since the subject term fails to refer to anything. But the sentence is obviously meaningful. Therefore its surface form is misleading. It does not have to be construed as a statement about a being that is king of France at present. Instead, it can be understood as a generalization that refers only to properties: 'The property of being king of France at present is possessed by exactly one thing, and whatever has that property is bald.' This move has been expanded by Quine into a way of getting rid of any reference to individuals at all, leaving us with just predicates and quantificational apparatus. Thus, metaphysically speaking, individuals have been reduced to properties.

(5) This list would be incomplete without mentioning the fact that reductions are sometimes undertaken in a spirit of "fun and games". It

can be a sporting challenge to show how one can get along with as few ontological commitments as possible. Thus one sets out to show that we can say everything we want to say without referring to any abstract entities, or to any substantial bearers of properties, or to events, or to intentional psychological states. One's response to such challenges may be largely a matter of taste. Those with a "taste for desert landscapes" will seek to get along with as little as possible. Those who prefer luxuriant jungles will tend to resist reductions and will seek to show how we can get along comfortably with a more crowded ontology.

iii Realism and Idealism

In thinking about reductive forms of antirealism, we should give a special place to those that seek to reduce the nonmental to the mental. What is called 'realism' is often concerned to assert that physical objects, universals, propositions, or whatever enjoy an "independent" existence. This is not taken to imply independence of any connections with anything. Presumably nothing except the whole of reality (and possibly God) enjoys that absolute an exception from dependence. It is independence of *mind* that is typically stressed. Hence the traditional opposition of REALISM and IDEALISM. Nor should we suppose that any kind of dependence on mind is incompatible with realism in this sense. Most obviously, the dependence of the mental on mind is not incompatible with being a realist about mental contents, properties, and states. No one would deny a philosopher the title of "realist" because he accorded mental states a place in the scheme of things. Even with respect to the nonmental it is not every kind of dependence on mind that derogates from "real existence". Causal dependence need not do so. Within the natural world human minds and their operations exercise a variety of impacts on the environment. The landscape of populated areas would not be what it is apart from the mind-directed activities of human beings and other animals; yet this doesn't count against realism with respect to the environment. More globally, theism is not necessarily an idealist position. Berkeley is paradigmatically an idealist, but most forms of theism are properly thought of as realist. And yet theism holds that everything other than God depends for its existence on the divine mind.

So what kind of dependence on mind is incompatible with a realist status? What is the difference between the way in which Berkeley thinks of physical things as dependent on God, and the way in which Aquinas, Descartes, and Leibniz do? The answer is that the kind of dependence that is incompatible with a realist status is what we may call *constitutive* dependence. If physical substances, space and time, universals, or whatever, depend on a relation to mind for being what they are, for their essential character, for their constitution, then they lack the kind of independence of mind that is required for realist status. There are various ways in which mind, minds, or MIND can play what I have called a "constitutive" role vis-à-vis, for example, physical objects. They can be identified with "ideas" in the divine mind, à la Berkeley. Panpsychism construes them as made up of (low-level, rudimentary) minds. They can be construed as aspects of the activity of the Absolute Spirit, as in Hegel and other forms of absolute idealism. All of the above are "absolute" modes of constitutive dependence on mind. The "constitutive" dependence is so complete that things realists take to be nonmental are mental through and through. But there are also views of partial dependence, the most renowned of which is Kant's. For Kant the structure of the physical world—spatiotemporal order, causal interconnection, division into substances with their attributes and interrelations—is what it is because of the conceptualizing activity of the human mind. Apart from the ways our conceptual and judgmental apparatus works none of these features have any place. And since these features enter into everything we find in the physical world, that world as we know it would not exist apart from the organizing activity of the human mind. Nevertheless, on Kant's view the human mind does not operate in a vacuum. It imposes structure on raw material contributed by "things in themselves". We can't know anything about that raw material in abstraction from the finished product, but we can be assured that it plays a role. This Kantian "partial constitutive dependence" is standardly taken to constitute a form of idealism. Kant himself said that on his view the physical world is "transcendentally ideal but empirically real". The physical world is shot through and through by the contributions of mind. But given this "wholesale" dependence on mental activity, particular physical facts are what they are, regardless of how we think of them or believe them to be.

It will be clear that what I have just been calling a "constitutive" dependence of the nonmental on mind belongs under the heading of reduction; it is reduction of the nonmental to the mental.[7] It deserves

----

7. If this formula is to be acceptable we will have to use 'reduction' in a somewhat wider sense than the one I explained above. Many idealists take physical objects, for example, not to *be* mental, but rather to be what they are by virtue of their relations to minds or to mental phenomena, or to items that are what they are by virtue of *their* relations to minds, or . . . . In this wider sense we can speak of reducing Xs to Ys when one of these latter relations is alleged, as well as to claims that Xs *are* Ys.

special treatment only because of its prominence in uses of the term 'realism' and its contraries. Well, almost "only". There is one other reason for special treatment. We have been talking all along about what might be called "departmental realisms"—realism about this or that kind of thing. But is there, or can there be, a global realism or antirealism, an unqualifiedly general metaphysical position, one that concerns whatever there is? Positions that stand in the realism–idealism contrast are typically so regarded. Let's consider that for a moment.

One can, of course, be realist or idealist about some domains and not others—idealist about physical objects (considering them to be mind-dependent) but not about properties, for example. Nevertheless, realism and idealism are often construed as more global positions. But how can this be? How can one recognize everything or nothing to be constituted by the mental? Well, one could recognize nothing to be constituted by the mental if one denied that there are any minds; but that is not taken to be a requirement for being a metaphysical realist. Perhaps the best way to represent the matter is this. Assuming that mind has a fundamental sort of reality, we think of idealism as the position that *everything else* is reducible in one way or another to mind. If you like, we could think of the dependence of the mental on itself as a limiting case of reduction to the mental, thereby getting a global idealism that takes *everything* to be reducible to the mental. A global realism holds, on the other hand, that everything not commonly regarded as mental is *not* constituted by, is not reducible to, the mental, but exists in its own right as a nonmental sort of reality.

To be sure, there could be a global realism that denies that minds exist, and a global idealism that flatly denies the existence of anything commonly regarded as nonmental, rather than taking it to be reducible to the mental. But these are much less common positions and are not what people have in mind when they contrast realism and idealism. Realists, so called, typically recognize the basic existence of minds; they just resist any imperialist pretensions for the mental. And idealists, so called, do not deny any reality to the physical world, abstract entities, space and time, and the like. They only insist that these items are somehow mental in nature.

iv The Boundary between Flat Denials and Reductions

When presenting the first way of being antirealist about Xs (flat-out denial of real existence), I said that I would wait to discuss it further until we had *reduction* on the table with which to compare it. I now want to suggest that the line between these modes of antirealism is by no means a sharp one. What is the difference between denying that physical objects exist, and saying that they are really congeries of sensations? What is the difference between saying that properties do not exist and saying that they are really classes of particulars bound together by similarity relations? What is the difference between saying that mental states do not really exist and saying that they are really dispositions to overt behavior? It is often not clear which way to jump. To be sure, not all cases are up for grabs. Your typical atheist is unequivocally denying that there is any such being as God, rather than proposing some iconoclastic view of the nature of God.[8] Whereas the typical relational theorist of space and time would never dream of claiming that space and time are not real; he simply propounds a certain view as to their nature. But often the classification could go either way, depending on various features of the case. Let's take a look at some of the factors that tip the balance one way or the other.

(1) First, if the theorist has no interest in preserving statements involving Xs, at least no interest in preserving them as literally true, then she is best taken as denying the existence of Xs. This is the case with the usual kind of atheists, with mechanists who have no use for any descriptions or explanations in terms of teleology, and with those who think that "theoretical entities" like positrons and quarks just aren't "out there" anywhere. On the other side, it is (in part) because people want to hold that there are many true statements about organizations, families, and nations that a reduction of such social entities to relations between individuals is construed as telling us what these social entities are, rather than as a denial that they exist.

(2) Among those who hold to the literal truth of various statements about Xs (and on that basis are on the reduction side of the divide) there are still important distinctions to be drawn. Perhaps the most important is this. It makes a big difference whether the view involves point-by-point correlations between particular Xs and particular Ys, or whether the two bodies of discourse are related in a more holistic way. With both behavioristic and neurophysiological reductions of mental states and processes, the usual view involves a case-by-case identification. Each mental state or process is deemed to be identical with a particular set of behavioral dispositions or a particular neurophysiological state or process. This tells in favor of classing the view as an attempt to provide

---

8. That is not to deny that some people do the latter.

a novel account of what mental states are, rather than a denial of their existence. At least it encourages such an interpretation. For it enables us to preserve the "demographics" of the reduced. After the reduction we wind up with just as many items as we had at the beginning, related in basically the same ways, just because each reduced item is linked up individually with a reducing item. Contrast this with the situation in which a recipe is provided for translating any statement putatively about Xs into a statement about Ys, but where there is no attempt to identify each individual X with an individual Y. Some reductive accounts of linguistic meaning are good examples. Statements that x "has the same meaning" as y are reduced to assertions of a synonymy relation (characterized without appealing to meanings as entities) between x and y. Statements to the effect that S "knows the meaning of x" are explicated in terms of how S is disposed to use x in various sorts of speech acts. And so on. Each context in which 'meaning' occurs is given an explication in which 'meaning' does not occur. But this battery of reductions provides no resources for picking out some entity with which a given meaning is identified. Meanings have *disappeared* in the reduction rather than having been *reidentified*.

(3) Perhaps the ontological "distance" between the reduced and the reducing also plays a role. The greater the distance, the more tendency, ceteris paribus, to think of the view as a denial of the existence of Xs. The lesser the distance, the more tendency to think of the view as an unorthodox account of what Xs are. Thus where numbers are reduced to classes of classes, both Xs and Ys are on, roughly, the same level of abstractness, and it can seem right to say that the view is telling us what numbers are rather than denying their existence. On the other hand, if physical objects are reduced to patterns of actual and possible sense data, the latter is so far from the way physical objects are commonsensically conceived that it can seem more natural to take the phenomenalist to be denying their existence.

v Logical Relations of Alethic Realism and Metaphysical Realisms

This will suffice, for purposes of this book, as a survey of metaphysical realisms, their varieties and interrelations. Now we are ready to tackle the question for which all the foregoing was background: How is alethic realism related to one or another of these metaphysical realisms? I will consider the question of implications or other significant connections in both directions. The discussion will focus exclusively on the first component of alethic realism, the claim that the realist account of truth correctly identifies our ordinary concept of propositional truth. I take it to be obvious on the face of it that the second component, that truth is important, has no special connection with any position on metaphysical realism or nonrealism.

First consider whether any metaphysical realism or nonrealism has any implications, positive or negative, for the realist account of truth. I take it to be clear that they do not. *Though a particular realist or antirealist metaphysical position (of the sorts we have been considering) has implications for what propositions are true or false, they have no implications for what it is for a proposition to be true or false.* And it is the latter with which the realist account of truth is concerned. Let's explore this point with a couple of examples.

Consider the opposition between a realist and a "flat denial" antirealist about theoretical entities. If there are no such things as quarks, then no proposition that requires the existence of quarks for its truth can be true; whereas realism about quarks would have the opposite result. But the resolution of this issue has no bearing at all on the correct answer to the question of what it is for a proposition to be true. How could it? In taking a position on what propositions are or are not true, the metaphysical positions presuppose an understanding of truth; they do not contribute to it. We get the same result with the issue between a realist account of theoretical entities and a reductionist form of antirealism, for example, one that reduces quarks and the like to regularities in what would be observed under certain observable conditions. This reductive account has direct bearing on the propositional content of statements about quarks, a different bearing from that of the realist position. But there is no reason to think that either position has any implications for what we are saying when we say that one of those propositions is true. The metaphysical realist or antirealist about quarks, like the rest of us, makes use of some concept of truth but is not concerned, qua metaphysical realist or antirealist, to determine its nature.

A similar point is to be made concerning the issue between a realist and a phenomenalist concerning physical objects. If physical objects are correctly viewed in terms of a phenomenalist reduction, that will affect the nature of the proposition that pine trees are coniferous (P), construed so that it has a chance of being true. The proposition will be much more complex in its structure than one might think. But whatever the constitution of the proposition that P, it will be true if and only if P. Or rather, since we are not presupposing the truth of alethic realism in this discussion, the phenomenalist reduction or its rejection has no bearing on whether alethic realism is true. Assuming sufficient reasons for accepting alethic realism, a decision on the phenomenalist form of antirealism about physical objects will have no tendency to shake that position. On alethic realism the proposition that there is a computer on my desk (understood in a commonsensically realist way) will be true if and only if there is a computer on my desk (understood in the same way). On a phenomenalist position, the closest proposition to that one that has any chance of being true will be some complex proposition as to what sensory experiences one would have under certain conditions. But then, assuming alethic realism, *that* proposition will be true if and only if one would have sensory experiences of those kinds under those conditions. Again, the decision on the metaphysical issue has a bearing on what propositions are true, but no bearing on what it is for a proposition to be true.

It is hardly necessary to add that a parallel point holds for the more global realism–antirealism contrasts that go under the heading of "realism vs. idealism". If everything other than minds are, as Berkeley supposed, congeries of ideas, then the proposition that a spruce tree is in front of my house, understood in a Berkeleyan way, will be true if and only if there certain ideas related in certain ways (i.e., if and only if *there is a spruce tree in front of my house,* where that is construed in the Berkeleyan fashion). Whereas on the realist position, the corresponding proposition will be true if and only if there is a spruce tree in front of my house, where that is understood in a more familiar realist way. Alethic realism is just as acceptable (or unacceptable) either way. A parallel point holds for other forms of idealism, for example, the form according to which a tree exists only as a certain stage in the development of the self-realization of the Absolute. On that construal (if the realist account of truth is correct) the proposition that beech trees are deciduous will be true if and only if some appropriate fact obtains with respect to the self-realization of the Absolute. Absolute idealist metaphysics is in no tension with a realist conception of truth.

Now let's consider the other direction of possible bearings. Does a realist account of truth carry any implications for metaphysical realism or nonrealism? Here the situation is rather more complex. I will suggest that the situation is basically the converse of the other direction, that alethic realism has no bearing on disputes between metaphysical realism and antirealism, but there are qualifications to be made. I will first present the case for an unqualified view that there is no significant connection and then proceed to consider possible qualifications.

The basic point is the mirror image of the previous one. Just as the issues between a metaphysical realism and a nonrealist opposition is *not* an issue about what truth is, so the question of how truth should be construed is *not* an issue over the existence, or metaphysical constitution or status, of one or another type of entity. Alethic realism is a view about what truth is, whereas the metaphysical positions in question have to do with what *kinds of propositions* are true. And just as we must not confuse the question of what virtue *is* with the question of what virtues there are, as Socrates liked to remind us, so we must not confuse the question of what truth *is* with the question of what truths there are.

But it may appear that this beautifully simple picture needs complicating at a couple of points. First, there is the question whether a particular account of truth, such as my own, has metaphysical presuppositions. I have presented my position as a way of spelling out what it is for a *proposition, statement,* or *belief* to be true. Moreover, I have insisted, against deflationists, that there is a *property* of truth. Doesn't this mean that my alethic realism is committed to a metaphysically realist position on propositions, statements, beliefs, and truth-value properties?[9]

I don't think there is much in this. First, as I have been at pains to claim in Chapter 1, section v, it makes no difference to the viability of my account of truth what metaphysical status we accord propositions, statements, and beliefs. As I said there, even an instrumentalist or fictionalist construal of propositions would leave the account of truth intact, as I mean it to be taken. I said that what is nonnegotiable in the position is the ability to use 'that' clauses to specify the contents of statements and beliefs, and to use them independently to identify particular truth-value bearers (as in 'It is true *that salt contains sodium*'). So long as we have that, the metaphysical chips can fall where they may, as far as alethic realism is concerned. And as for a commitment to there being a property of truth, I take that to be, most basically, a view as to how apparent truth-value attributions are to be understood (as really being of the form they appear to be), rather than any metaphysical commitment that can properly be considered a form of realism or nonrealism. The commitment to a property of truth does not, for example, involve a realist or nonrealist account of the metaphysical status of properties. It merely holds that, whatever metaphysical status properties have, truth and falsity are among them. Though this might be reckoned as an existential assumption, it is, I claim, no more "metaphysical" (and no more realist

9. I am indebted to the participants in Wolterstorff's seminar (at Yale) on the manuscript of this book for calling this problem to my attention.

or nonrealist) than the assumption that there is a property of flabbiness.[10]

But there is a reason for qualifying the position that alethic realism has no bearing on metaphysical realism, a reason that I will take more seriously. To get into this, let's consider the idea that realism about, for example, physical objects or abstract entities is more conducive to alethic realism than idealism or other reductionist views in these domains, just because the realist position is the one that takes truth makers to be "out there", enjoying a mode of existence independent of our thought, experience, or discourse. Well, there may be *something* to this. To determine what, if anything, that is, we have to be more explicit about certain distinctions.

First, let us set aside the oppositions in which the antirealist is flatly denying the reality of Xs, and those in which the antirealist is advocating a reduction (except for reductions of the apparently nonmental to the mental). In those cases no qualification is needed to the denial of any significant connection between alethic realism and the realist side of the metaphysical dispute. The nominalist about properties or the atheist can embrace alethic realism with as good a conscience as her realist rival. The proponent of a reduction of mental states to behavioral dispositions can be as staunch an alethic realist as one who takes mental states to have a basic, irreducible mode of reality.

It is in the oppositions that most felicitously go under the banner of realism vs. idealism that we will find some interesting connection with alethic realism, if anywhere. Those oppositions, at least the ones I am thinking of now, all have to do with some kind of reduction of the apparently nonmental to the mental. But here too there are distinctions that are crucial. The most important is between those forms of idealism that take various domains of reality to be independent of *human cognition* and those that do not. Among idealist positions that take most of reality to be independent of anything human are Berkeleyan idealism, Leibnizian and Whiteheadian panpsychism, and absolute idealism. Here, as pointed out above, the idealist can be as enthusiastic an alethic realist

10. Note that if my account of truth really did have substantial metaphysical commitments of a realist sort, this would also require qualification of the claim that metaphysical realisms and nonrealisms have no bearing on accounts of truth. For in that case a nonrealist denial of those commitments would imply that the account of truth is not acceptable by reason of the falsity of some of its presuppositions.

There is also the point that even if I were to accept the suggestion I have been rejecting, that would only show that alethic realism has a bearing on issues of metaphysical realism by virtue of what it *presupposes*. It would still not be the case that anything in the position itself that is erected on the basis of those presuppositions has any such bearing.

as his realist opponent. And even phenomenalism concerning physical objects takes them to be independent of human *cognition*. True, according to phenomenalism the reality of physical things is not independent of human *experience*, since what it is for there to be a bush outside my window is a matter of what sensory experiences we would have under certain conditions. But even here the reality of the physical is not at all constituted by our cognitive activity—how we think about the world or what conceptual scheme we use, or anything of the sort. The facts that make physical-object assertions true—facts about the conditions under which we would have sensory experiences of one or another sort—are just as objective vis-à-vis our thought as physical facts are on a realist construal.

But with the other group—those who take (all or much of) reality to be constitutively dependent on human cognition—the issue is not as clear. For a number of years I tended to think, without having thought hard enough about the matter, that alethic realism is committed to the (constitutive) independence of (most of) reality from human thought. After all, in most of our cognitive activity don't we mean to be talking and thinking about things that are what they are independent of us and our doings? And if so, alethic realism would hold that the truth values of these statements and beliefs are determined by what is independent of our cognition. Hence alethic realism is committed to the independent (of human cognition) reality of everything we think or talk about, except, of course, human cognition itself.

After having thought harder, I still find a grain of truth in this. But only a grain. The line of argument just sketched is defective for what should have been an obvious reason. Whether most, or any, of what we think and talk about is constitutively independent of human cognition depends on precisely the metaphysical issues involved here. Kant and his numerous progeny think that, aside from noumena about which little or nothing can be said, everything we are cognitively concerned with is what it is, at least in part, because of the structuring provided by the human mind. In Putnam's updated, relativized Kantianism, anything we have beliefs or make assertions about exists and is what it is only "within" or "relative to" some "conceptual scheme" or "theoretical scheme" of human devising.

Let's focus on a view like Putnam's, which is relativized Kantianism without the noumena, since it is a more extreme version of the constitutive dependence of what there is on human cognitive activity. Why isn't this view of Putnam's perfectly compatible with alethic realism? As we shall see, he denies that it is, or at least makes claims that imply such a denial. But I will, in turn, deny his denial. That discussion will be coming up in Chapter 6. For now the point is only that there is a prima facie case for the compatibility of alethic realism even with a view that holds that everything is constitutively dependent on human cognition. For doesn't this view, as much as the other forms of metaphysical antirealism, simply amount to a certain view as to the mode of reality of what makes our beliefs and statements true, not as to what that truth consists in? Isn't Putnam free to recognize that even though the statement that that tree has no leaves is one that can be true (indeed, can only exist) in a certain "conceptual scheme", still the statement is true if and only if *that tree does have no leaves* (in that conceptual scheme)? And if so, he is free to recognize that the necessary and sufficient conditions for its truth follow the pattern laid down by alethic realism. That is not Putnam's position on truth, but why couldn't it be? I can't see that his relativized Kantian metaphysics prevents him from being an alethic realist. As I said, this matter will be thrashed out in Chapter 6. But meanwhile this brief discussion will serve as an indication of why I will not maintain that alethic realism implies that (most of) what determines the truth values of propositions is (constitutively) independent of human cognition.

But then what is the grain of truth in the idea that alethic realism has such an implication? It goes like this. Alethic realism, together with an obvious truth, does imply that what makes a particular assertion (belief) of mine true or false is (almost always) constitutively independent of that assertion (belief) itself and its features. Since alethic realism holds that what it takes for an assertion to be true is determined by whether the state of affairs that constitutes its propositional content actually obtains, it is rarely, if ever, the case that that statement itself—its being issued, its epistemic status, its content—determines whether that propositional content obtains. In order for that to be so, the content would have to concern the statement itself, including its properties—its epistemic status or whatever. In other words the statement would have to be self-referential. And even where self-reference is coherent, we rarely make a statement about that statement itself. If we can coherently say something like "This statement is justified" (where the reference of 'this statement' is to the statement being made), then, on alethic realism the truth of the statement would depend on the epistemic status of that statement itself, for that is what the statement is about. But such cases are rare, at best. Almost invariably the truth value of a statement will depend on something other than features of the statement, or of the belief expressed by the statement, since its content concerns something other than that statement. This being the case, if truth is determined as alethic realism has it, then what determines the truth of almost any true statement, that is, the fact that makes it true, is constitutively independent of that statement. Hence alethic realism, together with the obvious fact that self-reference in statement or belief is rare at best, implies that (almost always) what confers a truth value on a statement is something independent of the cognitive-linguistic goings on that issued in that statement, including any epistemic status of those goings on. *To that extent,* alethic realism implies that what makes statements true or false is independent of our thought and talk. This could be taken as a minimal sense in which alethic realism carries with it a metaphysical realism concerning the status of truth makers. But that doesn't alter the main point I have been making—that alethic realism is neutral with respect to virtually all the controversies over the metaphysical status of this or that domain that go under the name of "realism vs. antirealism", including the relatively global ones.

So we are left with only the thinnest sort of significant connection between alethic realism and metaphysical realisms. Does that mean that since our focus is on the former, we can (almost entirely) ignore the latter? I'm afraid things are not that neat. The reason is that not all of those who discuss these matters agree with me on the relations between various modes of realism. More than one thinker, notably Putnam, brings metaphysically antirealist considerations to bear in attacking alethic realism. Hence, even though my policy is to stick to issues concerning alethic realism, I can ignore debates over certain forms of metaphysical realism only by ignoring some of the most important literature on the subject. Hence there will be discussion of one or another form of metaphysical realism in these pages, but only so far as that is relevant to the debates over alethic realism.

CHAPTER 3

An Epistemological Objection to Alethic Realism

I now begin my defense of alethic realism. Remember that it involves two theses—(1) the realist conception of truth is faithful to our standard concept of propositional truth, and (2) that concept is important; it is often very important to consider whether a given proposition is true in that sense. In Chapter 1 I alleged that (1) is overwhelmingly obvious on the face of it. That being the case, I consider it proper to omit any positive argument for the position and confine myself to rebutting objections to it, along with a criticism of alternatives. Where a position seems that obvious, this procedure constitutes sufficient support. Chapters 2–6 are devoted to rebutting criticisms of (1) and Chapter 7 to my critique of the most prominent alternative—an epistemic conception of truth. (In Chapter 1, section xi, I criticized another kind of alternative, "deflationary" views.) Chapter 8 is devoted to thesis (2). There I do seek to provide something that might be called positive support for the thesis, as well as rebutting criticism.

i The Alleged Impossibility of Comparing Judgments and Facts

I begin the case for (1) by considering one of the commonest criticisms of a realist conception of truth—that on that conception it is impossible to determine whether a given proposition is true. The present chapter will be devoted to this criticism. It is most often directed at a correspondence version of the realist conception, and I shall generally be discussing it in those terms. But we will see that if it has any force against that version, it tells equally against formulations that say nothing about correspondence.

The criticism can be briefly formulated as follows. "On the realist conception, in order to determine whether a proposition, statement, belief, or judgment is true we would have to ascertain whether it corresponds to some fact in the appropriate way. But this is impossible. We can never get 'outside' our thought (experience, discourse, beliefs . . .) and scrutinize reality itself. All our cognition of the world is mediated by our thoughts (experiences, statements, beliefs . . .); hence we can never get at the reality side of the relation so as to see how the two sides match up. No matter what we do, we are pinned inside the 'circle of our beliefs'." Here are some typical formulations of this claim.

> Each statement may be combined or compared with other statements, e.g., in order to draw conclusions from the combined statements, or to see if they are compatible with each other or not. But statements are never compared with a "reality", with "facts". None of those who support a cleavage between statements and reality is able to give a precise account of how a comparison between statements and facts may possibly be accomplished, and how we may possibly ascertain the structure of facts. (Hempel 1935, 50–51)

> If meanings are given by objective truth conditions there is a question how we can know that the conditions are satisfied, for this would appear to require a confrontation between what we believe and reality; and the idea of such a confrontation is absurd. (Davidson, "A Coherence Theory of Truth and Knowledge", in LePore, ed., 1986, 307)

> Justification is a matter of accommodating beliefs that are being questioned to a body of accepted beliefs. Justification always terminates with other *beliefs* and not with our confronting raw chunks of reality, for that idea is incoherent. (Michael Williams, 1977, 112)[1]

A short way with this objection would be to say that even if its claims are true they have no force against a realist theory of truth; for the theory aims only at saying what truth *is*—not at providing a way of determining what is true and what false. Thus Davidson, arguing against his earlier self as quoted above:

> This complaint against correspondence theories is not sound. One reason it is not sound is that it depends on assuming that some form

---

1. I abstain from citing remarks like the following. "In whatever way a man might attempt to justify his beliefs, whether to himself or to another, he must always appeal to some belief. There is nothing other than one's beliefs to which one can appeal in the justification of belief. There is no exit from the circle of one's beliefs" (Lehrer 1974, 187–88). For this thesis only has to do with what is involved in the activity of justifying one's beliefs, i.e., the activity of *showing* them to be true or to have some positive epistemic status. It has no implications for what is involved in any cognition of facts.

of epistemic theory is correct; therefore, it would be a legitimate complaint only if truth were an epistemic concept. If this were the only
reason for rejecting correspondence theories, the realist could simply
reply that his position is untouched; he always maintained truth was
independent of our beliefs or our ability to learn the truth. (Davidson,
1990, 302–3)

Though Davidson's point is accurate enough, I do not think it takes
all the sting out of the "no way of telling" objection. Even though an
account of what truth *is* is not an account of how one determines what
is true, it would still be a heavy cross for the realist to bear if it should
turn out that on the realist account of truth, no one could ever determine the truth value of any truth-value bearer. Certainly the realist conception of truth would be in a much happier state if that were not the
case. Hence I want to look into the question of whether the "no way of
telling" reproach is warranted. Why should anyone think that it is? In
the above quotes we have only the claim. We must see what arguments
are forthcoming.

ii Can We Cognize Anything Other Than Judgments?

The usual argument, only hinted at above, for the thesis that it is
impossible to "compare" beliefs (statements, judgments . . .) with "reality", "facts", "the world", to see whether they "correspond", "fit", or
"match", runs as follows. There is no pure, unmediated apprehension
of reality, things, objects, or facts as they are in themselves *apart from our
ways of conceptualizing them or "propositionalizing" them, apart from what we
judge them to be*. Hence, in seeking to apprehend the other term of the
correspondence relation to check its relation to the truth-value-bearing
term, we wind up, in spite of ourselves, with another belief, judgment,
or statement, rather than with the extracognitive and extralinguistic
item which we were seeking.

It will be useful to have a live example of this argument before us. I
choose a presentation by Brand Blanshard in his chapter entitled "The
Tests of Truth" (1939, vol. 2). This passage is typical of such arguments
in that it concentrates on sense perception. To be sure, the thesis argued
for ranges over all cognition. But it is natural to think that if we are
directly aware of facts anywhere, it would be in our perceptual awareness
of the environment. Hence it is understandable that those who pro-

pound the argument tend to concentrate on showing that facts are not directly given to us even there.[2]

In implementing this strategy Blanshard represents the advocate of a correspondence test as saying:

> When we turn to judgments where appeal to correspondence *is* possible, we find that it is always resorted to, and that in such cases uncertainty is banished. Take the judgement, "That bird is a cardinal". If you heard someone make that remark, how would you test it? You would look and see. If there was a correspondence between what was asserted and what you saw, you would call the judgement true; if not, false. That is the way we actually assure ourselves of the truth of all such judgements, and it is correspondence that assures us. (227–28)

Blanshard then responds as follows.

> Now plausible as this argument is, it goes to pieces on inspection. It assumes that, corresponding to our judgement, there is some solid chunk of fact, directly presented to sense and beyond all question, to which thought must adjust itself. And this "solid fact" is a fiction. What the theory takes as fact and actually uses as such is another judgement or set of judgements, and what provides the verification is the coherence between the initial judgement and these.
>
> Consider the cardinal. This is supposed to be fact, unadulterated brute fact, given directly to our senses and providing a solid reality to which our thought is to correspond. But no bird is a mere sense datum, or even a collection of sense data. Suppose that standing in our place were an animal with all our senses, each developed to the highest acuteness, but unable to attach meanings to sense data as we do, or note likenesses, implications, and differences. Would such a creature perceive what we perceive? Plainly not. To recognize a cardinal is a considerable intellectual achievement, for to do it one must grasp, implicitly but none the less really, the *concept* of cardinal, and this can only be done by a leap far out of the given into ideal classification. The most ignorant person among us who achieves such recognition could unpack from it a surprising wealth of contents. The idea of living organisms, the thought of the bird kingdom and its outstanding characteristics, the notions of flight and a peculiar song and a determinate colour—these and many other notions are so bound up

2. Introspective awareness of one's own conscious states would seem to be an even stronger candidate for direct awareness. But because the knowledge gained there can hardly be supposed to furnish an adequate foundation for knowledge generally, there is a tendency to concentrate on sense perception, the output of which has a stronger claim to undergird our knowledge generally.

with the identification that our thought would lose its character with the removal of any one of them. . . . They are elements in a theory, a theory of no little complexity, which is based on sense data if you will, but could not possibly consist of them.

Indeed, that the brute-fact view of perception is untrue is proved by this alone, that perception may be mistaken; I may take the cardinal for a robin. If the object were mere given fact, such a mistake would be impossible. A fact is what it is, and cannot possibly be something else. If it appears to be something else, the seeming must be in our thought, and the perception that involves such seemings has advanced beyond the given into the region of judgement. What makes the error possible is a theory of ours. (228–29)

Before isolating the nub of this argument I will set aside certain gratuitous and otherwise unfortunate elements in the passage.

(1) Blanshard identifies the thesis that the fact *that the bird in question is a cardinal* is an "unadulterated brute fact, given directly to our senses and providing a solid reality to which our thought is to correspond", with the thesis that the bird is a *sense datum* or a collection of sense data. But if 'sense datum' is used here in its usual philosophical sense to refer to *a nonphysical direct object of sensory awareness that carries the sensory properties and functions as an intermediary in the perception of external physical objects*, then one who holds that facts are directly presented to one's awareness in sense perception need not suppose that these are facts about sense data. Direct realists, at least some who wear that label, hold that external physical objects are directly presented to sensory awareness.

(2) Though Blanshard's main conclusion is that "What the theory [correspondence theory] takes as fact is another judgement or set of judgements", he neglects to specify what in this case are the judgments that play this role. Presumably he has something like this in mind. Whereas his opponents thinks that the belief that this bird is a cardinal is based on a direct sensory presentation of certain properties of the bird—its shape, coloration, etc.—that belief is really based on the *beliefs (judgments)* that the bird has those properties, and the former is adequately based on the latter if and only if it coheres sufficiently with them.

(3) The claims that all perception is shot through with *concepts*, and that it always involves *judgments* seem to be conflated in this presentation. The two theses are clearly distinct. I might be using concepts in a certain perception (e.g., seeing something *as* a bear) without making any judgment about the object or believing anything about it. At least, if this is not a possibility, if all application of concepts to something

necessarily involves judging, we need an argument to that effect. It can't be taken for granted. The details of Blanshard's argument are mostly in terms of the involvement of concepts, but it is the inescapability of judgments that Blanshard needs for his conclusion that instead of a given fact what we find is simply another judgment. So I will take Blanshard to be arguing that perception necessarily involves judgments as well as concepts.

With these bugs out of the way we can see that the nub of Blanshard's argument conforms to the sketch I gave above of this sort of argument. His argument can be summarized as follows:

(1) Perception essentially involves judgment. There is no pre- or sub-judgmental sense perception of anything.
(2) Therefore we are not directly presented with external facts (external to our thought) in sense perception.
(3) Therefore when we try to get a fact, a bit of non-judgmental reality, before the mind in order to see whether it "corresponds" with a judgment, we only succeed in getting at a different judgment.

The alleged comparison of judgment with reality turns out to be merely a comparison of judgment with judgment. There is no escape from the "circle of belief". Judgments, even perceptual judgments, can be supported only by coherence in a system of judgments.

What are we to say of this argument? My difficulties begin with the first step—the necessity of judgments, or even of concepts, for perceptual awareness. So far as I can see, there is such a phenomenon as the *presentation* or *givenness* of something to one's awareness. Speaking of vision in particular and following Dretske (1969), I would say that all that is required for my *seeing* something (my being aware of it in a distinctively visual way) is that I "visually discriminate" it from its background, that it stands out for me visually, and therefore *looks* a certain way to me (red, round, lumpy, or whatever). It is arguable that this mere presentation never exists alone, but is always *accompanied* by conceptualization (or even by judgment, though this is a further step), but I am not convinced by such arguments. No doubt, ordinary mature perception almost always involves conceptualization and judgment—*taking* perceived objects to be so-and-so. But it remains to be shown that there is *no* perception without concepts and judgments. I would suppose that in certain reduced states of visual consciousness—when just waking up, for example—and at the periphery of the visual field, one has pure presentation without the intrusion of higher cognitive processes. And perhaps the sensory experience of very young infants is barren of conceptualization.

It is worthy of note in this connection that when Blanshard argues for the concept and judgment ladenness of perception, he concentrates on judgments and other propositionally structured aspects of perception, rather than on the perceptual awareness of objects. Thus he writes. "To *recognize* a cardinal is a considerable intellectual achievement, for to do it one must grasp, implicitly but none the less really, the *concept* of cardinal, and this can only be done by a leap far out of the given into ideal classification." (Emphasis of "recognize" is mine.) Sure. To *recognize* a cardinal is to form the belief that it is a cardinal, and, like all beliefs, this involves using concepts. But this does *not* show that to be visually aware of a cardinal one must employ that concept. Indeed, it is obvious that one need not employ the concept of a cardinal in order to see a cardinal. I can see a cardinal (i.e., it can be that what I see is a cardinal), even though I do not recognize it as such, and even though I totally lack any such concept. Acknowledging in effect this last point, Blanshard writes: "Indeed, that the brute-fact view of perception is untrue is proved by this alone, that perception may be mistaken; I may take the cardinal for a robin. If the object were mere given fact, such a mistake would be impossible." But in speaking of a "mistaken" perception, Blanshard must be talking about the judgmental or doxastic element in perception. The mere visual awareness of a cardinal cannot be mistaken; it is not the sort of thing that can be correct or incorrect. It is the belief or judgment that what I see is a robin that is susceptible of mistake. The argument depends, at least in part, on focusing on the judgmental aspect of perception and ignoring the presentational aspect.

But I don't want my objections to Blanshard's argument to hang, even in part, on my reservations concerning step (1). There are two reasons for this. First, to make the above contentions convincing I would have to go into many issues concerning perception, a notoriously complex topic; and there is no space for that in this book. Second, and more importantly, the question of whether there is or can be subconceptual, subjudgmental perceptual awareness of *objects* is not the central issue here. Though Blanshard formulates his contentions as applying to perception *überhaupt* in an undiscriminating fashion (and here, too, he is typical of partisans of proposition-laden perception), the real concern is with the question whether there is any direct presentation of *facts* in perception. It is this possibility that Blanshard is concerned to dismiss. Hence he could accept my contentions concerning the perceptual awareness of objects and still maintain that there is no judgmentally unmediated awareness of *facts* in sense perception; and this would give him what he needs for step (1) of the argument.

To be sure, if I were discussing Blanshard's coherentist epistemology rather than his views on truth, it would be a different story. For it is certainly arguable, and I would be prepared to argue, that if a perceptual object is sensorily presented to me as so-and-so (as *looking, sounding, smelling,* etc. a certain way), that would give me a basis for judging that the object is so-and-so. And that would be a justification for perceptual judgments that is other than their coherence with other judgments.[3] But this is not the current topic. We are currently considering a certain argument against the view that it is possible to determine the truth value of a belief by determining whether there is a fact it "fits" or "matches". More specifically, we are interested in whether sense perception provides us with the facts we need for this purpose.

To return to this central concern, I will accept, for the sake of argument, Blanshard's step (1), where the awareness in question is awareness of facts. Let's rewrite (1) as follows.

(1) Perception of facts essentially involves judgment. There is no pre- or subjudgmental awareness of facts in sense perception.

Even if the tree can be visually presented to me without my taking it to be, for example, bare, still one cannot be perceptually aware of *the fact that the tree is bare* without wielding the concepts of *tree* and *bareness,* indeed, without entertaining the *proposition that the tree is bare.* Facts are not simply *given* to us. The world is not presented to our passive awareness already carved up into facts. We become aware of facts only by virtue of imposing a propositional structure on what is perceptually given. We have to think of what we are seeing as a tree's being bare before we can be said to be aware of the *fact* that it is bare.[4]

By accepting (1) I am thereby committed to accepting (2) as well, that we are not directly presented with external facts (external to our thought) in sense perception. Indeed, if we construe 'direct presentation' as presentation without the mediation of conceptualization and judgment, (2) is just a rewrite of (1) And so, if I am to contest the argument at all, it will have to be at the transition from (2) to (3)—*that when we try to get an external fact before the mind, all we succeed in getting is another judgment.* That I will now proceed to do.

Start with the point that even if sensory *presentation* of an object never

3. For a good presentation of this point see Van Cleve 1985.
4. Note that the only plausible examples of perception that does not involve concepts and/or judgments, like those mentioned above, are definitely *not* cases in which we are concerned to compare judgments with facts to see whether they match.

occurs alone, it is still an *element* of normal perceptual cognition that is different from any deployment of concepts or acts of judgment. This is clear from the mere fact that actually seeing something is strikingly different from merely applying concepts to it, having beliefs about it, or making judgments about it. Try the following simple experiment. Close your eyes, and think about the things and people around you. Remember what they are like, form judgments about them, speculate about where they will be tomorrow, wonder where they came from, and so on. Then open your eyes, and look at them. There is a world of difference in your cognitive consciousness before and after that eye-opening experience. What is the difference? It is felicitously put by saying that when you open your eyes these things and people are *presented* to your awareness, whereas before they were not. It is this element of perceptual presentation that makes the difference. While your eyes were closed, you were conceptualizing, judging, believing, and engaging in other cognitive acts with propositional content, just as you were after opening your eyes. That isn't what makes the difference. Indeed, you could have been using *just the same concepts* and making *just the same judgments* whether you were seeing anything or not. It is the *visual presentation* that makes the difference between seeing something and just thinking about it (remembering it, wondering about it . . .).

I must confess that in what I just said I employed my favorite way of bringing out what makes the difference between mere judgment and perceptual consciousness. On that view the extra element in perception is a sensory *presentation* of (what are usually) external objects in the environment. But although I take it to be absolutely undeniable that there is a crucial difference between merely thinking about an object and perceiving it, there are other accounts of what makes the difference, what is in the latter and not in the former. And on some of those accounts, unlike the "theory of appearing" account I favor, that additional element is itself propositionally structured.[5] So far as I can see, my objection to Blanshard's step (3) will go through just as well on any (not maximally implausible) view as to what makes perceiving an object different from just thinking about it, so long as the difference is recognized. I will continue to present my criticism in terms of the theory of appearing, with the tacit understanding that it could be carried through on other views that recognize something in perceptual cognition that is nonjudgmental in character.

Thus even if Blanshard is right in supposing that there is no sensory

5. For such views see, e.g., Searle 1983.

consciousness of a fact without judgment, that doesn't show that when I perceive that the bird is a cardinal I am *merely* judging it to be a cardinal. For the simple experiment just mentioned shows that that even if judgment is always involved in perception it is never the whole story; it isn't what makes perceptual cognition distinctively perceptual. Even if my perceptual awareness *that there is a robin on that branch* involves the judgment *that there is a robin on that branch*, it involves more, and must involve more if it is to be a perceptual cognition of the fact in question and not a *mere* judgment that the fact obtains. Therefore, the concept and judgment ladenness of perception is radically insufficient to show that in perception we do not (much less cannot) succeed in gaining knowledge of a fact that is something other than a judgment (belief, statement, proposition) and that is something with which a judgment can be compared for the assessment of its truth value. Why can't the whole perceptual package—sensory consciousness structured by conceptual-propositional-judgmental activity—be a way of cognizing external facts? It certainly seems that this is what is going on in perception, and the points Blanshard and other thinkers adduce fail to show otherwise. It is because the judgment informs and structures a *visual presentation* that I can be said, in this perception, to be aware of the extrajudgmental fact *that a robin is on the branch,* as well as judging this to be the case.

And so even if all perceptual awareness of facts involves judgment, it by no means follows that all we are aware *of* in such perception is a judgment. This is no better than arguing from the fact that all eating involves chewing and swallowing to the conclusion that the only things I can eat is my teeth, throat, and esophagus. Indeed, it doesn't even follow from the judgmental nature of perception that we are *perceptually* aware of judgments at all They may function as part of what *enables* us to be perceptually aware of something, rather than themselves functioning as objects of perception. The way is left open for perception to involve an awareness of facts that is different from, or at least not exhaustively comprised of, an awareness of our judgments.

Thus even if perception and other relatively "direct" modes of awareness of facts, such as introspection, always involve judgment, it by no means follows that when I perceive things in the physical environment, or when I am introspectively aware of my own conscious states, I am not aware of facts that make my judgments true or false. Hence it does not follow that I cannot inspect, examine, and scrutinize these facts to determine whether they are such as a given judgment takes them to be.

At the beginning of this chapter I quoted Hempel as denying the possibility of a comparison of statements with facts. Here is a wonderfully vigorous defense of this possibility by Moritz Schlick. It is occurs in a response by Schlick to the essay of Hempel's from which that quotation was taken.

> I have been accused of maintaining that statements can be compared with facts. I plead guilty. I have maintained this. But I protest against my punishment: I refuse to sit in the seat of the metaphysicians.[6] I have often compared propositions to facts; so I had no reason to say that it couldn't be done. I found, for instance, in my Baedeker the statement: "This cathedral has two spires." I was able to compare it with "reality" by looking at the cathedral, and this comparison convinced me that Baedeker's assertion was true. . . .
>
> Perhaps you say: "But if we analyze the process of verification of Baedeker's assertion we shall find that it amounts to a comparison of propositions." I answer: I don't know; it will depend on what you mean by "analysis'. But whatever the result of your analysis may be, at any rate we can distinguish between cases in which a written, printed or spoken sentence is compared with some other written, printed or spoken sentence, and cases like our example, where a sentence is compared with the thing of which it speaks. And it is this latter case which I took the liberty of describing as a "comparison of a proposition with a fact." . . .
>
> You insist that a statement cannot or must not be compared to anything but statements. But why? It is my humble opinion that we can compare anything to anything if we choose. Do you believe that propositions and facts are too far removed from each other? Too different? Is it a mysterious property of propositions that they cannot be compared with anything else? That would seem to be a rather mystical view. . . .
>
> Is it true that we are unable "to give a precise account of how a comparison between statements and facts may possibly be accomplished and how we may possibly ascertain the structure of facts"? I think it is not true. Or was the description faulty which I gave of such a comparison a little while ago? It consisted of the simplest empirical prescription of a kind which we carry out many times almost every day. (Schlick, in Macdonald 1954, 232–35)

In this passage Schlick does not respond to the argument Blanshard and others give in support of Hempel's claim. But I find his remarks a vivid example of the way in which it seems for all the world as if we really do

---

6. We are here in the heyday of logical positivism when the accusation of being a metaphysician was a capital charge.

have "external" facts (facts that are not aspects of our thought) before the mind in sense perception as items we can compare with other items.

At the beginning of section i I suggested that though the argument under consideration is directed specifically at a correspondence theory of truth, we can see that if it had any merit at all it would tell equally against any form of a realist account of truth, including the most minimal form that we have in XIII and XIV For what the argument is designed to show is that it is impossible to "get at" the other side of the supposed correspondence relationship so as to see whether there is a fact to which the judgment (belief) corresponds; the only things to which we have cognitive access are judgments (beliefs). But if that is so, it is equally impossible to determine whether the condition for the truth of the belief that sugar is sweet that is set out in the T-statement—'The belief that sugar is sweet is true if and only if sugar is sweet'—is satisfied. If we cannot get beyond our judgments to cognize anything else, we cannot apprehend the fact that sugar is sweet. And that means we cannot tell whether the belief that sugar is sweet is true by determining that sugar is sweet. There is no need to get into correspondence talk to set up a realist account of truth that would make it impossible to tell what is true if Blanshard's argument were cogent.

In what I just said I was, of course, assuming that knowing that sugar is sweet does not amount to knowing anything about *judgments*, whether they cohere with each other in certain ways or anything else. And this will be contested by the likes of Bradley and Blanshard. They take it to be a fundamental mistake to suppose that thought is (to a large extent) "about" a reality that is other than thought. The "reality" to which thought refers is simply thought itself in its ideal completion.[7] On this view the fact that sugar is sweet is a fact about the shape a fragment of thought will take when thought attains an ideally complete and coherent form. Thus if we accept this kind of absolute idealism, we can hold that we never cognize anything other than judgments and the like, while hanging on to the T-schema account of the concept of truth. So what my criticism shows is that it is only at the price of this kind of metaphysical commitment that the argument we have been discussing would fail to tell against a minimalist realism about truth.

There are, of course, other arguments that are directed specifically against correspondence theories of truth, and some of these have epistemological implications. It has often been argued, against a theory of propositional truth that makes it consist in a structural isomorphism

7. See Bradley 1914, chaps. 5, 11; Blanshard 1939, chap. 26.

between proposition and truth-making fact, that we cannot find extralinguistic, extramental correlates for all propositional constituents—not, for example, for the copula or quantifiers. And if the truth of a proposition requires such correlates in the world, it would follow that on this view it is impossible for us to determine the truth values of propositions. This argument definitely does not tell against the T-schema generated versions of my view or against the minimalist correspondence account (XVII). But the argument I have been criticizing is not of this sort. It does not trade on distinctive features of specific forms of correspondence theory. It aims to establish the more general point that it is impossible for us to get nonmental, nonlinguistic facts into our cognitive sights so as to use them to assess the truth value of propositions, judgments (beliefs), and statements. And this claim is incompatible with any sort of realist account of truth. I have limited the discussion to this argument because I have no interest in defending forms of correspondence theory that give rise to other arguments like the one just mentioned.

iii Counterattack by Blanshard

Blanshard might reply to the above as follows. "Even if what you say is correct, it fails to show that in perception we have direct, unmediated awareness of external facts. Since, as you concede for the sake of argument, all perception of facts involves judgments, our apprehension of those facts is achieved *through* those judgments. It is not a matter of our simply being *confronted* by the fact. It is not a matter of the fact's being directly presented to our awareness, with our role confined to *receiving* and registering what has been given to us. No, we make a more active contribution than that. Our judgmental, interpretive activity is crucially involved, shaping and molding what it is we come perceptually to know, shaping it in terms of the concepts we bring to the experience. We still don't have what the correspondence theorist needs for his project—a purely external fact that is what it is whatever our conceptual schemata, and which can therefore lay claim to be an independent standard against which our judgments can be tested for truth value."

By way of counterresponse, my first point is that I do not plead guilty to having conceded all that I am imagining Blanshard to have just said. In particular, I have not conceded that our conceptual-judgmental activity plays an essential role in determining (some of the content) of the facts we come to know perceptually. But let that pass.[8] In this Blanshardian response we have reached what I take to be the heart of the argument we have been considering. For the argument is based on the assumption that a correspondence theory, or other realist account of truth, requires a pure, unmediated presentation of facts to our awareness if it is to be viable.[9] And that is an assumption I will now proceed to challenge. Why should we suppose that I must be directly *confronted* with a certain fact, for example, *that there is a lamp on my desk*, in order to use that fact to test the belief *that there is a lamp on my desk* for truth value? What difference does it make *how* I come to know it, provided only that I do know it? The essential thing is that I come into (cognitive) possession of this fact, add it to the store of things I know. So long as that condition is satisfied I am in a position to use it as a check on my beliefs about what is on my desk, in accordance with a realist conception of truth. Any supposition to the contrary would appear to reflect a confusion between *what I know* and *how I come to know it*. So long as I know that there is a lamp on my desk, whether I learn it perceptually as that is construed by Blanshard, or I learn it by direct sensory presentation in terms of the "theory of appearing", or I learn it from reliable testimony, or I infer it from my knowledge that the lamp is somewhere in the house and it is not anywhere else in the house, or . . . , I will be in a position to assess my belief that there is a lamp on my desk for realist truth. I suspect that one source of the thesis I am criticizing is an attachment to picture thinking. There is a powerful tendency to picture realist truth in terms of an *immediate confrontation* with facts that are what they are in complete independence of the way we think of them. The independence part of this notion is certainly the heart of a familiar form of *metaphysical* realism, a position I argued in Chapter 2 to be independent of alethic realism.[10] But the idea that we can test a statement for realist truth value by reference to whether what it says to be the case is the case only if we enjoy an unmediated cognitive access to the relevant range of fact will not survive careful examination. And the picture thinking that is behind this, according to my diagnosis, is not worthy of serious philosophical thinking.

This is the point at which to note another feature of Blanshard's argu-

8. In Chapter 6 I will argue that Putnam's position of "conceptual relativity", which does hold that our conceptual-theoretical activity makes an essential contribution to what it is we come to know, is itself compatible with alethic realism.

9. This is a widely shared view among critics of realism. A recent influential example is Rorty 1979.

10. Once more the point made in n. 8 becomes relevant.

ment, again one that is widely shared by thinkers of his persuasion. He assumes that anything that would count as an apprehension of "external" fact—an awareness of extracognitive, extralinguistic reality—would have to be infallible, not susceptible of error. We found Blanshard saying "that the brute-fact view of perception is untrue is proved by this alone, that perception may be mistaken". He takes his realist opponent to be committed to a quest for a mistake-proof mode of cognition. And Hempel, in the essay from which I quoted earlier, writes: "The *third* and *last* phase of the logical evolution here considered [away from a correspondence theory of truth] may be characterized as the process of eliminating" the idea that there are "basic propositions which are conceived to be ultimate and not to admit of any doubt". (1935, 53). In other words, in order to hold a correspondence theory of truth one must take there to be indubitable statements. In the same essay he makes it clear that he takes the correspondence theory to be incompatible with supposing that "basic statements" are subject to confirmation or disconfirmation by considerations outside themselves. Thus Blanshard and Hempel between them saddle the correspondence theory with the requirement that our cognition enjoys the three basic "epistemic immunities"— infallibility, indubitability, and incorrigibility.[11]

Again, Otto Neurath in an essay, "Protocol Statements" (Ayer 1959), that is often taken to attack the notion of a thought-reality comparison (Davidson, for example, so takes it in 1990, 302), in fact says nothing that is explicitly on that point. Instead the whole burden of his argument is that "protocol statements" (i.e., reports of observation) cannot be taken to be incorrigible, or to "stand in no need of verification", cannot be regarded as acceptable just by virtue of the fact that they transcribe what has been given in immediate experience. And if one looks at F. H. Bradley's diatribes against a correspondence theory of truth (1914, chap. 7), they consist almost entirely of arguments that judgments of perception and memory are all fallible. Moreover, Schlick, on the other side of the debate, seems to go along with the assumption that a comparison of judgment and fact requires points in our experience where we apprehend facts in such a way that we cannot be mistaken, or at least in such a way that nothing could show that we are mistaken. At least, he assigns that epistemic status to the beliefs that record perceptions he supposes to give him the requisite access to the facts.

---

11. I term these 'epistemic *immunities*' because they constitute immunity to one or another epistemically undesirable condition—mistake, doubt, and being refuted. For an extended treatment of all three see my "Self-Warrant: A Neglected Form of Privileged Access" in Alston 1989.

> If all the scientists in the world told me that under certain experimental conditions I must see three black spots, and if under those conditions I saw only one spot, no power in the universe could induce me to think that the statement "there is now only one black spot in the field of vision" is false. (Macdonald 1954, 237)

The view that a correspondence theory of truth requires an assumption of infallibility, indubitability, and/or incorrigibility, is intimately connected with the view we have seen to be basic to the argument under discussion, the view that the correspondence theory requires a cognitive access to the world of fact beyond our thought and language that involves a "pure givenness" of fact, unmediated by any conceptualization, judgment, or "taking" on our part. The connection can be seen as follows. It is easy to suppose that such epistemic immunities are available only where some fact is directly presented to our awareness, in such a way that there are no mediating judgments, preconceptions, or background beliefs to introduce the possibility of error. If we simply passively receive the fact itself, what could go wrong? And so if we can show that there is no such "immaculate reception" of external fact, we have thereby shown that none of our cognitions enjoy these immunities from error, correction, or doubt.

I see no more merit in supposing that we can compare fact and proposition only if our cognition of the fact enjoys these epistemic immunities, than I do in the closely linked requirement of direct, unmediated apprehension of fact. Why should we suppose that we can get external facts into our cognitive sights in such a way as to appeal to them in determining the truth value of judgments, only if our cognition of those facts is so direct as to be infallible, incorrigible, and indubitable? Why should a fact have to be presented to us in a foolproof way in order for us to ascertain that the fact obtains? All that is required for us to "have" the fact that sugar is sweet (have it before the mind, have it as something we can examine) is that we know *in some way or other* that the fact obtains, that *sugar is sweet*.[12] To be sure, here as elsewhere, it would be a good

---

12. Some may feel that the requirement of *knowledge* is too stringent. Why wouldn't justified belief that *p* be sufficient to give us the fact that *p* to scrutinize in the way my opponents are declaring to be impossible? That wouldn't suffice to do the job just because it is possible for justified belief to be false. And if I have a false justified belief that *p* there is no fact that *p* as a possible object of my scrutiny. We could, of course, consider the idea that *true* justified belief would give us what we need. But then it would seem that the considerations that have led Gettier and others to deny that this is sufficient for knowledge would also tell against the idea that it is sufficient to do the job we are discussing. Think of a Gettier case like that of Smith, who believes falsely but justifiably that Jones will get the job and that Jones has ten coins in his pocket, and then infers validly that whoever will get the job has ten coins in his pocket. This latter belief is

thing to know what we know in a way that is minimally, if at all, subject to mistake by reason of distortion from a medium of transmission. But if we take this to be a requirement for all knowledge, we fall back into the "quest for certainty", into exaggerated requirements for knowledge of a Cartesian or Platonic sort that we are supposed to have gotten beyond by now. Using commonly accepted, workaday standards for knowledge, it is only an extreme skeptic who doubts that we know many things that go beyond our speech acts, beliefs, and their propositional contents. And that being the case, we are well supplied with facts that we can examine to determine whether any of them render this or that propositional attitude or assertion true. It doesn't matter how we came by this knowledge, or what credentials it exhibits, provided its credentials qualify it as genuine knowledge. We may have attained the knowledge by some relatively direct route, such as introspection or perception, or by some more indirect route, like induction, argument to the best explanation, or taking Y (a reliable sign of Z) to indicate that Z obtains. It doesn't matter. So long as we *know* that Z obtains, that is enough to give us a sufficient condition for the truth of Z, on a realist conception of truth. No doubt, we do not have as much knowledge of objective fact as we would like. But we are not as bereft of it as the likes of Blanshard would have us believe.

Once we appreciate the point that *any* knowledge of fact will serve the realist's purposes, we can see that there is no need to place such emphasis on relatively direct sources of knowledge like perception and introspection in considering whether facts can be appealed to in determining the truth value of judgments. Since any knowledge of objective fact will serve the correspondence theorist's, or other realist's, turn, the discussion may as well be directed on high-level scientific theories as on sightings of cardinals. If we really do know that nothing can move faster than the speed of light, then that suffices for grounding a judgment that the proposition that nothing can move faster than the speed of light is true, as surely as my perceptual knowledge that there is a lamp on my desk grounds the judgment that the proposition that there is a lamp on my

---

true and justified, even though Jones will not get the job, because Smith, unbeknownst to himself, will get the job and also has ten coins in his pocket. Here I think the right thing to do is to deny that Smith is in a position to "scrutinize" the fact that whoever will get the job has ten coins in his pocket, even if we agree that his belief in this is true and justified. Since what justifies his belief lacks the right kind of connection with the fact that makes the belief true, we should, I think, deny that Jones has cognitive access to that fact. But I am not confident about this. In any event, working with the stronger requirement of knowledge will be sufficient to make the point I am concerned to make, viz., that no particular kind of knowledge, and, more specifically, no ideally direct infallible cognition, is required to enable us to determine whether a realist sufficient condition of truth is satisfied.

desk is true. It is only the misguided supposition that direct, unmediated knowledge is required to make the realist's project go that leads to an undue preoccupation with perception and introspection.

The above discussion also enables us to see that it is only an extreme epistemological skepticism that will get Blanshard & Co. the desired conclusion. If any knowledge whatever will put the realist into a position to look at a fact and thereby determine whether a given judgment is true or false, it is only if *no* such knowledge is forthcoming that his project is doomed. So long as we have some knowledge of facts about which we make judgments, the realist way of determining truth value is viable. Thus, once we see the arbitrariness of the demand for unmediated apprehension, we see that Blanshard would have to embrace an extreme and unpalatable skepticism in order to support his strictures on a realist conception of truth.[13]

13. In Chapter 7, where I discuss and criticize at length an epistemic conception of truth, I compare the prospects of determining truth values on that conception with the prospects on a realist conception. The palm is awarded to the latter.

CHAPTER 4

Dummett's Verificationist Alternative to Alethic Realism

i Forms of Verificationism

At least since the early years of this century verificationism has been prominent in debates over realism. Verificationism is always concerned with linguistic meaning. Verificationist semantic doctrines differ along several dimensions. First and most fundamentally, there is the distinction between a verificationist *criterion of meaningfulness*, according to which a necessary condition for the (cognitive, factual) meaningfulness of a sentence is that there be some way of verifying or falsifying it, and a verificationist *theory of meaning*, according to which the meaning of a sentence consists of the "method of its verification (falsification)" or, alternatively, consists in the conditions under which the sentence would be verified or falsified.[1] Crosscutting this distinction is the distinction between conclusive verification (falsification), on the one hand, and some degree of *confirmation* (*disconfirmation*) on the other. My examples of a criterion and of a theory were stated in terms of verification (falsification), but they could be reformulated in terms of confirmation (disconfirmation). There are other important distinctions as well. Some verificationists claim to be depicting the ordinary, or at least some existing, conception of meaningfulness or meaning; while others put the position forward as a *proposal* for how these notions should be construed. In this chapter I will be thinking of verificationist theses in the former way. Again, there are different ways of explicating the notions of *cognitive* or *factual* meaning for which the criterion or theory is claimed to hold. For present purposes we can think of "factual" meaning as the kind of

---

1. Each of the forms of verificationism I am distinguishing is itself susceptible of various formulations. Except for the forms I will be discussing in detail I will give, in each case, only a representative formulation.

meaning a sentence must have to be usable to make statements that have truth values.

Before proceeding further I will clean up, in a certain respect, the usual way of talking about verificationism, of which the previous paragraph is a sample. As a thesis about *meaning*, verificationism is concerned with *sentences*, the linguistic bearers of meaning on which it concentrates. But it follows from the reasons I gave in Chapter 1 for denying that sentences are bearers of truth value that sentences are not subjects to *verification* or *falsification*, *confirmation* or *disconfirmation*. For to verify (falsify) X is to show that X is *true* (*false*). And to confirm (disconfirm) X is to show that X is probably *true* (*false*). Hence we cannot really hold, as the usual formulations of verificationism seem to suppose, that it is the same entities that are capable of possessing a certain kind of meaning *and* are subject to verification (falsification) and confirmation (disconfirmation). So what are we to do? Fortunately, a simple solution is ready to hand. When speaking of verification, etc., we can replace the *sentence* in question with a *statement* that an utterance of that sentence (in a certain context, where that qualification is needed) would be used to make if used correctly. Thus a sanitized formulation of the verificationist criterion of factual meaningfulness would go like this.

> (I) A sentence has a factual meaning *if and only if* a statement made by a correct utterance of it can be verified or falsified (confirmed or disconfirmed).

With this understanding of how to build a bridge from sentence talk to statement talk, I will freely oscillate between them in the sequel.

Though 'verification' ranges over any way of determining the truth value of a statement, the concern of most verificationists in this century has been with *empirical* verification, which we can think of as verification by observation or by observational data. (This restriction is often not made explicit.) However this chapter will focus on a verificationist position that is not so restricted—that of Michael Dummett, who comes to his version from the philosophy of mathematics. Thus we will be thinking of verificationism in a wider way than is customary.

In terms of the first distinction, my focus will be on verificationist *theories* of meaning. There is not even a prima facie case for the incompatibility of a verificationist *criterion* of factual meaning and a realist conception of truth. Why should we suppose that the restriction of statemental-truth bearers to those that are susceptible of verification (confirmation) runs into any conflict with the T-schema? Couldn't gold's being malleable be the necessary and sufficient condition for the truth of the statement that gold is malleable, even if that statement wouldn't be a candidate for a truth value unless it were susceptible of verification (falsification) or confirmation (disconfirmation)? I can think of no argument for incompatibility here that is even remotely plausible. Therefore I shall confine my attention to the thesis that a verificationist *theory* of factual meaning is incompatible with a realist conception of truth.

ii Dummett's Verificationist Semantics

This chapter will be almost entirely devoted to the most prominent avowedly antirealist verificationist on the contemporary scene—Michael Dummett. Dummett is not the easiest philosopher to interpret, and I will unavoidably be enmeshed to some extent in exegetical questions. It is not my aim, however, to deal with the whole of Dummett's philosophy or even the whole of his semantic theory. I am concerned only with those aspects of it that might seem to have a bearing on alethic realism. And that does simplify life somewhat.

I will begin with a summary statement, and then get into the sometimes prickly details. Dummett's view, in a word, is that the meaning of sentences is given, not by truth conditions as often (realistically) understood, but by verification conditions. "According to a theory of meaning in terms of verification, the content of an assertion is that the statement asserted has been, or is capable of being, verified" (1976, 117). This is in terms of the "content of an assertion"; and we have seen in Chapter 1 that sentence meaning does not, in general, suffice to determine that. Dummett, however, glosses over this point in presenting his views; he simply announces that he will neglect the frequent need for contextual support to turn the utterance of a sentence with a certain meaning into a definite assertion capable of truth value (1991, 30). Since this neglect has no bearing on the issues with which I am concerned here, I shall go along with him in this fiction.

Dummett begins with the idea that the truth conditions of sentences are crucial for their meaning, an idea found in different forms in various thinkers. Dummett pays most attention to Frege and Davidson, especially the former. He pays passing attention to the question of what to do about interrogatives, imperatives, and other sentences not standardly usable for making assertions that have truth values (1976, 73; 1991, 114–21), but he could hardly be thought to have dealt satisfactorily with the problem. Again I will pass this by and take his account to deal only with assertoric sentences. The simplest form of a truth-conditional semantics would be this: *The meaning of a sentence is given by the conditions that are necessary and sufficient for its truth.*

Dummett then lays down certain constraints on a theory of meaning, constraints that he takes to rule out an unqualified identification of meaning with truth conditions. (A) The theory must show how the understanding of a sentence is built up from the understanding of its meaningful parts (1976, 69; 1991, chap. 10). (B) The theory cannot be completely holistic (1975, 121, 127ff.; 1991, chap. 10). That is, it must not turn out that the meaning of every sentence presupposes the whole language. These two constraints will play no role in this discussion. I will be concentrating on what follows.

(C) The theory must explain in what the understanding of the language consists (1973, 92; 1975, 99–101; 1991, 108). If we are working with truth conditions, we must not only lay down those conditions but also show how one determines whether those conditions hold (1975, 118; 1991, 306–17). Thus truth conditions that constitute the meaning of some sentence we can understand must not be beyond human powers to grasp (1975, 133ff.). Dummett takes this to imply that a specification of what *manifests* the knowledge of truth conditions is essential (1991, 149, 313–14). Not all knowledge of the truth conditions of a sentence can consist in the ability to formulate those conditions, or else we are faced with an infinite regress in which the sentences used to formulate the truth conditions of a given sentence require yet other sentences to be used to formulate their truth conditions, . . . (1991, 150, 315). In at least some cases, the knowledge of the truth conditions of a sentence must consist in a practical ability—the ability to recognize that those conditions hold if and when they do.

Because of this third constraint we cannot rest content with an account of sentence meaning in terms of truth conditions that are independent of our means of ascertaining whether they hold (1973, 468, 470, 586; 1975, 101). To understand what it is for a sentence to be true (and hence to understand what it means) is to understand what it would be to *recognize* it as true.

> On this account, an understanding of a sentence consists in a capacity to recognize whatever is counted as verifying it, i.e., as conclusively establishing it as true. (1976, 110–111)

> A verificationist theory represents an understanding of a sentence as consisting in a knowledge of what counts as conclusive evidence for its truth. (1976, 132; see also 1976, 136; 1978, 155; 1991, 317)

And since, to spell out the the third constraint a bit further, an account of what it is to understand a sentence tells us what it is for a sentence to have a certain meaning, the meaning of a sentence is given by "verification conditions", conditions such that we can determine the truth of the sentence by ascertaining that those conditions hold, rather than by "realist"-truth conditions, that is, truth conditions that are specified without any attention as to how, if at all, we can tell whether they hold.

> [T]he sense of a sentence is thought of as being fixed by determining, not the conditions under which it is to be true, as Frege thought, but the conditions under which we are able to recognize it as true. (1973, 586)

> [T]he sense which we confer on the sentences of our language can be related only to the means of recognition of truth-value which we actually possess. (1973, 467)

In arguing from the conditions of *understanding* a sentence to conclusions about what it is for a sentence to *have a certain meaning*, Dummett assumes that understanding is the clue to meaning. And this is highly plausible. After all, to understand a sentence *is* to grasp its meaning. Moreover, it is crucial that the meaning(s) of a sentence is something that is accessible to speakers of the language. Sentence meaning, and more generally semantic and linguistic facts of all kinds, are not the sort of thing that might be totally unknowable by human beings with our present limitations. It is in this way unlike, say, the presence or absence of life elsewhere in the universe, which might conceivably remain forever unknown to us. For language is something that exists only by virtue of the use we make of it for communication and for the articulation of thought. And that use requires a grasp of the meanings of linguistic units. A sentence the meaning of which speakers of a language could not possibly grasp would be a sentence that is unusable for thought and discourse, and hence could not figure as part of a language.[2] Hence it is an eminently reasonable constraint on theories of meaning that they must depict meaning in such a way that it is possible for human beings to grasp those meanings, that is, to understand and use the linguistic items whose meanings they are.

Controversy enters when Dummett takes the further, verificationist

---

2. We have to qualify this argument to allow for sentences that are too complex for humans to grasp. If sentencehood is defined recursively, there is, in principle, no limit to the length and complexity of sentences in the language. Let the above argument be restricted to those sentences of the language that are simple enough to be usable by human beings.

step of maintaining that one can understand (know) what the truth conditions are for a sentence are only if one is able, in practice, to determine whether those conditions are satisfied. To understand a sentence is to be able to *recognize* what *verifies* it. What is the rationale for this further step? So far as I am aware, Dummett's reasons are two. (1) One could *learn* the meaning of a sentence only by learning how to tell whether it is true (1973, 467–68, 515). This could happen either by learning how to formulate truth conditions in sentences one already understands (and hence that are such that one already knows how to tell whether they are true), or by acquiring an unformulated, practical ability to recognize verifying conditions when and if they occur. But if I am just presented with a statement of truth conditions for a sentence, S, and I lack any capacity to determine whether those conditions hold, how does that help to me to understand S, to use it to communicate my thoughts to others, or to understand what someone is communicating to me by uttering S? All I have learned to do is to associate different forms of words; and that does not amount to understanding what any of them mean. (2) One could *manifest* one's understanding of a sentence only by showing that one recognized a verifying or falsifying condition, or by showing in some other way that one has the capacity to do so (1973, 467; 1976, 117; 1991, 149).

I will cast doubt on the capacity of these arguments to establish Dummett's position when I get to the critical portion of my remarks. For now I am trying to set out Dummett's position as clearly and completely as possible. The next point is that the verification (falsification) of which Dummett speaks has to be conclusive. (In addition to the last set of references, see 1975, 123; 1976, 132.) Dummett does not explain how he thinks of conclusiveness. He leaves it unclear whether he means to be presupposing very high standards such that we have not conclusively verified a statement unless we have presented grounds (evidence, reasons . . .) that are incompatible with its falsity, or unless we have presented grounds strong enough to exclude any reasonable doubt, or unless we have established it beyond any possibility of its being refuted or (reasonably) abandoned, or . . . Perhaps he is thinking in terms of more modest, everyday standards of conclusive verification, in which I can claim to have conclusively established that the water on the floor of my basement came from the hot water heater, even though my grounds for claiming this do not come up to any of the standards just mentioned. In any event, Dummett does place a great deal of emphasis on the distinction between conclusive and "defeasible" verification (confirmation, justification . . .), and roundly asserts that an ability to recognize the former is required for understanding a sentence.

This urgently raises the question of the status of sentences that fail this test. Let's say that theoretical principles in science, large scale historical accounts of the origin and nature of past social forms such as feudalism, and religious affirmations are not susceptible of conclusive verification. No one has the ability to recognize something as a conclusive verification of any such statement. Are we to say that no one understands them? Surely they are not meaningless gobbledygook, like "Rah-nem-zbk-ash". Perhaps they have some kind of meaning other than "factual meaning", a kind that will have to be delineated in some other way. The closest thing I have found to an answer to this question in Dummett is that a verificationist theory of meaning for such statements has to be given in terms of grounds that fall short of conclusiveness. Here is a passage from the preface to *Truth and Other Enigmas* (1978).

> As Putnam has recently pointed out [see "Realism and Reason" in Putnam (1978)], it is misleading to concentrate too heavily, as I have usually done, on a form of antirealist theory of meaning in which the meaning of a statement is given in terms of what conclusively verifies it; often such conclusive verification is not to be had. In "Realism" [an essay in Dummett (1978)] it is acknowledged that there may be no such thing as a conclusive verification, and that, in such a case, an anti-realist theory of meaning must be given in terms of grounds of assertion that fall short of being conclusive. (xxxviii)

In the essay "Realism" Dummett writes: "For him [the anti-realist] the meaning of a statement is intrinsically connected with that which we count as evidence for or against the statement; and there is nothing to prevent a statement's being so used that we do not treat anything as conclusively verifying it" (1978, 162).

Thus in the development of his thought Dummett recapitulates the movement of the Vienna Circle from requiring conclusive verifiability for factual meaningfulness to requiring merely "confirmability", that is, the possibility of finding considerations that count for or against the statement in question.[3] Dummett has not, to my knowledge, done anything to develop a verificationist semantics for non-conclusively verifiable sentences. Indeed, as indicated by the fact that he has little to say

---

3. Although Dummett thus feels that the difference between conclusively verifiable and non-conclusively verifiable sentences is of no great significance for the development of a verificationist theory of meaning, he does very definitely think, as we shall see, that this difference is crucial for truth-value attributions.

about how he conceives of conclusive verification, he has done little to develop verificationist semantics of any sort. He seems not to be interested in working out the details, with all the attention to epistemological issues that this would require. He is much more occupied with logical issues. In more than one passage Dummett frankly admits that he has not properly worked out the theory of meaning that he advocates.

> Whether a plausible theory of meaning in terms of verification can be constructed, I do not know; there are many problems which there is no space in this general discussion to investigate. (1976, 116)

> To replace a realistic theory of meaning by a verificationist one is to take a first step towards meeting the requirement that we incorporate into our theory of sense an account of the basis on which we judge the truth values of our sentences, since it does explain meanings in terms of actual human capacities for the recognition of truth. I have, however, already pointed out that this step does not, in itself, take us all the way towards meeting this requirement, and I have no clear idea how it may be met. (1976, 36–37)[4]

iii Critique of Verificationism

Before examining the bearing this semantics is claimed by Dummett to have, and the bearing it does have, on alethic realism, I will make some critical remarks on the semantics itself. I won't go into the matter as thoroughly as I would if I agreed with Dummett about its relevance to realism (see section v), but I do want to indicate why I think that his verificationism is neither adequate to the purpose, nor sufficiently motivated. But first a mild protest against Dummett's parochial concentration on a truth-conditions theory of sentence meaning as a starting point. When he says that "the most popular candidate" for a central role in the theory of meaning "is the notion of truth" (1973, 457; see also 1976, 67, 77), he is speaking from a severely limited perspective. A survey of all the accounts of linguistic meaning over the centuries would reveal that those featuring truth as the (a) central notion are in a tiny minority. Even in the twentieth century, this is by no means so common as a preoccupation with Frege, Carnap, and Davidson would lead one

4. In two essays, "Anti-realist Semantics: The Role of Criteria" and "Second Thoughts About Criteria", reprinted in Wright 1993, Crispin Wright explores the use of the Wittgensteinian notion of a criterion to give an account of sentence meaning in terms of defeasible assertibility conditions. The upshot of the second essay is that the notion will not do the job. Wright ends with a suggestion of an alternative approach but does not develop it.

to believe. There is also Grice and his progeny (Schiffer, Bennett) and illocutionary-act-based theories (Searle, Alston), not to mention a large variety of behavioristically oriented accounts. It is still more startling to hear Dummett say that "Philosophical theories of truth have usually been intended as contributions to delineating the outlines of some theory of meaning in which either the notions of truth and falsity themselves, or some closely related notion such as verification (establishing a statement as true) or acceptance (acknowledging a statement as true), have been taken as central" (1973, 457). It is a comparatively recent phenomenon that theories of truth have been oriented in this way.

To get back to the central issue, verificationist semantics has been criticized in many ways over the last few decades. Here I will confine myself to one basic difficulty, which I take to be fatal. Dummett thinks in terms of assigning meanings, one by one, to sentences in terms of what would (conclusively or inconclusively) verify the sentence. But with the possible exception of sentences usable for making observational or introspective reports (and even these are controversial), no empirical sentence can be empirically verified or confirmed unless we assume the truth of various other sentences. The reason for this is simple. Unless a sentence is wholly couched in observational terms, we cannot derive any observational statement from it alone. We require additional premises to make the derivation, without which no empirical test is possible. Take a simple example like "Jim is insecure". We would ordinarily try to decide the truth value of this by observing Jim's behavior and demeanor in a variety of situations. But the observable states of affairs that we ordinarily take to tell in favor of the statement, for example, nervously twisting his handkerchief before being called upon to speak, do not follow from "Jim is insecure" alone. We need further premises linking insecurity to such behavioral manifestations. We have to embed our target statement in a "minitheory of insecurity" before there is any possibility of our putting the statement to an empirical test. And there is a multiplicity of minitheories, some of which are incompatible with others, that can be used for this purpose. Thus what counts as an empirical verification (confirmation) of "Jim is insecure" does not depend on that sentence alone with its meaning.[5] It also depends on the further theoretical context in which it is embedded. Therefore the identification of verify-

---

5. To be sure, a verificationist can claim that nonobservational sentences like this come with a specification of what counts as empirical evidence for and against it as part of its meaning. This was the position of Operationalism. But it is generally agreed by now that this claim radically distorts the way in which nonobservational sentences function in science. Their meaning is much more loosely connected with observable indicators.

ing (confirming) conditions is not a function of the meaning alone, or vice versa. Hence the meaning of the sentence cannot be identified with any such set of conditions. And if the verificationist were to respond by saying that the meaning of 'Jim is insecure' consists of the contribution that sentence makes to verification conditions for various complexes in which it figures, he would have to give a much more complicated account of the meaning of the sentence than simply saying that the meaning is given by the conditions under which that sentence could be verified.[6]

The basic premise of this argument is generally credited nowadays to Quine:

> The notion lingers that to each statement, or each synthetic statement, there is associated a unique range of possible sensory events such that the occurrence of any of them would add to the likelihood of truth of the statement, and that there is associated also another unique range of possible sensory events whose occurrence would detract from that likelihood. . . . My counter suggestion . . . is that our statements about the external world face the tribunal of sense experience not individually but only as a corporate body. (1953, 40–41)

Actually the point goes back at least to Duhem, as Quine was quick to acknowledge. In any event, this thesis—that a nonobservational statement does not carry with it its distinctive set of confirmatory and disconfirmatory conditions—though it is one of the most often repeated platitudes in recent philosophy—is still persistently ignored by verificationists. Dummett makes a perfunctory acknowledgement of the Duhem–Quine point (1976, 111), but I can't see that he really takes account of it in working out his position. To do so would require him to say something much more complicated than he does. In Dummett's (1991, chap. 10) *The Logical Basis of Metaphysics* there is a chapter entitled "Holism", but the holism mostly criticized there is an extreme version according to which one cannot understand a given sentence without knowing the whole language.

By following out certain implications of the Duhem–Quine point we

6. It has been suggested to me by Alvin Plantinga that the verificationist might, so to say, complicate the view from another direction by taking the meaning of a single sentence to include all the verifying conditions for the additional statements that would be involved in providing empirical evidence for it. But this would render the specification of the meaning of any particular sentence unmanageably complex, since there is an indefinitely large plurality of ways of imbedding a given statement in a theoretical matrix for purposes of testing. It seems as clear as anything can be that when we grasp the meaning of a sentence we do not grasp anything nearly that complex.

can see not only that the meaning of a (nonobservational) sentence cannot be given in the way Dummett suggests, but that it is clear that we have the capacity to grasp the meaning (truth conditions if that is what is involved) of nonobservational sentences without being able to recognize verification conditions for them. Consider the status of speculative suggestions prior to the time at which someone figures out a way of empirical testing them, for example, the first glimmer of atomism in ancient Greece. When the idea first occurred to one that matter is composed of tiny, invisible, and indivisible particles with much empty space in between, no one had any idea of how to put the suggestion to the test because no one had developed ways of embedding this suggestion in a context that made possible the derivation of observationally testable consequences. In subsequent millenia, many such connections were hypothesized, of ever-increasing sophistication and complexity, and this brought the thesis within the range of empirical inquiry. But even at the beginning the sentence, 'All matter is composed of invisible, indivisible particles' had a meaning that was grasped by some people. It must have; otherwise those who worked on ways to connect *it* up with other suppositions so as to put it to the test would have had nothing to work on. It had a meaning and was understood before there were any "verification conditions" associated with it.

These same considerations show verificationist semantics to be poorly motivated. Consider Dummett's learning argument mentioned in the previous section—*one can learn the meaning of a sentence only by learning verification conditions.* But we don't acquire the "use" of sentences one by one in this way, attaching verification and falsification conditions separately to each one. Instead, once we have a leg up on the language, we use what we have already mastered to construct and understand indefinitely many new sentences, without having to appeal to anything outside the language to do so, whether "verification conditions" or otherwise. Thus, going back to atomism, having earlier mastered the use of terms like ''particle', 'composed of', 'visible', 'divisible', 'space', etc., along with negation and certain grammatical forms, we are able to understand and use 'All of matter is composed of invisible, indivisible particles with a lot of empty space in between', without learning any verification and falsification conditions for that particular sentence. Having acquired an initial stock of terms, sentence forms, etc., we can generate indefinitely many new sentences by various combinations of the stock we already have in hand. As another example, consider how we can use and extend terms like 'power', 'knowledge', 'create', 'person', 'body, 'finite', along, again, with negation and various grammatical forms, to generate an indefinitely large number of sentences about an infinite all-powerful and all-knowing personal creator of all other beings, again without having the foggiest idea of what the verification conditions for this statement might be. It does small credit to human powers of cognition to suppose that we can acquire the understanding and use of sentences only by associating something like "verification conditions" with them one by one.[7]

Indeed, Dummett himself recognizes the points I have just been making. He recognizes that once we have mastered a basic set of sentences we can exploit that knowledge to understand indefinitely many other sentences.

> The compositional principle demands that, for any given [subsentential] expression, we should distinguish between two kinds of sentence containing it. An understanding of the expression will consist in the ability to understand representative sentences of the first kind and does not, therefore, *precede* the understanding of sentences of that kind. By contrast, an antecedent understanding of the expression will combine with an understanding of the other constituent expressions to *yield* an understanding of a sentence of the second kind, which demands an understanding of the expression but is not demanded by it. (1991, 224; see also 1973, 515; 1975, 137)

This is clearly subversive of the claim that the understanding of *every* sentence consists in a grasp of what would verify or confirm that sentence. For what Dummett says here indicates that for many (most?) sentences, such as those I cited above in my minicritique of verificationist semantics, we have ways of understanding them other than grasping their verification conditions, namely, understanding the constituent expressions and grasping how they are combined in the sentence. My contentions and the views expressed in the above quotation are compatible, at most, with the claim that the understanding of (base) sentences, those that Dummett calls the "first kind", consists in a grasp of what would verify or falsify them. And this (much) more restricted verificationism is flatly inconsistent with Dummett's repeated assertions of an across-the-board verificationist semantics, as well as being subversive of his learning argument for this position.

7. In Dummett 1991, 341–48, he considers three realist replies to his verificationism, but the position adumbrated above is not among them. The closest is the third reply, in which the so-called realist claims that we can understand sentences we are not capable of showing to be true or false by an analogical conception of a subject that does have such a capacity. But this "realist" has already given the game away by conceding "the absurdity of supposing that a statement of any kind could be true if it was in principle impossible to know that it was true" (345).

The "manifestation argument" can be dismissed on the same grounds. Since our understanding of sentences is not, in general, a matter of knowing their verification conditions, we cannot expect a "manifestation" of that understanding to amount, in general, to showing that we know under what conditions they are verified or falsified. Just what does manifest linguistic understanding is a further, and complicated problem into which I cannot go in this book. But I will say this. Dummett seeks to support his semantics by contending that our linguistic understanding must show itself in how we *use* the language. I couldn't agree more. But Dummett, in effect, restricts "use" to our activity of accepting or rejecting statements as certain conditions are or are not satisfied; and that I cannot accept. This is only one bit of what is involved in our use of language. A more comprehensive view would lead to what I call an "illocutionary-act-potential" theory of sentence meaning, but that is a very long story—one for another occasion.[8]

Having seen that Dummett accepts a compositionality principle that has the effect of restricting his verificationist semantics to a basic stratum of language, we can further note that his learning and manifestation arguments are often stated in such a way as to support only this limited position. He more than once, in speaking of manifestations of understanding, points out that where we have formulations of truth conditions in antecedently understood terms our grasp of those conditions can consist in understanding those formulations, rather than in a practical capacity to recognize verification conditions (1976, 79–80, 97–98). And the claim that we learn to grasp sentences by learning verification conditions for them is sometimes explicitly restricted to a "fragment" of language (1973, 515). A further critical evaluation of Dummett's verificationist semantics would go into the question whether it is the right story even for a semantically basic stratum of language.

iv Verificationist Semantics and the Concept of Truth

So much for the claims of verificationist semantics. Now for the question of what bearing this has on realism—alethic and otherwise, but with special attention to the former.

Dummett certainly takes his semantics to have implications for how to think about truth. Indeed, he gives the impression of having entered onto the whole semantic project for the sake of these implications, to-

---

8. See Alston 1994 and my forthcoming book, *Illocutionary Acts and Sentence Meaning.*

gether with further implications as to how to understand the realism issue generally.

> [T]he notion of truth, when it is introduced, must be explained, in some manner, in terms of our capacity to recognize statements as true, and not in terms of a condition which transcends human capacities. (1976, 116)

> The anti-realist opposes to this [realism] the view that statements of the disputed class are to be understood only by reference to the sort of thing which we count as evidence for a statement of that class. . . . The anti-realist insists . . . that the meanings of these statements are tied directly to what we count as evidence for them, in such a way that a statement of the disputed class, if true at all, can be true only in virtue of something of which we could know and which we should count as evidence of its truth. (1978, 146)

Here Dummett purports to derive from his verificationist semantics a view about the concept of truth. But precisely how is this concept to be understood? The first quotation is quite unspecific. The second can hardly be credited with giving us a verificationist analysis of truth. What it presents as *that in virtue of which a statement is true* itself employs the (a) concept of truth ("something of which we could know and which we should count as evidence of its *truth*"). However, we should not make too much of this apparent circularity. Dummett tells us that "the central notions of a theory of meaning must . . . be those of verification and falsification rather than those of truth and falsity" (1973, 467). This dictum should not, of course, be read as a proposal to dispense with the terms 'true' and 'false' altogether, a project radically at variance with Dummett's practice. Rather it expresses an intention to explain 'true' and 'false' in terms of verification and falsification. Thus we should take the second quotation as telling us that, on a verificationist conception, a statement is true *if and only if* there are "verifying conditions" for it, that is, *conditions cognitively accessible to us and such that if we were aware of them we would be in a position to verify the statement.*[9] (Cf. "[T]he truth of the statement can consist only in the existence of the evidence", [1978, 155]; also, "On a verificationist account . . . our notions of truth and falsity, as applied to such a sentence, consist merely in the conception of a situation's occurring which would thus conclusively determine its truth-value" [1973, 514].)

---

9. To be sure, this avoids the circularity only if 'verify' is conceptually independent of truth, and this is doubtful, to say the least. Doesn't 'verify' mean *show to be true*? For more on this see the end of section v.

Before we are home free, we must disambiguate such formulations in an important respect. Look at the last quotation. A situation that would conclusively determine a statement's truth value could be understood in terms of our italicized formula, as a situation that involves verifying conditions that we *could* use to verify the statement. But it could also be construed as a situation in which an actual verification is carried out.* This last understanding would appear, on the surface, to be dominant in the following passage: "The truth of such a sentence can consist only in the occurrence of the sort of situation in which we have learned to recognize it as true, and its falsity in the occurrence of the sort of situation in which we have learned to recognize it as false" (1973, p. 468). For it is natural to think of the kind of situation described as one in which we have carried out a verification or falsification (a *recognition* of the sentence as true or false). Thus if we are to arrive at a single unambiguous Dummettian verificationist concept of truth, we must decide whether (a) it consists in the *existence* of a verifying condition (one that we *could* use to verify the statement, whether we have actually done so or not), or (b) it consists in the actual carrying out of a verification.

So far as I can see the weight of the textual evidence definitely favors (a). I have cited several passages that seem to be unambiguously on that side; and the last quote is the only one I know that is naturally read in terms of (b). But what I take to be a more decisive point is that (b) would make nonsense out of much of Dummett's discussion of truth. For one thing, although he wants to restrict the application of truth values much more than realists do (see the discussion below of his denial of bivalence), there is no hint that he has an idea of restricting truth-value bearers to statements that have actually been verified or falsified by some human being. And indeed the attempt to do so would short circuit a large part of our employment of 'true' and 'false'. We could not wonder, or look into, whether a hitherto uninvestigated hypothesis is true or false; instead we would have to set out trying to *make* it true or false. We could not issue generalizations involving 'true' and 'false', like "In a valid argument it is impossible for all the premises to be true and the conclusion false", that range over statements that have as yet been neither verified nor falsified. An explicit statement of Dummett's that bears on this matter, and that we shall be exploring shortly is that each "decidable" statement is either true or false. (See below for an explanation of 'decidable'.) But it is obvious that not all such statements have been, or ever will be, verified or falsified. Hence, of the two alternatives (a) is the one we must adopt.

Another feature of the account concerns the distinction between *de-*

cidable and *undecidable* statements, to which I now turn. This distinction has only a tangential relevance to my concerns here, but since it plays a large role in Dummett's presentation of his position, it will be necessary for me to relate it to my discussion. It will be useful to examine the following passage in some detail.

> From this point of view [verificationism] what we learn when we learn to use . . . sentences is not what it is for them to be true or false, but, rather, what counts for us as conclusively establishing them as true or as false: the central notions of a theory of meaning must, therefore, be those of verification and falsification rather than those of truth and falsity. In the case of a sentence for which we have no effective means of deciding its truth-value, the state of affairs which has, in general, to obtain for it to be true is, by hypothesis, one which we are not capable of recognizing as obtaining whenever it obtains. . . . [W]hen we are concerned with sentences of this kind, we should regard an understanding of them as consisting in an ability to do just what we actually learn to do when we learn to use them, that is, in certain circumstances to recognize them as having been verified and in others as having been falsified. The truth- and falsity-conditions for any sentence hence should instead be taken as ones which we are capable of recognizing effectively whenever they obtain: it is in just this that the difference resides between the realist conception of truth and falsity and the alternative conception of verification and falsification. An undecidable sentence is simply one whose sense is such that, though in certain effectively recognizable situations we acknowledge it as true, in others we acknowledge it as false, and in yet others no decision is possible, we possess no effective means for bringing about a situation which is one or other of the first two kinds. . . . The actual fact of our linguistic practice is that the only notions of truth and falsity which we have for such a sentence are ones which do not entitle us to regard the sentence as determinately true or false independently of our knowledge. The truth of such a sentence can consist only in the occurrence of the sort of situation in which we have learned to recognize it as true, and its falsity in the occurrence of the sort of situation in which we have learned to recognize it as false; since we have no guarantee either that a situation of one or other kind will occur, or that we can bring about such a situation at will, only a misleading picture of what we learned when we learned to use sentences of that form can give us the impression that we possess a notion of truth for that sentence relative to which it is determinately either true or false. (1973, 467–68)

As examples of undecidable sentences Dummett mentions open-ended universal generalizations, subjunctive conditionals and sentences containing components that are explained in terms of such conditionals, and statements about the past.

This passage may give the impression that Dummett thinks that the verificationist concept of truth applies only to undecidable sentences, but such is not his view. Consider the following passage.

> The conditions under which a sentence is recognized as true or as false . . . are conditions of quite another kind [from realist-truth conditions]; they have, by the nature of the case, to be conditions which we can recognize as obtaining when they obtain. Only in the very simplest of cases, perhaps such a statement as 'I have a toothache', does it hold even for one individual that either that condition in which the sentence is recognized as true obtains, or that condition obtains in which it is recognized as false. The most that we can normally hope for is that we have some effective method of bringing about a situation in which, relative to a given sentence, one or other of these two conditions must obtain: when such an effective method exists, the sentence is effectively decidable. (1973, 586)

This passage, and many others, should be read as indicating that decidable and undecidable sentences differ not in *what constitutes truth for them*, but in the kind or degree of access we have to that. In both cases, a sentence is true if and only if a "verifying condition" obtains. For decidable sentences we have the capacity to get ourselves, whenever we choose, into a situation in which we ascertain either a verifying or falsifying condition. For undecidable sentences we lack such a capacity, though for such a sentence, it may happen that we do encounter a verifying or falsifying condition.

One implication Dummett draws from his account of truth is this: "If a statement is true, it must be in principle possible to know that it is true" (1976, 99). Interestingly enough, he maintains that this is (must be) acceptable even to a realist, in a sense. Speaking of the principle just formulated he says:

> [I]ts application depends heavily on the way in which 'in principle possible' is construed. One who adopts a realistic view of any problematic class of statements will have to interpret 'in principle possible' in a fairly generous way. He will not hold that, whenever a statement is true, it must be possible, even in principle, for *us* to know that it is true, that is, for beings with our particular restricted observational and intellectual faculties and spatiotemporal viewpoint. . . . But even the most thoroughgoing realist must grant that we could hardly be said to

grasp what it is for a statement to be true if we had no conception whatever of how it might be known to be true; there would, in such a case, be no substance to our conception of its truth condition. Moreover, he would further grant that it would be useless to specify in a purely trivial manner the additional powers which a hypothetical being would have to have if he were to be capable of observing directly the truth or falsity of statements of some given class. We could not, for example, explain that a being who had a direct insight into counterfactual reality would be able to determine by direct observation the truth or falsity of any counterfactual conditional, because the expression 'a direct insight into counterfactual reality' provides no picture of what these powers consist in. Even the realist will concede that the picture of the required superhuman powers must always bear a recognizable relation to the powers which we in fact possess; they must be analogous to, or an extension of, our actual powers. (1976, 100)

I fear that Dummett has concocted a "thoroughgoing realist" for his own philosophical purposes. The thoroughgoing realist writing these lines, for one, does not fit his picture. In the explication of the concept of truth I gave in Chapter 1 I said nothing at any point about what it would be to know a statement to be true. Hence I flatly deny that "we could hardly grasp what it is for a statement to be true if we had no conception whatever of how it might be known to be true". Even if we have such a conception, it is not at all necessary for this to figure in our understanding of what it is for a statement to be true, as I fancy I showed in Chapter 1. Moreover, even though I have no hesitation in recognizing that an omniscient being would know the truth of every true proposition, I am not at all disposed to think that I have any insight into how such a being would know (much of) what it knows. Hence I feel under no pressure to suppose that its superhuman powers "bear a recognizable relation to powers which we in fact possess". To be sure, Dummett might point out that he meant the "must grant" in "even the most thoroughgoing realist must grant that . . ." to be normative rather than descriptive, and if I, for example, do not grant these points, I am thereby failing to conform to norms of rationality. That may be, but I would like to see a convincing argument for it.

This is the place at which to look at Dummett's notorious denial of the Principle of Bivalence for undecidable sentences. Dummett lays it down more than once that, on the verificationist account of truth, undecidable sentences cannot be depended on to have a determinate truth value. Thus in the long passage quoted above from *Frege: The Philosophy of Language* (1973), he writes:

[T]he only notions of truth and falsity which we have for such a sentence are ones which do not entitle us to regard the sentence as determinately true or false independently of our knowledge. The truth of such a sentence can consist only in the occurrence of the sort of situation in which we have learned to recognize it as true, and its falsity in the occurrence of the sort of situation in which we have learned to recognize it as false; since we have no guarantee either that a situation of one or other kind will occur, or that we can bring about such a situation at will, only a misleading picture of what we learned when we learned to use sentences of that form can give us the impression that we possess a notion of truth for that sentence relative to which it is determinately either true or false. (1973, 468)

And again:

On a verificationist account, an understanding of such a sentence, a grasp of its sense, consists merely in the capacity to recognize whatever would decide conclusively in favour of the truth or of the falsity of the sentence; and our notions of truth and falsity, as applied to such a sentence, consist merely in the conception of a situation's occurring which would thus conclusively determine its truth-value. From such a viewpoint, there would be no justification in saying, of such an undecidable sentence, that it must be either true or false, in advance of anything's occurring to enable us to recognize it as one or the other, or at least of information's becoming available which would provide us with what we previously lacked, an effective means of bringing about such a determining situation. (1973, 514; see also 1973, 586–87; 1976, 103, 105, 116)

The first of these passages, and others of the same ilk, might give the impression that Dummett is flatly denying truth value to undecidable sentences. But the second passage and others correct that misapprehension. The claim, rather, is that we cannot take any undecidable sentence to have a definite truth value, prior to showing that it does by encountering a verifying or falsifying situation. What is denied is that every undecidable assertoric sentence, just by virtue of being a meaningful assertoric sentence, *must* be true or false. Thus the position is often put as a denial of the Principle of Bivalence, the principle that every assertoric sentence *must* be either true or false.

Note that the denial of bivalence for undecidable sentences presupposes that there is no problem about their satisfying verificationist conditions of meaningfulness. If these sentences were not even meaningful, no question of their capacity for truth and falsity could arise. Then the position would be—not that they could not all be guaranteed to have a definite truth value, but rather that none of them could have a truth value. Going back again to the long quotation (1973), we see there that Dummett makes it quite explicit just how undecidable sentences conform to verificationist requirements for having a meaning: "[W]e should regard an understanding of them as consisting in an ability to do just what we actually learn to do when we learn to use them, that is, in certain circumstances to recognize them as having been verified and in others as having been falsified." A look back at Dummett's formulations of a verificationist account of sentence meaning will confirm that the undecidable sentences have what it takes. If we have a grasp of what *would* constitute a verifying (falsifying) condition for a sentence, then it has a verificationally approved meaning for us. And Dummett is at pains to underline this point from time to time. For example:

> On this account, an understanding of a statement consists in a capacity to recognize whatever is counted as verifying it, i.e., as conclusively establishing it as true. It is not necessary that we should have any means of deciding the truth or falsity of the statement, only that we be capable of recognizing when its truth has been established. (1976, 110–111; see also 1973, 514)

One might well wonder whether the sentences that Dummett regards as undecidable really are susceptible of conclusive verification. He holds, you will recall, that these sentences are such that there are circumstances in which we can apprehend verifying (falsifying) conditions, but that we lack an effective capacity to realize such circumstances at will. But are there such circumstances for, for example, open-ended universal generalizations and subjunctive conditionals? What would constitute a conclusively verifying condition, one that we are capable of recognizing on inspection, for an open-ended universal generalization? Is it within human powers to verify conclusively the generalization that all life, everywhere—past, present, and future—involves DNA? It is certainly conceivable that we should identify a falsifying condition. Would that satisfy the requirement? And how about counterfactual conditionals? What would conclusively verify or falsify the statement that if Britain and France had militarily opposed Hitler's military occupation of the Rhineland, his government would have collapsed? Until we hear more from Dummett on this, one may be pardoned for suggesting that much of what Dummett includes in the undecidable subclass of the conclusively verifiable should be ranked rather with, at best, the inconclusively verifiable.

v Compatibility of Verificationist Semantics and Realist Truth

I now want to suggest that, despite Dummett's asseverations, his verificationist account of sentence meaning by no means requires the abandonment of a realist conception of truth, at least the realist conception
I have been advocating. Let's focus on a particular set of verification
conditions. Consider the sentence, 'The orchestra is playing Beethoven's Fifth Symphony'. The verification condition for this, let's say, is
that the performance follows fairly closely an authentic score of that
symphony. Now according to Dummett's semantics the *content* of my
statement that the orchestra is playing Beethoven's Fifth Symphony is
just that the verification condition obtains. But then in satisfying the
Dummettian truth condition that the verification condition obtains, we
have simultaneously and *ipso facto* satisfied the *realist* truth condition that
what is being asserted is the case. In other words, if what we assert is
always that a verification condition for the assertion obtains, then that
condition's obtaining necessarily *amounts to* what the assertion asserts to
be the case. No wedge can be driven between them. In other words,
Dummett's verificationist semantics for sentences amounts to taking the
propositional content of what is asserted by uttering a sentence to be
the satisfaction of a verification condition. This is just a particular form
of a reductionist theory of propositional content—in this case a verificationist reduction. And like all reductions it is perfectly compatible with
an account of truth according to which the statement that p is true if
and only if p. It is just that we have a verificationist view of what p is in
each case.[10]

To be sure, in the essay, "Realism", Dummett says that "anti-realism
need not take the form of reductionism" (1978, 157). Be that as it may,
his verificationism obviously does take this form. Not only does he explicitly state, as we have seen, that the content of an assertion is that the
statement asserted can be verified. There is also this clinching consideration. Consider the statement of a verifying condition for the statement
that p. The statement of that must, on Dummett's semantics, have the
same content as the statement that p. Surely a verifying condition suffices to verify the statement that that very condition obtains. And so if
the verifying condition for p is C, the statement that C obtains has the
same verifying condition as the statement that p, and thereby has the

10. In Dummett 1991, 327–28 he acknowledges that reductionism is compatible with realism, but his reasons for this are very different from mine.

same propositional content. Thus the statement that p is the same statement as the statement that C obtains. Q.E.D.[11]

Look at the matter in still another way. We can abstractly imagine two ways in which a verificationist semantics might try to distinguish itself from a realist semantics, for a range of assertoric sentences. On the one hand, it might take a verificationist line on the propositional content of these statements. On the other hand, it might leave the propositional content alone and take a verificationist tack on what it is for a statement to be true. But it need not do both. Either move will give it a distinctively verificationist cast. What we have seen is that although Dummett says that his view is distinctively verificationist in the second way, he has already made it verificationist in the first way. That being the case, he is unwarranted in claiming that the verificationism *requires* the second way—adopting a different understanding of truth. The reductionist theory of content cuts the ground from under the demand for a nonrealist theory of truth.

Note too that it is only the first way of being verificationist that gives us a verificationist theory of sentence *meaning*. For the second way, which confines its verificationism to reshaping the concept of truth, "leaves the propositional content alone". It does not carry with it a verificationist interpretation of sentence meaning. Thus Dummett cannot take the second way *instead of the first way* without abandoning the verificationist account of sentence meaning, thus rendering his position unrecognizable. But he maintains the verificationist semantics at the price of rendering his concept of truth gratuitous. I do not deny that he could hold the verificationist account of truth, consistently with his verificationist semantics. I do not claim that the two views are incompatible. My point is only that the verificationist semantics does not provide a basis for the verificationist account of truth. Thus he needs a rationale for his account of truth other than the one he suggests.

In fairness, I should point out that Dummett's characterization of a realist conception of truth is by no means identical with mine.

> Realism I characterize as the belief that statements of the disputed
> class possess an objective truth-value, independently of our means of

---

11. We have to be careful how we formulate the idea that the statement that *p* is the statement that C. If the latter refers to the statement that *p* (if, for example, it is the statement that C is a verifying condition for the statement that *p*), then we are in the self-defeating position of taking the statement that *p* to be a statement about the statement that *p*, in which case we will never be able to say what the statement that *p* is. (It is a statement about a statement that is about a statement that is about . . . .) Hence the statement that C, in order to be identical to the statement that *p*, must be construed as a formulation of the verifying condition, not a statement that this is a verifying condition *for the statement that p*. See Chapter 7 for a similar puzzle posed for any explicitly epistemic analysis of truth.

knowing it; they are true or false in virtue of a reality existing independently of us . . . [;] that is, the realist holds that the meanings of statements of the disputed class are not directly tied to the kind of evidence for them that we have, but consist in the manner of their determination as true or false by states of affairs whose existence is not dependent on our possession of evidence for them. (1978, 146)

[F]or the realist, the statement can be true even though we have no means of recognizing it as true. (1978, 147)

The phrase "true or false in virtue of a reality existing independently of us" in the first quotation would seem to be a slip, as a way of characterizing what distinguishes the realist from the antirealist (verificationist). For as Dummett points out on the next page: "It is not, of course, simply a matter of whether or not the truth of a statement of the disputed class is something objective. The realist and the anti-realist may agree that it is an objective matter whether, in the case of any given statement of the class, the criteria we use for judging such a statement to be true are satisfied."

At least it was a slip if we can equate "existing independently of us" with "objective". The phrase "determination as true or false by states of affairs whose existence is not dependent on our possession of evidence for them" would seem to be a much better way of expressing Dummett's idea. The heart of the contrast, as Dummett sees it, is that for the realist a statement may have a determinate truth value whatever our position vis-à-vis verifying (falsifying) or evidential states of affairs, whereas for the antirealist, truth value is essentially tied to our access to what shows the statement to be true or false. By those lights it may well seem that verificationist semantics really does imply a nonrealist account of truth. But not so fast. The verificationist reduction of content does imply that whenever a statement is true on (my kind of) a realist conception of truth, there is a verifying condition accessible to us. But it does not follow from this that the accessibility is required by the *concept of truth*. It could still be that the truth of the statement that p only (conceptually) requires that it be the case that p; it would, then, be a further point that all the ps are such that whenever that condition is satisfied there is a verifying condition that we have the capacity to recognize.

One more point on the relation of verificationism and (my version of) realist truth. Doesn't the notion of verification presuppose a notion of truth, one that is independent of verifiability, independent in the sense of not being definable by verifiability, since verifiability, on the contrary has to be defined (partly) by truth? Looking back at Dummett's formulations of a verificationist conception of truth we have quoted, we see that he usually couches them in terms of the existence of conditions sufficient to establish the *truth* of the statement in question. And once we move out from the territory of conclusively verifiable statements and take in statements for which we can only pile up evidence that renders them more or less probable, isn't it still more undeniable that a concept of truth is presupposed? For if we say that the most we can do with respect to, for example, a theoretical statement in science is to adduce evidence that makes it more or less probable but cannot exhibit conclusively verifying evidence, by virtue of what do we make the judgment that the evidence available to us is insufficient to strictly verify? We must have some grasp of what is being asserted by the statement that goes beyond any possible evidence we can compile. And if, as Dummett assumes, such understanding consists in a grasp of either (realist) truth conditions or verification conditions, and since, ex hypothesi the latter are not available here, then what is presupposed here is a grasp of realist truth conditions for the statement.[12] It does not strictly follow from these considerations that it is a realist notion of truth (in my version) that is being presupposed, but that seems overwhelmingly the most likely supposition.

The idea just broached—that verification presupposes an independent notion of truth—may not be wholly repugnant to Dummett. He is not at all disposed to get rid of a realist concept of truth. On the contrary, he affirms that it is needed for certain purposes, for example to explicate the notion of validity of inferences (1976, 115). Moreover, it is no part of his program to give a reductive (verificationist) definition of the ordinary concept of truth, and thereby turn it into something else. On the contrary, his programme is to introduce a verificationist conception of truth, contrast it with the realist conception, and give it pride of place.

vi No Meaningful Sentences Are Only Defeasibly Verifiable

The discussion up to this point has been almost entirely restricted to conclusively verifiable sentences. But, as I've already noted, Dummett is well aware that not everything we succeed in asserting is subject to conclusive verification or falsification. He does not say much about this, and I am not aware of a passage in which he gives examples of such sen-

12. See Vision 1988, chap. 7 for a detailed presentation of this argument.

tences. Let's fill in for him and take theoretical statements in science, lawlike open-ended universal generalizations, and subjunctive conditionals to have this status.[13] It is clear that his position implies that such statements lack a truth value. Since there is no (conclusively) verifying condition the statement is not true, and since there is no (conclusively) falsifying condition the statement is not false. Whatever reason he has for denying bivalence to those conclusively verifiable sentences that are not "decidable" will apply in spades to those that can, at best, only receive defeasible evidence. It is not just that there is no guarantee that they have a truth value. There would seem to be a guarantee that they do not. And yet he displays no tendency to deny that they are understandable. He even suggests that an antirealist theory of meaning could be "given in terms of grounds of assertion that fall short of being conclusive" (1978, xxxviii). Presumably, if this project were carried out, we would take the understanding of a defeasibly confirmable sentence to consist of the ability to recognize defeasibly confirming conditions and defeasibly disconfirming conditions, on the model of his account of the understanding of undecidable conclusively verifiable sentences. And, presumably, this would give rise to an account of the meaning of such sentences as consisting in the confirming and disconfirming conditions in each case.

But if we think this position through, we get the very surprising conclusion that there can be no merely inconclusively verifiable meaningful sentences. For the basic principle of his semantics is that the meaning of a (conclusively verified) sentence is given by the verifying conditions. Transfer that to sentences that are putatively at most non-conclusively verifiable, and, as just pointed out, we get the result that the meaning of one of those sentences is given by its (allegedly nonconclusive) confirmation conditions. But these verifying or confirming conditions are, by hypothesis, such that we can, at least in favorable circumstances, recognize them to obtain when they do; they are, by their nature, the sort of things that are cognitively accessible to us. But then the statement of a set of confirming conditions, C, for a putatively non-conclusively verifiable sentence, S, is itself conclusively verifiable. But by the terms of verificationist semantics the statement of C is synonymous with S, since C is what specifies S's meaning. Therefore S is conclusively verifiable after all. Hence there can be no merely defeasibly verifiable meaningful sentences on this semantics. Q.E.D.

13. Dummett takes the latter two classes as examples of the undecidable subclass of conclusively verifiable sentences. But I have already expressed doubt about this.

vii Dummett on Realism

That completes my examination of the relation of Dummett's verificationism to alethic realism. I could take my leave at this point. But since Dummett makes such a point of claiming that realism–antirealism controversies are to be construed in terms of whether to adopt a realist or a verificationist conception of truth—along with the (allegedly) associated issue of whether the Principle of Bivalence holds for all statements—it will not be an intolerable digression to take a brief look at these claims.

In his essay, "Realism" (reprinted in 1978) Dummett points out differences in the way disputes between realists and antirealists about a given subject matter are presented. Sometimes it is a question whether entities of a certain type exist, or whether they are among the "ultimate constituents of reality". Linguistically construed, these would be questions about whether terms belonging to a certain range have a reference and about whether statements of a certain type can be reduced to statements of another type. He then presents his preferred way of construing the contrast. "Realism I characterize as the belief that statements of the disputed class possess an objective truth-value, independently of our means of knowing it; they are true or false in virtue of a reality existing independently of us" (1978, 146; see also 1973, 466; 1976, 101; 1978, xxx, 155).

Note that once more Dummett closely associates possessing a truth value independently of our means of knowing it and possessing a truth value in virtue of a reality existing independently of us. He seems not to notice that one of these conditions might hold and not the other. In particular, why couldn't our statements (mostly) be true or false in virtue of facts that are what they are independently of us, even though truth value also requires that we have cognitive access to that independently existing truth-value determiner? This is not Dummett's conception of how the first condition is satisfied; his conception of this is tied to verificationist semantics. But it is a (putative) possibility that should be considered.

Dummett goes on to characterize the antirealist foil to this position.

> The anti-realist opposes to this the view that statements of the disputed class are to be understood only by reference to the sort of thing which we count as evidence for a statement of that class. . . . The anti-realist insists . . . that the meanings of these statements are tied directly to what we count as evidence for them, in such a way that a statement

of the disputed class, if true at all, can be true only in virtue of something of which we could know and which we should count as evidence
for its truth. The dispute thus concerns the notion of truth appropriate for statements of the disputed class; and this means that it is a
dispute concerning the kind of *meaning* which these statements have.
(1978, 146)

Here again we have the claim that a verificationist account of the meaning of a statement carries with it a different conception of truth. (I have
already done what I can to shoot down this view.) Hence Dummett also
characterizes the dispute as one about the kind of meaning possessed
by the sentences in question. "The conflict between realism and antirealism is a conflict about the kind of meaning possessed by statements
of the disputed class" (1978, 155). And since Dummett holds that the
verificationist notion of truth is such that the Principle of Bivalence applies to none but decidable sentences, he is equally disposed to characterize realism as a commitment to bivalence for all statements. "We may,
in fact, characterize realism concerning a given class of statements as
the assumption that each statement of that class is determinately either
true or false" (1976, 93; see also 1973, 466; 1976, 93, 101; 1978, xxix–
xxxi).

Thus Dummett gives us three characterizations of the realist–
antirealist controversy concerning a given class of sentences: (1) the
kind of meaning these sentence have, (2) the notion of truth that is
applicable, and (3) whether the Principle of Bivalence holds across the
board. Since he takes these to be tightly connected, he feels comfortable
in freely oscillating between them. But since I have what I take to be
good and sufficient reason for denying these connections, the characterizations do not seem to me to be anywhere nearly equivalent. Be that as
it may, I want to look briefly at the extent to which any of these formulations captures what is at issue in what are termed realist–antirealist disputes. I will concentrate on the formulation in terms of truth, since that
is the one most intimately connected to the topic of this book, but with
side glances at the others.

Before doing that, I should note a couple of things that Dummett says
by way of explaining why he proceeds as he does. First, he is concerned
with the apparent heterogeneity of so-called realist–antirealist controversies, and he thinks that his formulation enables us to see a unifying
thread. Second, there is a general skepticism about traditional metaphysics. He thinks that metaphysical talk about something's "existing
independently of us", and the contrasting talk of being "constructed by

us" and the like, are simply expressions of "pictures"; and a "picture preference" is not a theoretical position that can be argued. "[T]he content of each picture lies in the conception of meaning that prompts it" (1978, xxviii–xxix). Thus behind Dummett's way of viewing realism is a familiar theme in twentieth-century philosophy—a substitution of linguistic issues for metaphysical issues. "[T]he whole point of my approach to these problems has been to show that the theory of meaning underlies metaphysics. If I have made any worthwhile contribution to philosophy, I think it must lie in having raised this issue in these terms" (1978, xl).

Let's turn now to the question of how fully Dummett's characterization(s) of realist–antirealist disputes covers the waterfront. I take the coverage to be very inadequate. Indeed, Dummett is careful to disclaim any complete coverage.

> I did not suppose that, by making acceptance of the principle of biva-
> lence the touchstone of a realist view, I was uncovering what underlay
> all traditional applications of the term 'realism'. I thought, rather, that
> the traditional use of the term covered a confusion between two quite
> different types of issue—whether statements of one kind could in any
> sense be reduced to statements of another kind, and whether state-
> ments of the one kind could be held to be determinately either true
> or false; and I thought that no progress could be made in discussing
> these problems until those issues were sharply distinguished. How,
> having clearly distinguished them, one then prefers to use the term
> 'realism' is a matter of secondary importance. (1978, xxxii)

So disputes over claimed reductions of, for example, physical-object statements to phenomenal statements are explicitly set to one side.[14] But there plenty of other counterexamples lurking in the underbrush. Consider the "flat denial of the existence of Xs" form of antirealism discussed in Chapter 2. Various thinkers have denied the real existence of all sorts of abstract entities—properties, propositions, classes, numbers—of temporal succession, space, material substance, and so on. If we think of a dispute between one who holds that propositions exist and one who denies this, it is difficult, if not impossible, to see that they differ over the kind of meaning possessed by "proposition sentences", or about the concept of truth applicable, or about the Principle of Biva-lence. These issues *can* be involved. A verificationist could deny the exis-

14. See Chapter 2 for a list of some other reductionist claims that are prominent in the literature.

tence of propositions because sentences putatively about propositions do not have the kind of meaning that would satisfy verificationist scruples. But that is only one among many reasons for denying the real existence of propositions. There is no excuse for thinking that Dummett's picture of what is at stake in realist–antirealist disputes captures what is always, or even usually or typically, involved in such controversies, even after controversies over reductionism have been set aside.

This is not to say that his proposals cover nothing. Most obviously, when someone takes what could naturally be regarded as an antirealist stance toward some subject matter on verificationist grounds, at least one of Dummett's characterizations will apply. And if an opposition to, say, moral realism takes the form of an expressivist account of moral discourse, then the dispute may well involve all of Dummett's touchstones—what kind of meaning the sentences in question have, what concept of truth, if any, is applicable to them, and whether each sentence in the domain in question is either true or false. But admitting that the characterization does have application is a far cry from agreeing that it makes explicit what is most deeply at issue in a large stretch of the field.

Perhaps it is the "linguistic turn" in the initial formulation of what a realist–antirealist issue is about, that is responsible for the relative lack of coverage of Dummett's proposal. "I shall take as my preferred characterization of a dispute between realists and antirealists one which represents it as relating, not to a class of entities or a class of terms, but to a class of *statements*" (1978, 146). (This could be more accurately put in terms of a class of *sentences*.) If what one may be realist or antirealist about is some domain of *sentences*—something linguistic, then the explanation in these terms of what differentiates the realist from the antirealist is bound to leave to one side disputes as to what exists, what is more or less ultimate in the scheme of things, or what the ultimate nature of a given class of entities is.[15]

15. See Devitt 1984 for a spirited argument along this line. See especially pt. 2 and chap. 12.

CHAPTER 5

Putnam's Model-Theoretic Argument

i The Argument

Hilary Putnam, who earlier had been a prominent defender of realism, underwent a major change of heart in the midseventies, and has since been among the most prominent critic of what many of us regard as realism. Putnam, sensibly enough, does not accept the idea that there is a unique position properly called 'realism'. He attacks what he calls "metaphysical realism" and defends what he, at one point, called "internal realism". Though Putnam's thought does not present the formidable difficulties of exegesis one finds in Dummett, it is certainly not clear sailing. One thing that makes for problems is Putnam's penchant for giving brief presentations of a position or argument on a number of occasions, rather than a more extended exposition. Another is that his thought is in more or less continuous flux, so that today he does not fully accept what he wrote in the late seventies and early eighties, the period at which he was espousing and arguing for the nonrealist views I will be criticizing. And even if we stick to that period it is by no means easy to determine just what his "internal realism" comes to. However, just as with Dummett, I will not aspire here to give a comprehensive treatment of Putnam's thought. My aim is only to consider his arguments that can be construed as directed against alethic realism, and to criticize his form of an epistemic conception of truth. But to do this properly I will have to look at the wider context in which these aspects of his thought are set.

Putnam's break with his earlier realism comes in his 1976 presidential address to the Eastern Division of the American Philosophical Association, "Realism and Reason" (reprinted in Putnam 1978), and, a year later, in his presidential address to the Association for Symbolic Logic,

"Models and Reality" (reprinted in Putnam 1983). Essentially the same argument against "metaphysical realism" is presented in both addresses. But the target is not very fully described in either. For that we must go to *Reason, Truth, and History* (Putnam 1981), where he explicitly contrasts metaphysical realism and what he there calls the "internalist perspective" (elsewhere "internal realism").

> One of these perspectives is the perspective of metaphysical realism. On this perspective, the world consists of some fixed totality of mind-independent objects. There is exactly one true and complete description of 'the way the world is'. Truth involves some sort of correspondence relation between words or thought-signs and external things and sets of things. I shall call this perspective the *externalist* perspective, because its favorite point of view is a God's Eye point of view.
>
> The perspective I shall defend has no unambiguous name . . . I shall refer to it as the *internalist* perspective, because it is characteristic of this view to hold that *what objects does the world consist of?* is a question that it only makes sense to ask *within* a theory or description. Many 'internalist' philosophers, though not all, hold further that there is more than one 'true' theory or description of the world. 'Truth', in an internalist view, is some sort of (idealized) rational acceptability— some sort of ideal coherence of our beliefs with each other and with our experiences *as those experiences are themselves represented in our belief system*—and not correspondence with mind-independent or discourse-independent 'states of affairs'. There is no God's Eye point of view that we can know or usefully imagine; there are only the various points of view of actual persons reflecting various interests and purposes that their descriptions and theories subserve. (49–50)

This contrast between the "perspectives" impinges most directly on alethic realism in their differing views on truth. To be sure, the externalist is depicted as taking truth to consist in "some sort of correspondence relation", whereas I have argued that we can have a distinctively realist conception of truth without getting into that. But the internalist conception of truth as "some sort of (idealized) rational acceptability" is clearly incompatible with even a minimalist form of the realist conception, as will come out more fully in Chapter 7. And since Putnam's arguments against the externalist conception take the form of a defense of the internalist conception, and are not aimed solely at the notion of correspondence, one can easily see them as directed against any realist, nonepistemic conception of truth.

What about the more clearly metaphysical constituents of "metaphysical realism"? First, the doctrine that "the world consists of some fixed totality of mind-independent objects".[1] I argued in Chapter 2 that many idealist denials of this are compatible with the acceptance of a realist conception of truth. It is just that the idealist has a different interpretation of the content of truth-value bearers. Nevertheless, Putnam's way of denying this, as we shall see, makes *what exists* relative to our conceptual or theoretical schemes for dealing with the world; and the relation of this to alethic realism will be discussed in the next chapter. Second, what about "There is exactly one true and complete description of 'the way the world is' "? That depends on our criteria for individuating descriptions. The most hard-nosed realist can allow some variation in true descriptions of a given state of affairs. We can report a temperature on either the Fahrenheit or the Celsius scale. Putnam presumably means this second doctrine of metaphysical realism to rule out the kind of conceptual relativity he advocates, which recognizes the possibility of different descriptions that look clearly incompatible being, all of them, true and rationally acceptable ways of saying what there is. This notion will be taken up in the next chapter. Putnam thinks that the various components of each of these "perspectives" are tightly interconnected, but I have already hinted at reasons for doubting this, reasons that will, again, be explored in the next chapter.

What I want to focus on in this chapter is Putnam's arguments against a realist conception of truth and in support of an epistemic conception. The argument that is most explicitly so directed is the one that occupies center stage in "Realism and Reason".[2] It is specifically directed against what Putnam calls "the most important consequence of metaphysical realism", namely, that "*truth* is supposed to be *radically nonepistemic*", that "the theory that is 'ideal' from the point of view of operational utility, inner beauty, and elegance, 'plausibility', simplicity, 'conservatism', etc., *might be false.* 'Verified' (in any operational sense) does not imply 'true', on the metaphysical realist picture, even in the ideal limit." Putnam says, "[I]t is this feature that I shall attack!" (1978, 125). His argument is designed to show that where a theory is epistemically ideal

---

1. This formulation obviously requires qualification if it is to be taken seriously. For no "metaphysical realist" who recognizes minds—their states, activities, and contents—is going to think that the world consists solely of mind-independent objects. The qualification could be in terms of the kind of independence—independence of being an object of cognition, something that could apply to the mental as well as the nonmental. Or it could consist of exempting the mental from the scope of the thesis. The world, in addition to minds and their states, etc., consists of some fixed totality of mind-independent objects.

2. We must take care not to confuse this APA presidential address with the third volume of Putnam's *Philosophical Papers* (1983), which bears the same title.

it is not the case that it might false, that is, that it is impossible that it should not be true.

So let T_1 be an ideal theory, by our lights. Lifting restrictions on our actual all-too-finite powers, we can imagine T_1 to have every property *except objective truth*—which is left open—that we like. E.g., T_1 can be imagined complete, consistent, to predict correctly all observation sentences (as far as we can tell), to meet whatever 'operational constraints' there are . . . to be 'beautiful', 'simple', 'plausible', etc. The supposition under consideration is that T_1 might be all this *and still be* (in reality) *false.*

I assume THE WORLD has (or can be broken into) infinitely many pieces. I also assume T_1 says there are infinitely many things (so in *this* respect T_1 is 'objectively right' about THE WORLD). Now T_1 is *consistent* (by hypothesis) and has (only) infinite models. So by the completeness theorem (in its model-theoretic form), T_1 has a model of every infinite cardinality. Pick a model M of the same cardinality as THE WORLD. Map the individuals of M one-to-one into the pieces of THE WORLD, then use the mapping to define relations of M directly in THE WORLD. The result is a satisfaction relation SAT—a 'correspondence' between the terms of L [the language in which the theory is stated] and sets of pieces of THE WORLD—such that the theory T_1 comes out *true*—true of THE WORLD—provided we just interpret 'true' as TRUE (SAT). So what becomes of the claim that even the *ideal* theory T_1 might *really* be false? (1978, 125–26)

That is, there will be a way of assigning singular terms of T_1 to individuals, and general terms of T_1 to sets of individuals, such that every sentence of T_1 comes out true. So much, says Putnam, is guaranteed by model theory.

Whether this is true depends, inter alia, on just how the "constraints" are construed. Putnam doesn't say much about the operational constraints in this essay, but he is more forthcoming in "Models and Reality".

To describe our operational constraints we shall need three things. First, we shall have to fix a sufficiently large 'observational vocabulary'; . . . call it the set of 'O-terms'. . . . Second, we shall assume that there *exists* (whether we can define it or not) a set of S which can be taken to be the set of macroscopically observable things and events . . . The third thing we shall assume given is a valuation (call it, once again 'OP') which assigns the correct truth value to each n-place O-term . . . on each n-tuple of elements of S on which it is defined. . . . Thus OP is a *partial* valuation in a double sense; it is defined on only a subset of the predicates of the language, namely the O-terms, and even on these it only fixes a part of the extension, namely the extension of T/S (the restriction of T to S) for each O-term T. (1983, 11–12)

Presumably the "operational constraint" puts constraints on the *meaning* of O-terms (the only ones with whose meaning it is in any way concerned) only to the extent of specifying which attributions of a given term to an observable object is true and which are false. This underdetermines meaning to the extent that we can have terms with different meanings that are coextensive over the range of observable objects.

How plausible is it that there will be an admissible interpretation of T_1 such that on that interpretation all sentences of T_1 come out true? In other words, how plausible is it that the operational and theoretical constraints can be guaranteed to leave room for such an interpretation? Though Putnam, so far as I know, does not specifically consider this question, I believe the answer would have to go something like this. All that is required is that the interpretation assign individuals to singular terms of the theory, and sets to the general terms, in such a way as to make all statements of the theory come out true. *And the constraints give us a free hand in this.* The operational constraint provides truth values for all observation sentences. The theoretical constraint presumably includes the requirement that the theory implies all the true observation sentences but none of the false ones. Does this prevent an assignment of truth for all the theoretical sentences? One doesn't see how it could. It doesn't mandate such an assignment, nor does Putnam suppose it does. The thesis of the underdetermination of theory by empirical evidence would prevent an entailment of the claims of the theory by the true observation reports. But surely if the theory entails all and only true observation statements, we can find *some* assignment of referents to the terms so that the theoretical statements all come out true.

ii Initial Difficulties with the Argument

What should we say about the model-theoretic (MT) argument? There have been a number of criticisms in the literature, and I find some of the critical points to be cogent. My main reactions to the argument, however, are rather different from anything I have found in the literature, and hence this section will not simply repeat what one can read elsewhere.

The first point to note is that the argument employs a realist conception of truth. This occurs at two places. First in the premises, most obviously in the "operational constraints", one of which is a "valuation" that "assigns the correct truth value to each n-place O-term . . . on each n-tuple of elements of S on which it is defined". We have to construe this as "realist correctness" for two reasons. First, this is an ad hominem argument directed against the realist. It is designed to show that *even on his own terms* he cannot hold that an ideal theory might be false. Hence the premises must embody a realist way of looking at things. And, second, if Putnam were to think of the "correct truth value" for observation statements in epistemic terms, he would have to tell us much more about the epistemology of observation statements than he does, namely nothing.

But the fact that the premises of the argument make use of a realist notion of truth is nothing against it. That simply reflects the fact that it is an ad hominem argument. A more serious problem concerns the conclusion. The conclusion is that since there is an acceptable model-theoretic satisfaction relation that makes all the sentences of the theory come out true, it is not the case that the theory might be false. Leaving aside, for the moment, the question whether the latter really does follow from the former, the present point is that the kind of truth Putnam claims to show that the theory cannot lack is the kind that is involved in the realist apparatus in terms of which the ad hominem argument is set up—namely, realist truth. And so at most the argument shows that an ideal theory cannot lack realist truth. Thus the argument, even on its most favorable valuation, does nothing to support the *replacement* of a realist conception of truth with the epistemic conception Putnam advocates.[3]

But this is all preliminary skirmishing. A more crucial defect of the argument is that the conclusion—*it is not the case that an ideal theory might be false,* that is *an ideal theory must be true*—simply doesn't follow from the model-theoretic result—that *the operational and theoretic constraints allow an interpretation in which all of its sentences come out true.* There are two ways of seeing this.

(1) Although Putnam does not emphasize the point, there will also be many admissible interpretations on which the theory is false. If this weren't the case, the truth of the theory would follow logically from the constraints, and Putnam obviously does not suppose (nor would it be at

---

3. As we shall see in Chapter 7, he later moderates his claims for an epistemic conception of truth.

all plausible to suppose) that the constraints have that power. And so if the existence of an admissible interpretation that makes the theory true shows that it must be true, by the same token the existence of an admissible interpretation that makes the theory false shows that it must be false. So the argument shows both that the theory must be true and that it must be false! As this result indicates, the argument, unless it is even more defective than I take it to be, establishes neither truth nor falsity. It only shows that it is *logically possible* (logically consistent with the constraints satisfaction of which make the theory ideal) that the theory be true (false). That is, the existence of an interpretation allowed by the constraints that render it true (false) merely shows that the constraints leave open the possibility of truth (falsity). And metaphysical realism, as depicted by Putnam, provides no motivation whatever for denying that. Still less would my alethic realism be moved to deny it. Why should a realist of any stripe deny that it is *possible* for an ideal theory to be true?

(2) If the argument were sound, wouldn't it be possible to show that any consistent theory is true? For if the operational and theoretical constraints on an ideal theory leave room for interpretations that make the theory true, why shouldn't an unideal theory, as unideal as you like, enjoy the same benefit? To be sure, if the theory entailed false observation statements, there would be no acceptable model in which all of its sentences are true. If all true observation statements are included in the theory, as Putnam supposes (1978, 126), then the theory would be inconsistent—including both a true observation statement and its contradictory, and the above claim is restricted to consistent unideal theories. And even if we don't include true observation statements in the theory, some of the theoretical premises used in the entailment of a false observation statement would have to be false. So to illustrate the present point, let's take nonideal theories to be defective in the theoretical constraints—simplicity, plausibility, etc. In moving to an unideal theory we make it complicated rather than simple and implausible rather than plausible. It seems clear that if an ideal theory has at least one interpretation that makes it true, a diminution of ideality in the ways just specified would not change the picture. How would the fact that the theory is complicated or implausible rule out the possibility of an assignment of designata and extensions that make all the sentences of the theory come out true? But then the argument has no special tendency to show that an ideal theory can't be false. It shows, if it shows anything, that no consistent theory that doesn't have any false entailments can be false. And if that's the way the wind blows, the argument does nothing to support an identification of truth with rational accept-

ability. It will be just as much a support for a "rational unacceptability" theory of truth. We can apply the results of the first point to illuminate this situation. Since the argument only shows, at most, that it is *possible* for an ideal theory to be true, it comes as no great surprise that it can also show that it is *possible* for a variety of unideal theories to be true.

Here is another indication that something is amiss with the MT argument. We don't have to delve far below the surface to see that this is a kind of indeterminacy of reference argument. Unlike an argument I will be considering later in the chapter, this one doesn't have indeterminacy of reference as its conclusion, but it does depend on its being the case that the constraints Putnam recognizes leave open a wide variety of interpretations. That is why it is possible to find an interpretation that renders the theory true. But if that is so, then we don't yet have anything on our hands that is capable of either truth or falsity. Before we can sensibly raise the question of truth value we must have a truth bearer that is more definite than this, one that expresses a proposition that is determinate enough to have a unique truth value. If the best we can say is that on a number of possible interpretations the theory is true and on a number of other possible interpretations the theory is false, we are still a long way from showing either that the "theory" is true or that it is false. We must go back to the drawing board and make the "theory" more definite before any such question can be significantly raised. This indeterminacy at the heart of the argument is responsible for my first criticism—that if the argument establishes truth it also establishes falsity. In other words, it establishes neither but only the possibility of either, depending on how the "theory" is further firmed up.

Putnam might respond that his "operational and theoretical constraints" make the theory as definite as it is possible for humans to make it. I don't accept that at all, as will become clear shortly. But if that were the case, then I think the reasonable conclusion would be not that we must adopt an epistemic conception of truth, but that we should abandon any attempt to evaluate theories for truth or falsity.

iii Another Reading of the Argument

In "Realism and Reason", after concluding the MT argument with "So what becomes of the claim that even the *ideal* theory T_1 might *really* be false?", Putnam continues.

Well, it might be claimed that SAT is not the *intended* correspondence between L and THE WORLD. What does 'intended' come to here?

T_1 has the property of meeting all *operational* constraints. . . . But the interpretation of 'reference' as SAT certainly meets all *theoretical* constraints on reference—it makes the *ideal* theory, T_1 come out *true*.

So what *further* constraints on reference are there that could single out some other interpretation as (uniquely) 'intended', and SAT as an 'unintended' interpretation (in the model-theoretic sense of 'interpretation')? The supposition that even an 'ideal' theory (from a pragmatic point of view) might *really* be false appears to collapse into *unintelligibility.* (1978, 126)

This passage suggests a different interpretation of the argument. I have been criticizing the argument for not showing the impossibility of the ideal theory's being false. But perhaps, rather than trying to prove that the ideal theory must be true, Putnam is simply throwing down a challenge to the metaphysical realist. "You say that it is possible for the ideal theory to be false. But show me that it is so intended (i.e., that an interpretation is so intended) as to make this a possibility. I can show you an interpretation (or show you that there is an interpretation) allowed by the operational and theoretical constraints on which it is true. What can you do to show me that this is not the intended interpretation, and that the intended interpretation instead is one on which there is a possibility of falsity? The interpretation that makes it true satisfies all operational and theoretical constraints (1978, 126). What other devices do you have to pick out a model that would leave open the possibility of falsity?"

We must recognize that on this understanding of the argument it doesn't do what Putnam said he was setting out to do: refute the supposition that an ideal theory might be false. Just posing a challenge to the realist to show that an interpretation is intended on which it might be false falls far short of showing that it is not the case that it might be false. But I will evaluate the argument on this weaker construal nonetheless.

Before considering various possible responses to the challenge, we had better look at the following complication. Suppose that an interpretation that makes the theory true is "intended". Does that show that the theory *might not* (*could not*) be false? Doesn't it show only that it *is* true, not that it *must* be true? But we have to be sensitive here to various orders of modality. Of course, showing that on the intended interpretation a theory is true doesn't show that it is *logically* impossible for it to be false. But it does show that falsity is impossible, *consistent with that interpretation*; the interpretation logically entails truth. And so the challenge to the realist is to show that an interpretation is intended that leaves open the possibility of falsity.

Let's be clear about the difference between this construal of the argument and the one I have been criticizing. Putnam, of course, does not purport to show that an interpretation on which the theory is true *is* the intended interpretation (by whom?). That would be to revert to the original construal, as an attempt to show that the theory *must* be true. No, on this reading, he is challenging the metaphysical realist to show that no interpretation that makes all the sentences of the theory come out true is intended. And if we ask, "Intended by whom?", that turns out to be irrelevant. For Putnam aspires to show that no one *can* intend an interpretation on which the possibility of falsity (consistent with that interpretation) is left open. His argument is that we lack resources for doing so, that doing so is not a human possibility.[4]

Continuing with this version of the argument, Putnam imagines various ways in which the realist might seek to meet the challenge. She might appeal to a causal theory of reference to reduce, or wholly eliminate, the indeterminacy of reference left by the constraints with which Putnam is working.[5] If the referents of singular terms and the extensions of general terms are fixed by causal relations between things in the world and the speaker, then it would be an open question, to be determined by what the world is like, whether the theory containing terms with those referents is true or not. But Putnam responds:

"Notice that a 'causal' theory of reference is not (would not be) of any help here: for how 'causes' can uniquely refer is as much of a puzzle as how 'cat' can, on the metaphysical realist picture" (1978, 126).

Unfortunately, for Putnam, this response rests on a conflation of *fixing reference* with *showing that reference has been fixed*, or at least *specifying how reference has been fixed*. The most that Putnam's remark (or an expansion of it into a full-blown argument) could show is that the attempt to specify or show how reference is fixed raises problems about the reference of terms used to do that, problems that parallel the problems about reference raised by the use of any other terms. But that by no means

---

4. As will appear in due course, this implies that the resources Putnam allows us—the "operational and theoretical constraints"—leave the theory indeterminate to a considerable extent.

5. Putnam follows what is, in my judgment, the very bad, albeit widespread, practice of (mis)using the term 'refer' both for the relation of a singular term to what it designates and for the relation of a general predicate to the set of things of which it can be truly asserted (what used to be called its "extension"). The term 'refer' is (most) properly used to indicate what a speaker does when she specifies something as what she is talking about. Despite my disapproval I will from time to time go along with the more general practice.

shows that causal relations do not, in fact, determine reference.[6] To be sure, it hasn't been shown that causal relations do determine reference either. But that is not to the point. Putnam is seeking to show that the realist *cannot* intend an interpretation on which the ideal theory might be false. And even if he could show that the realist cannot show that he can have such an intention, that by no means amounts to showing that the realist cannot have such an intention. We can, and do, have all sorts of abilities that we cannot prove we have.

In various places Putnam considers, and dismisses, various other possible realist responses to the challenge, such as a "direct (and mysterious) grasp of Forms" (1978, 127) or a "magical" theory of reference [it just happens!] (1981, 3). The question of what it is by virtue of which singular terms refer to what they do and general terms have the extensions they have is a fundamental, deep, and enormously difficult question. I have views on the subject, but this is not the place to go into them. The present point is that what Putnam needs for his project of disposing of metaphysical realism (so far as this construal of his argument is concerned) is a demonstration that there is no way in which a realist could "intend an interpretation" of the ideal theory that leaves open the possibility of its falsity. And he is a very long way from having done that.

iv What Is an "Interpretation"?

Although I am convinced that the last two sections conclusively show that Putnam's argument fails to do what he expects of it, on either interpretation of that expectation, I fear that we have only been gliding over the surface of the issues involved. We will have to dig deeper if we are to see the most fundamental problems with Putnam's way of approaching the matter, and to see our way clear to a more adequate grasp of the situation.

The deep reason for the failure of the MT argument has to do with the extensional model of "interpretation" that is involved. In this argument and elsewhere (e.g., the indeterminacy of reference argument in chapter 2 of *Reason, Truth, and History*) Putnam is following a massive tradition in twentieth century logic, and in philosophy influenced by that logic, in talking as if we "interpret" sentences, a body of discourse, or a whole language *extensionally*—by assigning designata to singular terms and extensions to general terms. The use of "models" to give an

6. For an elaboration of this point see Lewis 1984 and Heller 1988.

interpretation of a "theory" is along these lines. We have given a definite interpretation of a theory if and only if we have carried out such assignments for every nonlogical term of the theory. (We also presuppose grammatical structure, of course.) Indeed, Putnam saddles the metaphysical realist with a commitment to such an approach.[7]

> The predicament [for the metaphysical realist] only is a predicament because we did two things: first, we gave an account of understanding the language in terms of programs and procedures for *using* the language (what else?); and then, secondly, we asked what the possible 'models' for the language were, thinking of the models as existing 'out there' *independent of any description.* At this point, something really weird had already happened, had we stopped to notice. On any view, the understanding of the language must determine the reference of the terms, or, rather, must determine the reference given the context of use. If the use, even in a fixed context, doesn't determine reference, then use isn't understanding. The language, on the perspective we talked ourselves into, has a full program of use; but it still lacks an *interpretation.*
>
> This is the fatal step. To adopt a theory of meaning according to which a language whose whole use is specific still lacks something—namely its 'interpretation'—is to accept a problem which *can* only have crazy solutions. To speak as if *this* were my problem, 'I know how to use my language, but, now, how shall I single out an interpretation?' is to speak nonsense. Either the use *already* fixes the 'interpretation', or *nothing* can. (1983, 23–24)

Well, suppose we agree with Putnam that the metaphysical realist has no way of specifying a unique intended *extensional* interpretation of the terms in the theory, where that would involve hooking up the terms to things and sets of things in an independently existing, real world. And suppose we further agree that this shows that the realist cannot satisfy the demand to show that the intended (extensional) interpretation of the ideal theory leaves open the possibility of falsity? How discomfited should the realist feel about this?

Let's grant Putnam that *on the terms he has set,* the realist is in a highly unfavorable position. But why should we suppose that these terms are appropriate? Why should we think that the realist must successfully carry out the herculean task Putnam has assigned her in order to achieve

---

7. Putnam denies (1978, 124) that he is assuming that the metaphysical realist takes it that *understanding* a term amounts to knowing what its designatum or extension is; but I can't see how the argument is supposed to go without that assumption.

determinacy of reference? Why should we suppose that the realist must specify the items in the independently existing world that constitute the designata or extensions of the terms of the theory in order that the theory have a definite interpretation? *So far from this demand being rooted in the realist position, it runs directly counter to that position.* It is true that the metaphysical realist holds that most meaningful general terms have extensions made up (where not empty) of independently existing objects, and usable singular terms designate (where successful) independently existing objects. But she is far from holding, or holding anything that implies, that a definite interpretation of a language or a theory must specify *what* the designatum of each singular term is and *what* the extension of each general term is. On the contrary, it is fundamental to realism to hold that it is not up to us to determine what is included in the extension of, for example, 'cat'. It is fundamental to realism to deny Putnam's oft repeated assertion: "Either the use *already* fixes the interpretation or *nothing* can". At least it is basic to realism to deny this if we are thinking of interpretation along the lines of model theory— "interpreting" the language (theory) by listing designata for singular terms and members of extensions for general terms. Although realism recognizes that the "interpretation" (understanding, meaning) makes an important contribution to the determination of its extension, it is crucial to realism to deny that this is the whole story. It depends not (just) on our understanding (use) of language but also on how things are in the world just what is included in the extension of 'cat', that is, how many cats there are, and which of the individuals in the world have what it takes to be a cat. Therefore it comes as no shock to the realist that the "operational and theoretical" constraints laid out by Putnam do not fix the "reference" of terms in the theory. That is just what the realist would expect.[8]

Let me spell out more explicitly how a sensible realist thinks of this situation. I start with an unspecific formulation. The extension of a general term is jointly determined by the meaning of the term and facts of the world, the latter being nonlinguistic facts except in those special cases in which the term is a metalinguistic one. The meaning lays down necessary and sufficient conditions for something's falling in the exten-

---

8. These unrealistic requirements of Putnam's are connected with the extremely widespread tendency to speak of "use (meaning) *determining* reference". It may be that many of those who use this locution are guilty of nothing worse than using a sloppy way of saying that use (meaning), *together with relevant facts of the world* determine reference. But habitual sloppiness is not without its dangers, as we see by witnessing the lengths to which this kind of talk has carried Putnam.

sion of the term; and the way the (largely nonlinguistic) world is determines what objects satisfy those conditions. This formulation strictly applies only to terms with perfectly precise meanings. Suitable adjustments are required for terms whose meanings are less than completely precise, but the general outlines of the account are the same.

This is an unspecific formulation because it does not make explicit what it is for a term to have a certain meaning. There are, of course, many competing positions on this, and a realist is not restricted to any particular theory of meaning, though her realism may be incompatible with some. I agree with Putnam in holding that "use" theories of meaning are the only games in town, though I certainly don't claim that this is implied by realism, and I don't agree with Putnam's restrictions on what aspects of *use* determine meaning. I use the term 'use theory of meaning' for any account that takes linguistic meaning to be supervenient on aspects of what users of the language do with it in communication and in the articulation of thought. At the time he put forward the antirealist arguments we are considering Putnam favored a verificationist kind of use theory, one that is in the same ball park as the account of Dummett's we discussed in the last chapter.[9] I have already explained why I regard this account as unacceptable. Other prominent versions of use theory are the Grice-Schiffer-Bennett account in terms of speaker intentions to produce effects in addressees, and the illocutionary-act-potential account put forward by Searle and myself. I have no space here to go into theories of meaning. I will only say that I take it to be a necessary condition of adequacy for such a theory that it explain how it is that, by virtue of having a certain meaning, a general term embodies (more or less precise) necessary and sufficient conditions for something's falling within its extension.

What I have just said by no means rules out views, like Putnam's in "The Meaning of 'Meaning' " (in Gunderson 1975), according to which the meaning of a general term has a certain "indexical" feature. In that essay Putnam attacked the view that the requirements for membership in the extension of a term are all given by general properties that make up a concept expressed by the term. "Meanings ain't all in the head" was Putnam's slogan. Thus the meaning of 'gold' (what it takes for something to be gold) is not given solely by a set of properties that people typically have in mind as definitive of gold—yellowness, ductility, malleability, etc. Rather, what it takes to be gold is that something have the same essential nature (chemical composition) as socially ac-

9. See, 1978, 127–29 and 1983, 20, for endorsements of Dummett.

cepted paradigms of gold. Reference to this latter is where the "indexical" element comes in. The most basic component of the meaning of 'gold' is, to be sure, a property (though Putnam does not emphasize this), but it is an "impure" property, one with a relation to particular paradigms built into it. This most basic component is something like: *having the same chemical constitution as things in the paradigm.* The meaning (of the ordinary, commonsense term) does not include a specification of what that chemical constitution is, only a requirement that it meet this condition. We can also, as Putnam does in this essay, include a "stereotype" in the meaning—such standard properties as yellowness, malleability, and so on. But these are not necessary conditions for being gold. The only strictly semantically (conceptually) necessary condition is the one just given in italics. I go into the view at this length to underline the point that the condition of adequacy for a theory of meaning I have laid down (explaining how the meaning of a general term embodies conditions for membership in the extension) does not require us to hold that the meaning is exhaustively given by a set of purely general properties and does not rule out a view like the one he sets out in (Gunderson 1975).

This brief discussion has been restricted to general terms, since one can say something fairly definite about them in a short compass. Singular terms present thornier problems. With "indexical" terms and proper names, the meaning (what on the best semantic description of the language counts as the meaning) does not suffice to constitute necessary and sufficient conditions for being the designatum of the term. Designata vary on different occasions of use; the context of use and intentions of the speaker come into the picture. But these are aspects of "use" also. So at the most general level the picture is the same. Aspects of the use of the term determine what it takes for something to be designated by the term. It is then "up to the way the world is" what, if anything, satisfies those conditions.

So what the realist wants to say is that we should not understand an "interpretation" of a theory or a language as an assignment of "referents" to the terms involved. A theory is interpreted when (in addition to grammatical structure) all meaningful terms are assigned meanings. That is all that is needed to *understand* the theory. A grasp of meanings is all that is needed to equip one to use the sentences of the theory to make definite statements. It is then in the lap of the gods just what falls within the extensions of the general terms involved and whether what one says in uttering a given sentence is true.

Therefore the fact that the metaphysical realist is not in a position to derive a unique intended *extensional* "interpretation" from his "use" of the language involved should not be taken as a reproach to the position. It is, rather a confirmation of that view. Putnam's idea that the metaphysical realist is, by virtue of his position, faced with an extra step of hooking up each term of the theory with things and sets of things in the world rests on a radical misunderstanding of the situation. Not only is there nothing in the realist position that engenders any such requirement; the most basic facts of language, and our use thereof, make that requirement thoroughly gratuitous. The acquisition, use, and understanding of language just doesn't work that way. People do not learn general terms by having the extension of each laid out for them. If that were necessary, a first (or any subsequent) language would never be acquired. It is not within human powers to teach someone the meaning (use) of 'cat' by enumerating or pointing out all cats—past, present,and future, throughout the whole universe. Hence our mastery of the term, our ability to make use of what we learned when we learned the term, does not involve the employment of any such "interpretation". Suppositions to the contrary come from hypnotic fascination with the procedure of formal logic in describing (not, usually, actually carrying out) the procedure of setting up formal, artificial "languages" by such an extensional "interpretation". If one allows this model to blind one to the most obvious facts of the human use of actual languages, one may be led to suppose that something like this is what a realist would have to do to attach a definite meaning to a language. But once we get the actual facts of real language use before us, this supposition vanishes like the morning mist with the noonday sun.

At the risk of overexposure, let me bring out explicitly the bearing the above considerations have on Putnam's claim that the realist is in no position to maintain that an "interpretation" on which the ideal theory comes out true is not the "intended" interpretation. Putnam supports this by suggesting that the "operational and theoretical constraints" he mentions are the only things that can enter into what it is to *intend* a certain (extensional) interpretation. There are two ways in which the above discussion bears on this. First, I have pointed out that there are a number of other "use" theories of meaning according to which the kinds of constraints Putnam singles out are by no means the only aspects of use that enter into determining an interpretation (and hence not the only features an intention to include which could figure in what makes a certain interpretation "intended"). But second and more importantly, I have pointed out that, by the terms of the human condition, none of us can be in a position to *intend* an *extensional* interpretation of the sort envisaged in model theory. Hence the fact that the realist is unable to show that one such interpretation is not the *intended* interpretation has no significance for the merits or demerits of realism. In being unable to do this the realist is merely sharing in the common human lot, and that constitutes no reason for rejecting her position.

There is something else behind Putnam's supposition that the MT argument tells against metaphysical realism. The whole discussion hinges on an unwarranted picture of the metaphysical realist vainly struggling to connect his terms with items in a wholly transcendent realm. If we think of the metaphysical realist as committed to a domain of "transcendent" entities, out of any contact with our thought, experience, and discourse, then it can look as if he is faced with an extra, and insuperable, task of relating the terms of our thought and discourse to that transcendent reality. But this is, at best, constructing an artificial position in order to have a target for refutation. No living, breathing realist, to my knowledge, takes any such stand. I certainly do not. I don't think of realism as implying that one must, by some supreme metaphysical effort, "reach outside" our experience, thought, and discourse, to make contact with a transcendent realm. On the contrary, the real, independently existing world, the nature of which makes our statements true or false, is one with which we are in contact already *through* our experience, thought, and discourse. The constituents of that world—people, trees, animals, buildings, oceans, galaxies, God—are things we perceive or otherwise experience, think about, and talk about. They are not wholly external to us and our cognitive and linguistic doings, though they don't depend (for the most part) on those doings for what they are. No sensible realism supposes or implies that the realist is faced with the task Putnam takes the position to require.

Let me summarize the most crucial points of this rather complex criticism of the MT argument. (1) Even if the argument were wholly successful, it would only show the logical possibility of an ideal theory's being true, and leave open the logical possibility of the theory's being false— something the metaphysical realist is happy to accept. (2) If the argument shows anything, it shows that any theory we can construct is too indeterminate to be susceptible of truth or falsity. Hence it is far from showing that we can't deny that the ideal theory is true. (3) If the argument is construed as merely throwing down a challenge to the realist to show that an "interpretation" on which the ideal theory is true is not the "intended" interpretation, it suffers from using a purely extensional sense of "interpretation" (a) that the realist will, in principle, reject, and (b) which is such that no human being is in a position to "interpret" her language or theory in this sense. (4) Putnam's idea that the argument tells against the metaphysical realist is based on a wholly gratuitous supposition that the former is faced with the task of connecting terms of a language or theory with a completely transcendent reality.

v Indeterminacy of Reference

I have already noted that a claim of indeterminacy of reference is involved in the MT argument, although it is not an argument for such indeterminacy, nor is it directly an argument from indeterminacy to the denial of metaphysical realism. Nevertheless, Putnam does suggest, especially in "Models and Reality", that the indeterminacy involved tells against metaphysical realism but not against internal realism.

> We need, therefore, a standpoint which links use and reference in just the way that the metaphysical realist standpoint refuses to do. The standpoint of 'non-realist semantics' is precisely that standpoint. From that standpoint, it is trivial to say that a model in which, as it might be, the set of cats and set of dogs are permuted (i.e., 'cat' is assigned the set of dogs as its extension, and 'dog' is assigned the set of cats) is 'unintended' even if corresponding adjustments in the extensions of all the other predicates make it end up that the operational and theoretical constraints of total science or total belief are all 'preserved'. Such a model would be unintended because *we didn't intend the word 'cat' to refer to dogs.* From the metaphysical realist standpoint, this answer doesn't work; it just pushes the question back to the metalanguage. The axiom of the metalanguage, ' "cat" refers to cats' can't rule out such an unintended interpretation of the object language, unless the metalanguage itself already has had its intended interpretation singled out; but we are in the same predicament with respect to the metalanguage that we are in with respect to the object language, from that standpoint, so all is in vain. However, from the viewpoint of 'non-realist' semantics, the metalanguage is completely understood, and so is the object language. So we can *say and understand,* ' "cat" refers to cats'. Even though the model referred to [in which dogs and cats are interchanged] satisfies the theory, etc., it is 'unintended'; and we recognize that it is unintended *from the description through which it is given.* . . . Models are not lost noumenal waifs looking for someone to name them; they are constructions within our theory itself, and they have names from birth. (1983, 24–25)

The argument suggested by this passage is clearly different from the MT argument that we have been discussing, the one that is directed either to showing that the ideal theory cannot be false or to showing that the metaphysical realist cannot intend some interpretation on which it might be false. Here the suggestion is rather that the "operational" and "theoretical" constraints laid out by Putnam leave reference indeterminate for the metaphysical realist but not for the internal realist. Let's call this the MR ("Models and Reality") argument.[10] It is closely related to an argument for referential indeterminacy presented in *Reason, Truth, and History* (1981). There Putnam works with a much stronger constraint—the fixing of the truth values of all sentences of the theory in all possible worlds; and he argues that even this will leave indefinitely many alternatives open for the reference of terms (33–38). Determinacy at the sentence level does not trickle down to determinacy at the term level. The intuitive idea is that we can change any given "reference" if we make enough compensatory changes elsewhere. Call this the RTH argument. Putnam gives a formal presentation in an appendix, and I will accept it as valid.[11] Though the two arguments differ with respect to the constraints that are said to leave reference indeterminate, a number of points apply to both, and for the most part I will treat them together. My discussion falls into two parts. First, I will argue that neither argument succeeds in showing that the metaphysical realist is faced with a crippling referential indeterminacy. This is the part that directly bears on my basic aim in this book—to defend alethic realism. Second, I will explore Putnam's reasons for thinking that even though the arguments saddle the metaphysical realist with referential indeterminacy they leave the internal realist untouched. This discussion is not really germane to the defense of alethic realism, but it has important implications for the understanding of Putnam's alternative to metaphysical realism.

Do these arguments really show that reference must be indeterminate for the metaphysical realist? The reader might well expect me at this point to recur to the contention of section iv that Putnam is working with a thoroughly unrealistic conception of what is involved in "interpreting" a theory or a language, namely, assigning particular designata to singular terms and enumerating extensions of general terms, à la model theory. But in both these arguments we have a different approach to extensions. Look at how Putnam specifies extensions in the above passage from "Models and Reality": "[T]he set of cats and set of dogs

10. I don't mean this label to imply that this is the only argument to be found in "Models and Reality". The MT argument is explicitly presented there as well.

11. Though Putnam does not say in so many words that this is an argument against metaphysical realism, the subsequent course of the discussion in 1981 seems to indicate that this is the way he is thinking of it.

are permuted (i.e., 'cat' is assigned the set of dogs as its extension, and 'dog' is assigned the set of cats)". When he gives examples of divergent extensions for a given term that are all left open by the constraints in question, he does so, not by enumerating the members of each extension in the spirit of model theory, but by *using* a general term (the same or a different one) to do so. 'Cat' might refer to the class of cats or the class of dogs. Or again, in RTH: ' "Cow" refers to cows' follows immediately from the definition of 'refers' " (136). This is what we might call an "intensional" rather than an "extensional" way of specifying extensions. The extension is specified by using a general term we assume that we understand well enough for this purpose. This procedure is identical with the one I said, in section iv, is used by the realist (and anyone else for that matter) to "get at" extensions. The extension of a general term, I said, is determined by the meaning of the term, which lays down a criterion for membership in the extension, plus facts of the world that determine just what items, if any, satisfy that criterion. When we specify an extension, as Putnam does in these passages, by using a general term to do so, this is what we are doing. We suppose that the term in question embodies a criterion for membership in the extension and thereby, together with the way the world is, uniquely (insofar as the criterion is precise) determines a class of things to which the term truly applies. Putnam does not evince awareness of this difference between extensional and intensional ways of specifying extensions. But since he has, however unconsciously, moved from the former to the latter in these indeterminacy of reference arguments, I cannot criticize them on the grounds that the enumerative way of determining extensions is not viable.

But one critical point made in section iii against the MT argument does apply here—namely, Putnam's conflation of *referring to something* and *showing that one has done so or specifying how one has done so*. That conflation appears in the MR argument when Putnam claims that in order for the metaphysical realist to intend 'cat' to refer to cats, she must adopt an axiom of the metalanguage that lays this down. But the term 'cat', as used in this axiom, itself is in need of an intended interpretation, and so requires a parallel axiom in a meta-metalanguage. And in turn. . . . An infinite regress looms, and the poor realist never succeeds in forming the intention.[12] But the regress gets started only because of the assumption that the realist cannot intend to refer to cats by 'cat'

12. Later in this section I will consider why Putnam thinks that this regress does not arise for the internal realist.

(and so cannot succeed in doing so) unless she can spell out those referential intentions (and perhaps show that they are carried out, or specify how they are carried out). And this assumption is wholly unjustified, being a special case of the conflation between *doing something* and *saying (thinking, proving) that one is doing it, or explaining how one manages to do it.* We do things all the time without being able to specify what we are doing or explaining how we get them done. Why should referring be an exception to this generalization? Again, in making this point I don't mean for a moment to deny that there are interesting and important questions about reference—what it is by virtue of which one uses a singular term to refer to one individual rather than others, and what it is by virtue of which one uses a general term with one extension rather than another—or that philosophers are quite properly concerned with such questions. But the fact remains that it is an egregious error to suppose that referential success depends on being able to answer such questions, either in general or in application to particular cases.

Although this point is, I believe, fatal to the specific argument quoted above from "Models and Reality", there is a more basic defect that attaches to both referential indeterminacy arguments. *The constraints relative to which reference is said to be indeterminate do not exhaust the resources available to the metaphysical realist for securing determinate reference.* Since the two arguments work with different constraints, we will have to take each in turn. First the RTH argument. I have already accepted Putnam's proof that fixing truth values in all possible worlds does not suffice to determine the references of terms. But why should this bother the metaphysical realist? Why can't she respond by saying that what this shows is that this approach to semantics fails to cut things finely enough to handle the semantics of terms? I noted in Chapter 1 that the identification of propositions with sets of possible worlds (roughly a proposition *is* the set of worlds in which it is true) individuates propositions much too broadly. All logically equivalent propositions turn out to be identical. The present point is allied to that one. Putnam's argument shows that this possible-worlds approach individuates things much too broadly for the semantics of terms as well. The argument is really directed against a certain program in semantics and has no bearing on metaphysical realism at all. To be sure, Putnam seems to think that the metaphysical realist is committed by her position to this kind of truth-based semantics, but, so far as I can see, that supposition is wholly gratuitous. Even if no viable alternative semantics were available—and in section iv I suggested that this is not the case[13]—it doesn't follow that the metaphysical realist

13. None of the semantic approaches I suggested for the realist in section iv are based on the notion of fixing truth values of sentences in all possible worlds.

is committed to this one. Even if no good apples are available I am not required to eat a rotten one.

Now for the MR argument. Putnam points out that "the most common view of how interpretations of our language are fixed by us . . . is associated with the notions of an operational constraint and a theoretical constraint" (1981, 29). Nevertheless, such constraints are far from being exhaustive of our resources for attaching meaning to terms and hence for providing the linguistic contribution to fixing their references. One additional resource is our capacity to develop new concepts (word meanings) by analogical extension from concepts we already possess. There is an extensive literature on the role of analogy in the development of theoretical concepts in science.[14] Because of this there are features of the meanings of theoretical terms that are not captured by either operational or theoretical constraints. In my brief criticism of Dummett's verificationist semantics in Chapter 4, section iii, I gave both scientific and theological examples of this sort of thing. Hence from the fact that the "operational and theoretical constraints" of a certain theory fail to yield different meanings for 'particle' and 'wave' (to vastly oversimplify a certain well-known example), it doesn't follow that they are indistinguishable in meaning and reference. For other contributions to their meaning, illustrated by the points just made, might render them semantically distinguishable.

I now turn to what seems to me the most puzzling thing about these arguments, Putnam's claim that they show the metaphysical realist to be faced with an indeterminacy of reference *while leaving the internal realist free of any such liability*.[15] How can this be? If the constraints in each case constitute all we have to work with in rendering reference determinate, how can it be that these constraints don't leave reference as indeterminate for the internalist as for the metaphysical realist?[16]

Though Putnam's thought on this point is not wholly clear to me, I take his basic claim to be that the internal realist, but not the metaphysical realist, has resources for determining reference over and above the

14. For a good discussion of this see Hesse 1966.

15. This problem does not arise for the MT argument. Obviously, the internal realist is not bothered by the conclusion that an ideal theory cannot be false. That is a cornerstone of his position.

16. As for the RTH argument, I can imagine Putnam saying that the argument doesn't apply to the internal realist because it employs a metaphysically realist conception of truth. That would make it an ad hominem argument like the MT argument, one that is designed to reveal difficulties implied by the metaphysical realist's own assumptions. But Putnam nowhere says this. Perhaps he doesn't because the argument would not seem to employ anything (with respect to truth) that goes beyond Tarskian constraints on truth, and Putnam is on record as holding that the Tarski constraints are acceptable to any theory of truth, including his own.

constraints laid down in the arguments. Let's recall a bit from the section of "Models and Reality" quoted at the beginning of this section.

> From that standpoint [of 'non-realist semantics'], it is trivial to say that a model in which, as it might be, the set of cats and set of dogs are permuted (i.e., 'cat' is assigned the set of dogs as its extension, and 'dog' is assigned the set of cats) is 'unintended' even if corresponding adjustments in the extension of all the other predicates make it end up that the operational and theoretical constraints of total science or total belief are all 'preserved'. Such a model would be unintended *because we didn't intend the word 'cat' to refer to dogs.* . . . Even though the model referred to [in which dogs and cats are interchanged] satisfies the theory, etc., it is 'unintended'; and we recognize that it is unintended *from the description through which it is given.* (1983, 24–25)

This passage raises more questions than it answers. The non-realist is accorded the ability to intend an interpretation that goes beyond what is fixed by the operational and theoretical constraints, but the metaphysical realist isn't. But why this discrimination? Is it sheerly arbitrary? Is Putnam revoking the bars against a "magical" theory of reference for the internalist but not for the metaphysical realist? Here is his attempt to justify the unequal treatment.

> From the metaphysical realist standpoint, this answer doesn't work; it just pushes the question back to the metalanguage. The axiom of the metalanguage, ' "cat" refers to cats' can't rule out such an unintended interpretation of the object language, unless the metalanguage itself already has had *its* intended interpretation singled out; but we are in the same predicament with respect to the metalanguage that we are in with respect to the object language, from that standpoint, so all is in vain. However, from the viewpoint of 'non-realist' semantics, the metalanguage is completely understood, and so is the object language. So we can *say and understand,* ' "cat" refers to cats'.

But again this raises more questions than it answers. Why is it incumbent on the metaphysical realist to fix the interpretation of terms in the metalanguage by still higher level languages in order to escape indeterminacy of reference in the object language, while no such liability is incurred by the internal realist, who has no trouble at all in just *saying and understanding* that 'cat' refers to cats? Again, why this preferential treatment? For light on this we must turn to a discussion in "Realism and Reason" (1978) and its continuation in *Reason, Truth, and History* (1981). In a section of the former entitled "Why All This Doesn't Refute

Internal Realism", Putnam tells us that for the internal realist: " ' "Cow" refers to cows' follows immediately from the definition of 'refers' . . . ' "Cow" refers to cows' is a logical truth" (1978, 136). Of course, this isn't strictly a logical truth. Logical truths are necessarily true, whereas it is only contingently true that 'cow' refers to cows. 'Cow' might have had some quite different meaning, in which case its extension would have been something other than the class of cows. Nevertheless, Putnam has a point here, which could be put correctly by saying that when we make a statement by using a term to say what that term refers to, the meaning of our sentence guarantees that the statement is true. Such statements are "guaranteed true", as we might say. So the point is that the internal realist has no problem with indeterminacy of reference, because he uses 'refer' in such a way that it always turns out to be true that a given term can be used to specify what that term refers to. (See also 1981, 52.) But can't the metaphysical realist take advantage of the same bonus? Why isn't it the case for him too that " 'Cow' refers to cows" is guaranteed to be true? Here is Putnam's response:

> Of course the externalist agrees that the extension of 'rabbit' is the set of rabbits and the extension of 'extraterrestrial' is the set of extraterrestrials. But he does not regard such statements as telling us what reference *is*. For him finding out what reference *is*, i.e., what the *nature* of the 'correspondence' between words and things is, is a pressing problem. . . . For me there is little to say about what reference is within a conceptual system other than these tautologies. (1981, 52)

That is, for the realist reference is a *substantial* relation. Something other than the way we use terms has to obtain in order that one of our words gets hooked up with an object or a kind in order to be usable to talk about *that* rather than something else. But there is no such "transcendent" dimension to reference for the internal realist.

I don't find this at all convincing. I can't see that Putnam has distinguished the metaphysical and the internal realist in the way he supposes. Both sides of the distinction are misdescribed. Why can't the metaphysical realist recognize that " 'cow' refers to cows" is "guaranteed true" by the meaning of the sentence? Because he thinks that there is a problem as to what reference *is*? But how does that prevent him from recognizing that, whatever the nature of reference might be, the meaning of 'refer' is such that ' "Cow' refers to cows" is guaranteed to be true? That could be a *feature* of the meaning of 'refer', even though there are still important questions left over as to what reference *is*, questions as to how a singular term has to be related to an individual in order that the latter be the designatum of the former, and how a general term has to be related to a class in order that the latter be the extension of the former. This is parallel to a fundamental claim of this book, namely, that it is by virtue of what 'true' means that any statement of the form 'It is true that *p if and only if p*' is true, even though that doesn't answer all the important questions about truth, especially the question of how a statement has to be related to a fact in order for that fact to make the statement true.

This same point—that the self-guaranteeing character of " 'Cow' refers to cows" leaves open important questions as to what reference is—shows the other side of the distinction to be misdescribed as well. The fact that the internal realist takes advantage of that self-guarantee does not imply that there is no problem for him as to what reference is. The question as to how a general term has to be related to a class in order that the latter be the extension of the former arises for anyone who ascribes extensions to general terms. How could it not?[17]

But even if the contrast between the two realisms with respect to whether there is a substantial problem as to what reference is were sound, it would not show that or how the internal realist is not faced with an indeterminacy of reference while the metaphysical realist is. Suppose that the latter, but not the former, does have a problem as to what reference is, over and above the point that statements of the form *'T' refers to Ts* are guaranteed true. How would that show that they are in a different position vis-à-vis determinacy of reference? The idea seems to be that the guaranteed truth of such statements renders, or carries the possibility of rendering, reference determinate unless there is a further problem as to what reference is. But how does that additional condition neutralize the efficacy of the "guaranteed true" point to ward off indeterminacy? If determinacy of reference is (at least prima facie) effected by the fact that any statement of the form *'T' refers to Ts* is guaranteed to be true, how would that be queered by the fact that there is a

17. The move Putnam tries to make here is similar to one he makes at one point in "Realism and Reason". He argues that there is no indeterminacy of reference for a verificationist semantics like that of Dummett. Since the meaning of a sentence is given by verifying and/or falsifying conditions, "the realist concepts of truth and falsity are not used in this semantics at all". And that means that "the notion of 'reference' is not used in the semantics" (1978, 128). This leaves me wondering why indeterminacy of reference isn't still a problem for the verificationist if it is for the metaphysical realist, even if the notion of reference isn't used in his semantics. Doesn't the verificationist still have to recognize that the words 'cow' or 'tree' must have one particular set of objects as their extension rather than any other, if we are to use them to say what we mean to be saying? And isn't he still faced with the question of what endows them with that determinate extension, given that the constraints in question leave them open?

further problem as to what reference is? What does that have to do with it? The only supposed connection I can imagine involves another example of the conflation between doing it and talking about it. If we think that someone who is faced with the problem of what reference is can't secure definite reference until that problem has been solved, and furthermore think that it cannot be solved, then we will draw the conclusion that such a person cannot secure definite reference. But the first and crucial premise of this argument is just our old conflation of *referring* and *showing that or how one refers.* Clear that up, and the metaphysical realist is in no inferior position to anyone else, so far as these considerations go.

But perhaps we have been looking in the wrong place for the clue to Putnam's supposition that the internal realist is not subject to indeterminacy of reference, though the metaphysical realist is. Perhaps that conviction really rests on some form of the picture, exposed and denigrated in section iv, of the metaphysical realist as struggling with the impossible task of connecting words with the constituents of a wholly transcendent reality, completely outside our thought and experience. In a passage from "Models and Reality" Putnam hints at a rationale along those lines. "Models are not lost noumenal waifs looking for someone to name them; they are constructions within our theory itself, and they have names from birth" (1983, 25).

The hint is further developed in this passage.

> For an internalist like myself, the situation is quite different. . . . [A] sign that is actually employed in a particular way by a particular community of users can correspond to particular objects within the conceptual scheme of those users . 'Objects' do not exist independently of conceptual schemes. We cut up the world into objects when we introduce one or another scheme of description. Since the objects and the signs are alike internal to the scheme of description, it is possible to say what matches what. (1981, 52)

This quotation, unlike the other passages we have been discussing, brings a metaphysical difference between the two realisms to bear on the issue. For the internalist, objects do not exist independently of conceptual schemes. The objects and the language are alike *internal* to the scheme. While the metaphysical realist thinks of us as seeking to get the truth about some antecedently existing and independently determinate external reality, the internalist thinks of us as *creating* the lineaments of reality (or of one reality among others) by working with a certain conceptual/theoretical scheme. To be sure, Putnam not infrequently disavows the view that we create reality out of whole cloth or that we can make anything we like to be the case just by choosing to do so. He recognizes that we are subject to constraints from outside as to how we can "set up" a world.[18] Nevertheless, a striking contrast between the "perspectives" remains. For the metaphysical realist, of an Aristotelian stripe, *rabbits* are "out there" as little furry mammals, whatever conceptual or cognitive operations we or other intelligent subjects engage in. They are what they are antecedently to all that, and it is up to us to find out what that is, if we are concerned about the matter, and to conform our beliefs and statements to that. For the internalist realist, on the other hand, though we can't make up any world we choose, whether one of our terms refers to rabbits or to rabbit stages depends on fundamental features of the conceptual scheme with which we are working. Roughly speaking, if we use a substance ontology, we are referring to rabbits; if we use an event ontology, we are referring to something in the neighborhood of rabbit stages. The identity of the referent is given, so Putnam claims, by the structure of our conceptual scheme and not by any relation of items in that scheme to items outside the scheme. Hence the metaphysical realist is confronted with problems and difficulties about reference from which the internal realist is spared.

Thus, not surprisingly, in the end the claim that the metaphysical realist is in a different position from the internal realist vis-à-vis reference can be seen to turn on *metaphysical* differences. The point is that the metaphysical realist is faced with an extra step of hooking terms up with designata and extensions, just because he takes the latter to exist independently of thought, experience, and "conceptual schemes". But no such step is required of the "internal realist" just because on that view objects are "internal" to conceptual schemes, not beyond or independent of them. But so far this is just a picture. In the next chapter I will explore various readings of, and alternatives to, Putnam's "reality as internal to conceptual schemes" view. For now I will only make a few points that are designed to cast doubt on the claim that this metaphysical contrast has the consequences for reference that Putnam supposes it to have.

First, note that it will help the internalist, at most, only with broad, ontological aspects of reference. It will, at most, help him with the sort of issue just mentioned, whether 'rabbit' refers to (substantial) rabbits or to rabbit stages. But the problem that Putnam posed in *Reason, Truth,*

18. See, e.g., Putnam 1981, xi, 54; 1987, 4, 17. These are all quoted in Chapter 6, section v.

and History (1981, chap. 2), concerned more radical indeterminacies. There he argued that, having fixed the truth values of all statements in all possible worlds, it is still indeterminate whether 'cat' refers to cats or to robins. And internality to a conceptual scheme is not going to help with that if the conceptual scheme in question involves both cats and robins, as our commonsense scheme does.

Second, even if this metaphysical difference does have implications for reference, it remains to be shown that it implies *indeterminacy of reference* for the metaphysical realist but not for the internal realist. More specifically, it remains to be shown that determinacy of reference is not a real possibility for both. At this point I need to recur to the earlier contention that the MR and RTH arguments do not saddle the metaphysical realist with indeterminacy of reference just because she is not confined to the constraints on reference assumed by the arguments. If the metaphysical realist is not condemned to indeterminacy by those arguments, the question that remains is whether she is condemned to this fate by the fact that (most of) the referents of her terms exist independently of our cognitive doings. And that, in turn, hangs on whether such referents are cognitively inaccessible to us. Barring some extreme form of skepticism, I see no reason to suppose that they are. I see no reason to suppose that we are capable of cognizing only what has been "parboiled" for our consumption by our own cognitive activity. Nor has Putnam attempted to provide such a reason. Hence, until such time as I see a convincing argument to the contrary, I will continue to assume that we are capable of conceptualizing, referring to, directing illocutionary acts and propositional attitudes to, and knowing about a realm that exists and is what it is independent of that cognitive activity. If this is a sound assumption, there is no case for the conclusion that the metaphysical realist is saddled with indeterminacy of reference.

One final point. If there is any hope of a "conceptual-scheme internalism" helping with a reference problem, there is a question as to how radical that internalism has to be to do the job. Putnam does not want a complete idealism in which reality (within a conceptual scheme) is wholly our work, unconstrained by other influences. But it may be that Putnam would have to go all the way with Hegel and other absolute idealists to secure the results he is after. The discussion in Chapter 6 will be relevant to that issue.

vi Putnam's "Brain in a Vat" Argument

Finally, in this catalogue of Putnam's arguments directed at a realist conception of truth, we must take a look at the "Brain in a Vat" argument, which is set out most fully in chapter 1 of *Reason, Truth, and History* (1981). The argument is designed to discredit a standard skeptical scenario that runs as follows. "For all I know, I am merely a brain, being kept alive and functioning by being submerged in a nutrient solution and artificially fed neural stimulation that produces the kinds of sensory impressions and thoughts that I would have if I were an ordinary embodied human being. If this were my situation, practically all my beliefs—even those I take to be best grounded—would be false. Since I wouldn't be perceiving the things I think I am perceiving, all my beliefs that derive their credibility—directly or indirectly—from those perceptual beliefs would be unjustified. Since I don't know that this is not my situation, most of what I believe is radically unjustified." Putnam argues that this alleged possibility is not really possible. Since a term of mine refers to Xs only if my use of that term is under the causal control of Xs, if I am a brain in a vat and I form a belief expressed by the words "I am seated at a table", I can't be said to mistakenly suppose that I am seated at a table. For since my use of the word 'table' (or the corresponding "word" in my language of thought) is not causally connected in the right way with tables, that word doesn't really refer to tables. And so what the skeptic claims I am mistaken about I can't even entertain. On a causal theory, what my word 'table' refers to is either mental images or neural processes, and perhaps what I say about these things is true. Since it is not possible that I should be a brain in a vat and still make mistaken statements about the normal physical environment of real people, there is no possibility that I should always or usually be mistaken in my beliefs by reason of being a brain in a vat. For if I were a brain in a vat, I wouldn't be having the beliefs that I do have.

I don't agree that this argument succeeds in disposing of the brain-in-a-vat version of skepticism. For the argument presupposes that I do have beliefs of the sort I suppose myself to have. But on Putnam's own showing, that presupposition in turn presupposes that I am not in a brain in a vat; for if I were I couldn't be having beliefs with those contents. Hence the argument shows that I couldn't be a brain in a vat only by virtue of presupposing that I am not a brain in a vat. However, what I am interested in here is whether the disposal of brain-in-a-vat skepticism tells against the realist. In "Realism and Reason" Putnam casually associates the possibility that we are brains in a vat with the idea that truth is "radically nonepistemic", and hence that even an ideal theory might be false (1978, 125). But is this justified? Van Inwagen (1988) trenchantly points out that it is not. The point is this. (I am putting it my way.) The alethic realist is not committed by his position to accept the possibility that we are all, or any one of us is, a brain in a vat. Suppose the realist goes along with Putnam's attempt to discredit this alleged possibility. In that case the realist can agree that the ideal theory could not be false *for this reason*. But the brain-in-a-vat (alleged) possibility is not the only possible reason for the falsity of an epistemically ideal theory. One doesn't have to be an extreme skeptic about knowledge to maintain the possibility of an epistemically ideal theory's being false. One could, as realist, simply hold that epistemic credentials never *entail* truth, and so no matter how strong the epistemic credentials of a theory, there is still the logical possibility that it is false. To suppose that one who takes that position is committed to even the logical possibility that we are all brains in a vat, is to confuse sufficiency with necessity. The possibility that we are brains in a vat is *sufficient* to undergird the possibility of an ideal theory's being false, but it is not the only possible undergirding; and hence it is not necessary as a support for the realist position. The alethic realist can cheerfully toss brain-in-a-vat skepticism in the wastebasket and still take truth to be "radically nonepistemic".

CHAPTER 6

Putnam on "Conceptual Relativity"

i Putnam's Conceptual Relativity

The other antirealist line of argument in Putnam I want to consider stems from a position that he usually terms "conceptual relativity".[1] It would, I think, better be called "ontological relativity", a term Putnam avoids, I suspect, because he wants to distinguish his position from the well known view of Quine's that is so labelled.[2] This despite the fact that, as we shall see, Putnam's position is more properly called "ontological relativity" than Quine's.

Putnam's position is most directly opposed to the clearly metaphysical components of what he calls "metaphysical realism", namely, (1) "the world consists of some fixed totality of mind-independent objects", and (2) "there is exactly one true and complete description of 'the way the world is'" (1981, 49). But Putnam, who takes the realist account of truth to be tightly bound up with these convictions in an indissoluble package, thinks that his relativity tells against the realist conception of truth as well. Deciding whether it does will be one of my main concerns in this chapter.

Putnam's central contention is that there is a plurality of apparently incompatible ways of dividing the world into objects, and that there is

1. Putnam studiously avoids the term 'conceptual *relativism*', since he is concerned to insist that his doctrine is distinct from relativism.
2. The main distinction, so far as I can see, is that Quine's view, unlike Putnam, is based on, and embodies an *indeterminacy of reference* doctrine. To be sure, in the last chapter we saw Putnam presenting arguments that had an indeterminacy of reference as a conclusion. But, let's remember, that argument was supposed to be based on premises taken from the "metaphysical realist", premises from which Putnam withheld his assent. Indeterminacy of reference was presented as something that the metaphysical realist was stuck with; the internal realist was deemed to be free of its clutches. (I presented reasons for denying these claims of Putnam's, but at the moment I am concerned only to present Putnam's understanding of "conceptual relativity".)

nothing in the nature of things, in "the world" or in "the facts", apart from us and our cognitive activity, that makes one of these the "right way", or even reduces the field to an easily manageable plurality. These ways are incompatible if, but only if, they are each taken as "absolute", as depicting the one unique constitution of reality. But if we give up the dogma that there is "exactly one true and complete description of the 'the way the world is' ", we can recognize all of these different ontologies as "right" or "correct".

His favorite examples of this are taken from mathematics, pure and applied, and abstract ontology. In the first category he considers the difference between taking points as fundamental entities in geometry, and taking points to be logical constructions out of lines or out of volumes (1978, 130–33). He also points out that: "One can construe space-time points as objects . . . or as properties. One can construe fields as objects, or do everything with particles acting at a distance (using retarded potentials)" (1978, 133).

Putnam's favorite ontological example has to do with mereology. In *Representation and Reality* (1989, 110), he imagines taking "someone into a room with a chair, a table on which there are a lamp and a notebook and a ballpoint pen, and nothing else, and I ask, 'How many objects are there in this room?' My companion answers, let us suppose, 'Five'." But then Putnam asks about mereological sums, entities the identity conditions for which are given completely by what their constituents are. What about the "object" that is the mereological sum of my nose and the lamp? And so for all possible mereological sums of the objects originally recognized, for the mereological sums of those composite objects, etc. etc. (See also 1987, 18–19; 1992, 120.) This is supposed to illustrate the point that there are alternative ways of counting objects between which no objectively based choice is possible. Whether all (or some) mereological sums are "objects" can be settled as we like, if not in terms of taste or whim then in terms of what is more convenient or useful for one or another purpose.

It may be thought that such abstract ontological differences are not significant enough to motivate sweeping metaphysical conclusions. Sure, we are free either to quantify over mereological sums or not, but so what? And the mathematical examples may seem to bear only on the question of how best to systematize specialized branches of mathematics and mathematical physics and to have no more pervasive metaphysical consequences. But this is just the tip of the iceberg. There are much juicier candidates out there for alternative ontologies. Putnam mentions some of these, too. He points out that there is no unique right way to relate "ordinary objects" and "scientific objects". "We can speak as if such ordinary objects were identical with scientific objects, or as if they were distinct from the physical systems which constitute their matter, or we can say that which physical system a given common sense object is identical with is to some degree vague" (1992a, 109–10). And there are many others. One with deep roots in the history of philosophy concerns the difference between an Aristotelian substance ontology and one or another version of an event or process ontology (Whitehead, Russell, Bergson . . .). Faint echoes of this are heard in Quine's contention that it is indeterminate whether 'gavagai' (and indeed 'rabbit') refers to rabbits or to "rabbit stages". It certainly looks as if Aristotle and Whitehead, to concentrate on these two protagonists, divide up the world into basic constituents in fundamentally different ways. For the former the basic individuals are substances that remain identical through change of location, size, shape, and many other properties, whereas for Whitehead the basic individuals are momentary events (momentary "acts" of feeling on his construal). What Aristotle would take to be an enduring substance is taken by Whitehead to be a "society" of "actual occasions" connected by spatial, temporal, and causal relations. Add one more player to this contest—Goodman's earlier nominalistic ontology of "scattered particulars". Each such particular would be taken by a realist (in the antinominalist sense of that term) to be the sum of exemplifications of a property. Thus what would more ordinarily be taken to be the sum total of blue things, past, present, and future was construed by Goodman as a "scattered particular" called "Blue".

If there can be no objective rational basis for declaring one of these ontologies the winner (one out of a much more numerous diversity of which these three are only representative), this is more grist for Putnam's mill. He would maintain that there is no objective fact of the matter as to which ontology is the correct one, no fact as to which one gives us the true story as to how the world is actually structured. What counts as objective facts, and hence what counts as true statements, will differ from one ontology, one "conceptual scheme", to another. There is no such thing as the "fixed totality of mind-independent objects" of which the world consists. And it is not just what objects there are that is relative to the ontology. The properties of objects will differ as well. Whiteheadian actual occasions (and rabbit stages) just don't have the same properties as substantial rabbits. Rabbits run, have size and shape and weight, are furry; none of this is true of momentary rabbity events. Thus, as Putnam frequently says, what objects there are is relative to a theory or a description, one that has many equally correct alternatives, and there are no theory-independent "facts of the matter".

> [W]hat objects does the world consist of? is a question that it only makes sense to ask within a theory or description. (1981, 49)
>
> 'Objects' do not exist independently of conceptual schemes. (1981, 52)
>
> [W]hat is (by commonsense standards) the same situation can be described in many different ways. (1989, p. 114)
> In my picture, objects are theory-dependent in the sense that theories with incompatible ontologies can both be right. (1990, 40)
>
> [A]ccording to me, how many objects there are in the world (and even whether certain objects . . . exist at all as individual 'particulars') is relative to the choice of a conceptual scheme. (1987, 32)
>
> What we **cannot** say . . . is what the facts are **independent of all conceptual choices**. (1987, 33)

Within the Aristotelian conceptual scheme it is true, it is a fact, that there are rabbits that are furry, run fast, like to eat lettuce, etc. None of this is true, or is a fact, in a Whiteheadian or Goodmanian conceptual scheme, though unfortunately for present purposes it is a much more complex affair to set out useful examples of what would be true or a fact in or for those schemes. (This last point is due, no doubt, to the fact that our language reflects an Aristotelian ontology.)

Someone who is an even more hard-nosed realist than I might doubt or deny that this "conceptual relativity" makes any sense. How could what is a fact of the matter be relative to some particular conceptual scheme? Either it is a fact that the milk is sour or it isn't. What conceptual frameworks we do or do not use is totally beside the point. Before dismissing Putnam's claim this easily, such a critic might ponder the following consideration.

Putnam's ontological relativity is based on his diagnosis of certain classical ontological oppositions. His contention, to repeat it once more, is that since there is no possibility of any objective rational settlement of the conflict, the best diagnosis is that the differences between the positions simply amount to differences in the conceptual frameworks used for representing reality rather than disagreements as to what the one reality is like. And what Putnam is claiming with respect to these oppositions is what everyone, however realist, recognizes with respect to many surface incompatibilities. There are many familiar cases in which what look on the surface to be incompatible statements reflect differences in ways of representing the facts rather than differences in the facts themselves. One observer reports the temperature of the liquid as 39, the other as 4. Sounds as if they contradict each other. But if the first is employing a Fahrenheit scale, the second a Celsius scale, their statements are quite compatible. They are reporting the same thermal state of affairs relative to different systems of measurement. Again, I telephone two people in Tel Aviv and ask each of them what time it is there. One says 4:00 P.M. and the other says 5:00 P.M. Are they contradicting each other? Not if one is reporting standard time and the other daylight saving time. They are giving the "same information" represented in different ways.

I drag out these obvious examples to suggest that Putnam can be viewed as proposing an extension, a rather drastic extension, of something we all accept in some cases. The extension is so drastic as to carry the claim that everything we say falls under this rubric. Every true statement we make reflects a certain mode of representation, a certain scheme of conceptualization and/or of dividing the domain into objects, one for which there are equally acceptable alternatives—as well as reflecting the nature of that domain itself. And that is quite an extension! By universalizing the phenomenon Putnam blocks any neutral way of specifying the fact that is being represented in different ways. In our uncontroversial examples, we could give a basic physical description of the thermal fact that is reported differently in the Fahrenheit and Celsius scales, and we could specify the relative position of the sun and Tel Aviv that is reported differently by giving standard or daylight saving time. But if, as Putnam would have it, everything we say reflects some replaceable mode of representation, we are forever debarred from reaching a pure, unadulterated specification of the objective fact itself, uncontaminated by any way of conceptualizing it. Putnam denies that there is any way of displaying the "dough" that we use our "cookie cutters" to shape in different ways.

> A metaphor which is often employed to explain this is the metaphor of the cookie cutter. The things independent of all conceptual choices are the dough; our conceptual contribution is the shape of the cookie cutter. Unfortunately, this metaphor is of no real assistance in understanding the phenomenon of conceptual relativity. Take it seriously, and you are at once forced to answer the question "What are the various parts of the dough?" (1989, 113–14; see also 1987, 33–36)

And to answer this question we have to be working within some particular conceptual scheme, rather than getting at something behind all such schemes.

> What the cookie-cutter metaphor tries to preserve is the naive idea that at least one Category—the ancient category of Object or Substance—has an absolute interpretation. The alternative to this idea is not the view that it's all just language. We can and should insist that some facts are there to be discovered and not legislated by us. But this is something to be said when one has adopted a way of speaking, a language, a "conceptual scheme". To talk of "facts" without specifying the language to be used is to talk of nothing; the word "fact" no more has its use fixed by the world itself than does the word "exist" or the word "object". (1989, 114)

Note too that in this passage Putnam reiterates the point that we are not free to stipulate any old facts we choose. I can't just decide that my net assets are five billion dollars or that my house is situated on the Amalfi coast by manipulating my conceptual scheme in a certain way. Truth is not just a matter of how my modes of representation work.[3] It is constrained by the way the world is independently of me, as well as by how I conceptualize it. But I can't separate out these constraints and formulate each of them alone. Everything I can say or think is said or thought from within some conceptual scheme for which there are alternatives. And when I "discover" a fact, or respond to the way the facts are—as they impinge on my cognitive apparatus—I do so in terms of one or another conceptual scheme, between which there are choices.

Putnam takes these claims to oppose the view that "the world consists of some fixed totality of mind-independent objects" and "there is exactly one true and complete description of 'the way the world is' ", the first two of the three theses of "metaphysical realism" listed in *Reason, Truth, and History* (1981, 49). And so they do. His conceptual relativity takes everything to be mind-dependent (i.e., dependent on our modes of conceptualization and theorizing) to a certain extent. And the view also includes the claim that that there is a plurality of alternative, equally correct ways of describing what there is. But with respect to the rejection of the first thesis of metaphysical realism, I must emphasize that Putnam's espouses mind dependence in a very specific way. He doesn't embrace a disjunction of Leibnizian panpsychism, Berkeleyan idealism, and Hegelian absolute idealism. None of these idealists need embrace

3. See, e.g., 1981, 54; 1989, 114.

conceptual relativity by virtue of their idealism, and, presumably, none of them did (though there can be arguments about Hegel's position on this issue, as on many other issues). Putnam's view features a particular sort of "mind-dependence"—dependence on the very cognitive-conceptual activity that takes the objects (and their properties and relations) as its objects. It is relativity *to a way of conceptualizing the world* that is the gist of the position. And so the metaphysical realism it opposes is one that denies that. As just indicated, that metaphysical realism will include many varieties of idealism as well—any that are committed to the objective reality of one unique way the world is and one unique way of telling the truth about the world. Hence the opponent of Putnam's conceptual relativity is better termed an "ontological *absolutist* ". I will, however, slip from time to time into following Putnam's lead and referring to his opponent as "metaphysical realist".

ii Hard-Nosed Absolutist Rejoinders

Now we must see how an ontological absolutist might respond to Putnam's position. There are several possibilities.

(1) He can deny Putnam's crucial premise to the effect that there is no rational, objective way of deciding between ontological oppositions of the sort in question. If there is the possibility, in each case, of showing one of the contending parties to have it right and the others to have it wrong, Putnam's argument runs out of gas. All the plausibility of his position derives from the claim that there is no way of deciding between the alternatives. How do we decide who is right in *this* metadebate? How do we decide whether it is possible to settle the ontological oppositions to which Putnam appeals?

In support of his position Putnam can cite the fact that on these issues no one position has ever commanded universal assent for any considerable time. There have been periods in which a particular position has been dominant, but this eventually changes. In the later middle ages Aristotelian metaphysics was the received doctrine, but that quickly crumbled with the development of modern physics in the sixteenth and seventeenth centuries. At the present moment it looks as if the opposition between substance and process metaphysics, between realism and nominalism, between parsimonious and profligate views on mereological sums, will continue ad indefinitum, with the contenders brandishing arguments, replies to arguments of their opponents, replies to replies to . . . , etc., with no one permanently withdrawing from the field. This is an old charge against philosophy—that nothing ever gets settled. Nor can we see anything on the horizon that will alter the situation.

But one who maintains that we cannot dismiss the possibility of a rational settlement of the mereological sums problem, for example, does not have to deny the above points. She can say: "Yes, there is still plenty of disagreement; but that doesn't show that conclusive reasons have not been presented by one side or the other—much less that none will be in the future. It is unjustified to tie 'settling the matter' that closely to consensus. No doubt, a massive consensus among those who have considered the matter thoroughly is a good reason for supposing the matter to have been decided. But it is not a necessary condition, not the only possible good reason. We have to recognize that an issue can be settled de jure, but not de facto. Many factors can prevent someone from appreciating the strength of an argument. It may be difficult to hold it before the mind all at once and grasp the way in which the parts fit together. There may be strong contrary prejudices from group opinion or early training. Furthermore, philosophical argumentation, especially in metaphysics, is the opposite of cut-and-dried. It takes mature, sensitive judgment to appreciate its force. And finally, there may be truths that some people are simply not capable of seeing. These are some of the factors that can prevent a general consensus, even if there is a conclusive case for one of the contending parties.

"And even if no such case exists at present, that does not imply that one will not be developed at some later date. The future of any intellectual endeavor is notoriously impossible to predict. Who in the nineteenth century could have predicted the astounding developments in physics in the twentieth? Indeed, predicting fundamental scientific or other theoretical advances is not merely difficult; the very idea of such prediction is inconsistent. If one were to succeed in predicting relativity theory, she would have already developed that theory, and the "prediction" would be no prediction but the accomplished fact. Thus it is difficult, if not impossible, to be justified in supposing that there is no real *possibility* of a decisive case for one of the contending parties in the ontological disputes on which Putnam's argument is based."

(2) In this way the absolutist can, with some show of reason, contend that Putnam is unjustified in supposing that there is no real possibility of showing which of the contending parties has it right about the way the world is. But there are other responses open to him as well. He can agree with Putnam about that and still maintain that there is a unique fact of the matter as to whether, for example, rabbits are enduring substances or societies of Whiteheadian actual occasions. In fact this is the

standard hard-nosed realist's response. It is a cardinal tenet of realism that truth is distinct from epistemic status. And, as opponents like Putnam and Dummett are fond of pointing out, this implies that there is a real possibility of truths that we are incapable of recognizing as such, "evidence transcendent" truths. This being the case, why should a realist be moved by even the strongest arguments for ontological relativity[4] that are based on the premise that there are questions about whether p or not-p is true that we are incapable of decisively answering? Why should a realist be moved by this consideration to deny that the world really is such that either p or not-p, but not both, is the case? This is just what the realist is prepared by his position to accept.

So run the most intransigent realist responses to Putnam's ontological relativity. But though I have considerable sympathy with these responses, I also feel that it is a bit insensitive to dismiss so flatly the case Putnam makes. It is important to distinguish two ways in which truth might be evidence transcendent. First there is the possibility of truths (facts) to which we have no cognitive access whatever, of any sort. We cannot entertain them; they lie wholly outside our ken.[5] Realism is definitely committed to this possibility. To abandon it would be a betrayal of its opposition to the "man is the measure of all things" doctrine. But it is not this sort of evidence transcendence that Putnam takes as supporting his ontological relativity. He focuses on cases in which we can envisage the alternatives clearly enough, but in which we are unable to find sufficient objective grounds for preferring one to the other.

Is realism as firmly committed to the possibility of unique facts of the matter in these kinds of cases? I cannot see that it is. The crucial difference is this. For the first kind, since we have no capacity even to entertain them, we are in no position to take seriously an interpretation contrary to the realist one. To be sure, we can conceive of the abstract possibility that there are unthinkable (by us) alternative ways the world might be such that one of them has as much right to that title as its alternatives. But since we can't put any flesh on this skeleton, we have no basis for reading the (possible) situation in a relativist rather than an absolutist way. But where, as in Putnam's cases, we can spell out what the alternatives are, and, we are now supposing, recognize our inability to ever decide between them, we are thereby in a position to consider an account contrary to absolutism. And it may be that, on sufficient

4. I am deliberately using this term for Putnam's position, despite his disavowal of it, because I find it apt.

5. This possibility is exploited in Chapter 7, section v.

reflection, even a committed realist might decide that the ontological relativist construal is a reasonable one. These considerations motivate me to look for more concessive realist responses to Putnam's position.

(3) Before coming to that I will mention one other relatively intransigent response that looks to be a possibility for at least some of Putnam's cases. Think back on the mereology example. Is there a mereological sum of any already recognized objects whatever? Suppose we agree with Putnam that there is no sufficient rational basis for choosing between various positions on this issue, ranging from no mereological sums to all possible sums, but suppose we also maintain that there is no genuine issue here just because there is no rational bar to accepting the existence of any of the contending candidates. Why deny that there is a composite entity consisting of my computer, the Taj Mahal and the number 16? What harm does it do? It isn't taking up any room that isn't already occupied. It isn't in competition for scarce resources. It isn't polluting the atmosphere. More seriously, it looks like overscrupulous nit-picking to make an issue out of whether there is such an object as that sum or not. If someone cares to refer to this object, why should we object? Admittedly, we seldom have occasion to refer to such entities, but if someone does take it upon himself to single them out for attention, what is there to be said against it? Let a thousand flowers bloom!

It may seem that the orientation just sketched is indistinguishable from taking a position on the ontological issue in question, the one that acknowledges all possible mereological sums. But the former differs from the latter by its lack of ontological seriousness. It doesn't hold either that there *really are* all these mereological sums or that there aren't. It refuses to admit that there is any significant issue here. It says, "If you want to talk in terms of mereological sums, go ahead. If you don't, that's all right too. Nothing of any moment hangs on the decision."

This position is not so latitudinarian as to give carte blanche to any hare-brained metaphysical position anyone puts forward. It does not take the same attitude toward demons, psychic atmospheres, or the *élan vital*. (I don't mean that it necessarily denies such things; only that it doesn't deny that there is a serious issue in these cases as to whether the alleged entities exist.) The position is highly selective in its permissiveness.

And that is just why this latitudinarian position cannot claim to apply to the whole range of Putnam's cases. In addition to the mereological sums issue, it *may* be plausible for debates over various "abstract objects"—properties, classes, sets, propositions, and the like. These also take up no room, don't interfere with the way we conduct our lives, etc. Here too it is tempting to think that there can be no objection to recognizing their "existence", if anyone cares to. But not all prominent ontological oppositions can be handled in this way. Go back to the contrast between a substance metaphysics, a process metaphysics, and a metaphysics of Goodmanian scattered particulars. This debate differs from the one concerning mereology in a crucial respect. Here it is not a matter of whether entities are acknowledged that constitute an addition to what all parties to the discussion accept—the latter being left just as they are whatever the decision on those proposed additions. It is rather a matter of several different ways of conceptualizing what intuitively is the same range of fact. It is not as if the Aristotelian recognizes everything the Whiteheadian posits but only wants to make some additional commitments, or vice versa. Here there can be no question of welcoming all comers with open arms, trusting them to find some way to live in harmony in a common world. There can be no coexistence between Aristotle and Whitehead. Either the rabbit is an enduring substance that retains its self-identity through change, or it is a society of momentary actual occasions, each of which perishes in the moment of self-creation. We can't have it both ways. For another example consider the opposition between phenomenalism and substantial realism about physical objects. The basic thrust of phenomenalism is to deny the reality of what realism about material substances claims to be the fundamental constituents of the physical world and to replace them with constructions out of sense data or sensory experiences. Here too it is not a matter of agreement up to a certain point and then an argument over whether some addition to this should be recognized. It is rather a disagreement concerning how to metaphysically construe a large area of reality.[6]

For that matter, we should not suppose that all metaphysical arguments over whether something should be added to an area of metaphysical agreement can be plausibly handled in the latitudinarian way. Consider the opposition between theism and naturalism. If the theist should agree with the naturalist on the metaphysics of the natural world and differ only in whether there is a supernatural reality over and above

6. To be sure, the mereologist and her opponent will handle the same range of facts, e.g., the contents of the room, differently too. And so will the nominalist and realist about universals; they will represent differently the facts reported by predications. Nevertheless, the crucial difference remains. In these cases there is an area of metaphysical agreement, the controversy being over whether items of certain sorts should be *added* to that. With oppositions like that between substance and event ontologies, however, the disagreement does not concern a possible addition to a ground level of metaphysical agreement.

that, we would still have an obviously serious difference. It cannot be said that it makes no difference to the conduct of our lives whether what theism posits exists or not. This indicates that there are two conditions for the plausibility of a latitudinarian approach. (a) The opposition concerns an addition to an area of agreement. (b) It makes no important difference whether that addition is correct. Since we have seen that there are metaphysical oppositions that do not satisfy both of these conditions, the latitudinarian option is not a serious candidate for an across-the-board response to Putnam.

iii More Moderate Absolutist Rejoinders

I have suggested that there is more to be said for Putnam's conceptual relativity than the above reactions are prepared to admit. Although I take each of the first two responses to be reasonable ones, I also think that they are far from being supported by conclusive reasons, and that something like Putnam's position remains a live option. Thus I take his conceptual relativity argument to count more heavily against metaphysical realism than any of the other antirealist arguments I have considered. That may be damning with faint praise, since I have judged the other arguments to possess no significant merit whatsoever—give or take a jot and tittle. Nevertheless, I do take the ontological-relativity position seriously, and hence I am motivated to examine positions that retain some of the thrust of realism while, at the same time, making concessions to Putnam in a relativist direction.

(4) The most concessive reaction that retains any significant realist thrust is this. "It is true that every 'objective fact' is what it is partly because of our conceptual and theoretical choices. But this doesn't show that there is no unique and conceptual-scheme-independent way the world is. It is just that this independent way is more abstract and less specific than we may have thought. Ontological relativity leaves us able to affirm that the one real world is such as to accommodate all the conceptualizations that we can successfully work with, and is such as to ground discriminations between true and false statements inside each conceptual scheme. Nor is this a wholly trivial claim. Not all conceivable conceptual schemes will work—will fit the world as it is. Construing the world as wholly consisting of real numbers, paper,[7] rodents or caloric fluid, will not enable us to get around efficiently in our environment,

7. See O. K. Bouwsma, "Descartes' Evil Genius", in 1965.

not to mention winding up with ideally justified beliefs. Moreover it is by no means insignificant that within a given useful conceptual scheme, the world permits us to make distinctions between true and false statements using the concepts of that scheme. You might think that whereas the first feature (the world supports some schemes and not others) is conceptual scheme independent, the second (there is a difference between true and false statements within a scheme) is not. But that would be a mistake. Consider this analogy. Animal life requires oxygen in the actual world, but not in all possible worlds.[8] But *life requires oxygen in the actual world* is true in all possible worlds. Similarly, though *my desk is crowded* is true in a substance-conceptual scheme but not in an event scheme (and hence is not a conceptual-scheme-independent fact), still the fact that *the world is such that "my desk is crowded" is true in a substance scheme,* (while *the world is not such that "my desk is bare" is true in a substance scheme,*) is a fact that owes none of its status to any particular conceptual scheme. No doubt, we have to use some particular set of concepts to formulate it or think it, but the fact that the world is such that things work out that way with respect to the substance scheme is not something that is relative to one or another scheme, the way the fact that *my desk is crowded* is. The former is something that any conceptual scheme has to recognize in one way or another.

Thus one can hold that there are ways the world is independent of conceptual schemes, while still recognizing that these ways are such that they require reference to a conceptual scheme being built into the "first-order" facts of the world. The standard Putnam reply to suggestions of this sort is that the independent real world has, on this view, dissipated into an unknowable *Ding an sich*.[9] And that is the right reaction where the suggestion is merely that behind all our beliefs and theories about the world there is *the world*, of which it can only be said that it is what all the aforementioned are "about" or "of", but concerning which no further, conceptual-scheme-independent information can be given. But the suggestion of my maximally concessive realist was not of this ilk. She claimed to be able to formulate indefinitely many conceptual-scheme-independent truths concerning the real world. She may be mistaken in this claim, but at least she is not simply gesturing at an unknowable *Ding an sich*.

Still, I must confess that it is not completely clear that what this posi-

8. If you think that the requirement of oxygen for animal life is a metaphysically necessary truth, substitute your favorite contingent truth.

9. See, e.g., Putnam 1978, 132.

tion claims to be conceptual-scheme-independent truths really do have that status. Given that we have to use one rather than another scheme to articulate them, and given, what the position also admits, that there will always be alternative schemes between which there is no objective rational choice, it can always be claimed that even these very abstract, higher-level truths are each relative to some conceptual scheme as soon as each is given a definite enough propositional content (in some conceptual scheme, naturally) to be a candidate for a truth value. That is, it may be that in the final analysis this attempt to combine a full recognition of Putnam's claims about alternative conceptual schemes with the thesis that there are scheme-independent facts will not fly. This motivates me to look for other mediating positions in which not so much is conceded to Putnam.

(5) Consider a position that admits a contribution to every fact from a conceptual scheme with equally acceptable alternatives, but makes a distinction within each fact between an aspect that depends on the conceptual scheme and one that does not. The choice between conceptual schemes affects only the most fundamental aspect of a given fact—the ontology that it exhibits, and leaves the more substantive part untouched. Consider the fact that my car is now snow covered. That precise fact obtains, let us say, only relative to an ontology that divides the world up into enduring substances like automobiles and works with a scheme of properties and activities exhibitable by such substances. There are equally acceptable ontologies in which no fact that involves such an entity as an automobile and such a relation as "covered by" would appear. In a pure event ontology, for example, what it is natural to regard as "the same state of affairs" would be structured in a quite different way. But once the ontology within which we are working is specified, it is in no way a matter of our theoretical or conceptual choices that the facts assume one specific form rather than another. Within a substance ontology it is not as if I could bring it about by a "conceptual choice" that my car is clear of snow. Snow removal is not that easy! And within an event ontology, the details of the way events happen will be what they are, whatever my theoretical or other cognitive activity.

Unlike realist (4) realist (5) does not purport to specify any facts that obtain absolutely rather than "in" or relative to some conceptual scheme. She admits that any "complete" fact will exhibit both scheme relative and non-scheme-relative aspects, and she makes no pretense of being able to state the latter separately. Hence she is not vulnerable to the objections lodged against (4)'s attempt to do this. But this talk of "aspects" may well be judged too nebulous, too lacking in determinateness to form the basis for a position that unmistakably contrasts with Putnam in a realist direction. What can realist (5) do to make the position more definite?

I think her best move is an appeal to patterns of contrast, a familiar technique from linguistics and other disciplines. The syntactical-category membership of a word is specified in terms of what other words are or are not substitutable for that word *salve* grammaticality. Here too we might say that the specific, non-conceptual-scheme-relative aspect of the fact that my car is snow covered can be exhibited by considering the way this fact contrasts with the (possible) fact that my car is wet, that my car is free of any encumbrance, that my car is in the garage, that your house is snow covered, that my house is made of brick, and so on. The ways in which the original proposition differs from the others within the same scheme constitutes the substantive, non-conceptual-scheme-relative aspect of its content. To exhibit the conceptual-scheme-relative aspects we display contrasts between the way in which the "same" fact is reported in different conceptual schemes.[10] Imagine yourself in the original situation and using an event scheme or a scattered-particular scheme to report what is reported in the Aristotelian scheme by saying "My car is covered with snow". This set of contrasts exhibits the conceptual-scheme-relative aspect of the original fact.

I have been thinking of our concentrating on the *differences* between the statements in each set. That is the way to use the first set (different statements in the same scheme) to exhibit the more specific aspect and the second set (reports of the "same fact" in different schemes) to exhibit the more ontological, conceptual-scheme-determined aspect. But we can also look at the *commonalities* in each set, thereby using each set to display the opposite aspect. If we focus on what all the statements in the same scheme have in common, that will display the conceptual-scheme-relative aspect of each statement. Whereas by looking at what the "same fact" in different schemes have in common, that will, of course, enable us to see the more specific aspect.

10. One may doubt that this can be done, on the grounds that there is no nonarbitrary way of saying what state of affairs in the event scheme is the "same one" as, or the unique counterpart of, the original state of affairs in the substance scheme. But doesn't it seem obvious in what direction to go to begin constructing the Spinozistic or the Whiteheadian correlate of the attribution of the property of being snow covered to a particular substance? To be sure, it may be difficult to spell out the details in these other metaphysical systems, but *if* they are viable it must be possible in principle. Moreover Putnam is certainly committed to this. If it can't be done, then talk of there being equally acceptable schemes, each of which can handle everything there is to be handled, becomes empty.

This technique is obviously a particular form of the "It can't be stated; it can only be *shown*" position made famous by the early Wittgenstein. But it is by no means confined to the eccentricities of the *Tractatus*. As the example from linguistics illustrates, the procedure is used in various disciplines. If, as the above suggests, it is applicable here, it succeeds in bringing out a significant qualification to Putnam's thesis that there is no escape from conceptual scheme relativity. It concedes that relativity to the extent of acknowledging that we can't make a definite, complete statement—can't express a complete proposition—except by the use of some conceptual scheme that represents a choice from alternatives. But it brings out a way in which each complete proposition (state of affairs, fact) can be analyzed into a conceptual-scheme-variable aspect, and an aspect that is not so variable, the latter being (where the proposition is true) an absolute feature of the world.

(6) We are now reaching the other end of the continuum of mediating positions, the end at which the concessions to Putnam are minimal. The final stage in this progression (regression?) is one that takes realist (5) one step further. Instead of conceding to Putnam the conceptual-scheme relativity of every complete fact, and then distinguishing aspects of each fact, depending on whether the aspect is scheme relative or not, our last position plumps for the status of full facthood for these "aspects", thus avoiding the concession just mentioned. Remember that Putnam's position can be viewed as an extension to every fact of the theory- or conceptual-scheme-relativity that everyone recognizes in some cases. This suggests that someone who appreciates the force of Putnam's case for ontological relativity, but is disinclined to depart from absolutist realism to the extent Putnam does, might grant Putnam some extension of generally accepted relativities but not a universal one. Here is a possibility along those lines. Recognize the theory relativity of ontology (what the "ultimate furniture of the universe" is, what enjoys the special metaphysical status of being most fundamental) but deny that this affects the constitution of most facts and the content of most statements. Whatever the ontological truth as to whether substances or events, lines or points, physical substances or sense data, are more fundamental, most of our commonsense and even scientific assertions about the world can remain the same. Our cognitive and linguistic intentions are such that what we mean to be saying when we say that the leaves on the tree are red or that lead melts at 327 degrees is neutral with respect to those ontological differences. We aren't concerned with ontological issues in most of our thought and talk about the world. That doesn't just mean that we are not actively thinking about the ontological issues; it is rather that how

these ontological issues are resolved, or what position one takes on them, has no bearing on the truth or falsity of what we are asserting most of the time.[11]

To spell this out further, even though the form of what I am saying when I say, in the usual way, that *the leaves on the tree are red* appears to carry with it a commitment to a substance-property ontology, I need not intend it in that way, and it is not usually so intended. In most of what people say or think, they are only concerned to commit themselves to the more specific aspects of what is being said or thought—leaving the choice of one ontological framework rather than another up for grabs. It is as if we were always asserting a large disjunction containing all the ways in which the specific empirical content of "the leaves on the tree are red" can appear in alternative ontologies. We, so to say, represent that disjunction by explicitly formulating one disjunct, together with the attitude that we don't care which other disjunct is substituted for it, so long as the same empirical content is preserved.[12] If something like that can be carried through, the alethic realist can acknowledge ontological relativity, but leave the truth conditions of most statements unaffected by it, and hence free of theory- or conceptual-scheme relativity.

As already indicated, this last way of giving Putnam half a loaf differs from its immediate predecessor in "dividing up" into separate statements the aspects deemed by (5) to attach to every statement. Most of what we believe, and are concerned to assert, carries no real ontological commitment; despite appearances it is neutral on ontological issues, including the ones that, according to Putnam, there is no objective way of deciding. So realist (6) grants Putnam's "conceptual relativity" only for a special, rarefied class of statements, those that are ontological in the strictest sense, thus converting Putnam's relativity into an *ontological* relativity strictly so called. If, unlike a traditionally minded metaphysician, one is willing to throw ontology to the relativist, that will enable one to combine a substantial agreement with Putnam's relativism with an insistence that virtually all of what we believe and assert is true or false in an absolute, non-conceptual-scheme-relative way.

11. In a recent writing Putnam takes back the view that conceptual relativity affects all commitment to objects. "Certain things are paradigmatically objects, for example tables and chairs, but other uses of the term, 'object' are, to a greater or a lesser degree, optional. Thus there is no fact of the matter as to whether numbers, or mereological sums, are objects or not" (Putnam 1992, 367). This statement is definitely in the direction of my mediating position (6).

12. Note the similarity to the Berkeleyan view that a "general idea" is a particular image used with the intention of representing all similar images.

iv Conceptual Relativity and the Nature of Truth

It should be clear to the reader by now that I have no intention of trying to decide whether Putnam's "conceptual relativity" is warranted, in whole or in part. My excuse for this cowardly evasion is twofold. First, I am genuinely undecided as to just what to say about it. Second, since I am about to argue that even the full-blown Putnamian form (on at least one reasonable construal) is compatible with adherence to a realist conception of truth, and since the defense of that conception is my central concern in this book, it is not necessary for present purposes to reach a definitive position on the ontological issue. Instead, I have presented a variety of (more or less) realist responses, ranging from outright rejection of ontological relativity ((1) and (2)) through almost total acceptance of Putnam's contentions (4) to mediating positions that yield quite a bit to Putnam but modify his view, to a greater or lesser extent, in an absolutist direction ((5) and (6)). I have sought to show that each of these positions enjoys some rational support, but I have not attempted to pick one of them as the most rational choice.

Now for the argument that conceptual relativity is compatible with the use of a realist conception of truth. I will begin by thinking of the latter in its most minimal form, in which it amounts simply to embracing the T-schema—It is true that p if and only if p—taking every instance of it to be a necessary, conceptual truth, or more explicitly accepting its universal generalization, XIII.

The basic point is this. Putnam's conceptual relativism tells us that *every fact is a fact only "within" or relative to a conceptual scheme to which there are acceptable alternatives.* Facts are scheme relative; they don't hold independently of one way, among many ways, we have of conceptualizing things and theorizing about them. Because of the necessary relationship of *truth* and *fact*, this implies that what is true is not independent of a choice of conceptual-theoretical scheme. Just as it is a fact that *the car is snow covered* only relative to a substance scheme, so it is true that *the car is snow covered* only relative to such a scheme. But that in itself doesn't tell us what truth is, how to conceptualize it. And, given the case made in this book for taking the realist conception to be *the* reigning conception of propositional truth, why can't that conception be applied here? To be sure, what truths there are depends, at least in part, on what conceptual schemes we work with. That fact that would make a given (possible) statement true obtains only within a certain way of conceptualizing, and theorizing about, the world. But within a given scheme why can't the truth of a proposition (statement, belief) amount simply to things being, in or relative to that scheme, as the proposition would have them to be? Why can't it be the case, within a substance-property conceptual scheme, that whether it is true that my dining room table is rectangular depends on whether it is a fact, within that conceptual scheme, that my dining room table is rectangular? After all, as we have repeatedly had occasion to note, Putnam often explicitly disavows any supposition that we can "manufacture" facts at will. Things are as they are, by and large, independently of our desires, hopes, aspirations, and preferences. Wishes are not horses. The conceptual relativity comes in not to make the facts of the matter infinitely malleable *within a given scheme*, but only to affirm the multiplicity of acceptable schemes within which whatever facts there are obtain. Hence this position presents no bar to our recognizing that *within a scheme* what makes a statement true is whether, within that scheme, what the statement is about is as the statement says it to be. Conceptual relativity does rule out the claim that the truth of a statement consists in a reality that is wholly independent of our conceptual-cognitive activity being as the statement says it to be. But the incompatibility comes from the metaphysical aspect of this realist position—its insistence that what makes for truth is the disposition of something(s) *totally independent of our conceptual-cognitive activity*. And, as I argued in Chapter 2, that metaphysical commitment is not implied by a realist conception of truth. Truth can still hang on whether what we are talking about is as we say it is, even if what we are talking about does not have the complete mind independence that Putnam's "metaphysical realist" supposes it to have.

Now if Putnam's view included a conceptual-scheme relativity of truth itself, that would be incompatible with a realist account of the conception of truth. For on that conception it is necessarily the case that the proposition that p is true if and only if p. This implies that there is no possibility that a proposition should vary its truth value from one conceptual scheme to another. On the realist conception the *same* proposition can't be true in one scheme and false in another. But if truth itself were scheme relative, that is just what we would have. That is what I meant by truth itself being scheme relative. If the realist conception of truth is to be compatible with Putnam's conceptual relativity, as I believe it to be, then things will have to be set up so that the same propositions don't change truth value across schemes. The simplest way to ensure this, and I believe this is wholly in the spirit of Putnam's position, is to hold that every proposition contains as part of its content an "index" something like 'in conceptual scheme C_1'. This will usually not be needed, since conceptual schemes, as the term implies, are *schemes of concepts*. And different conceptual schemes will, at least in part, involve different sets of concepts. To be sure, all this talk is at a very programmatic stage, and we are far from having a developed way of individuating conceptual schemes. But suppose that the most plausible mode of individuation will involve some conceptual overlap between schemes, even if no two schemes contain precisely the same set of concepts. In that case we would need the indexing of propositions to conceptual scheme in order to prevent the same proposition occurring in different conceptual schemes, thereby ensuring that no proposition has different truth values in different schemes.

I can see no grounds for supposing that Putnam has ever taken truth to be conceptual-scheme-relative in this way. I have searched the passages known to me in which conceptual relativity is expounded and defended, and in none of them does he espouse a relativity of propositional truth. He does occasionally speak of a *sentence's* changing truth value in different schemes, but it is always stipulated that this is because constituent terms change their meaning or use.[13] In terms of propositions, this is to say that the sentence expresses different propositions in the different schemes, and this is why the truth value has altered. Indeed there is at least one passage in which Putnam forthrightly applies my "minimalist" version of a realist conception of truth in connection with conceptual relativity.

> How we go about answering the question, 'How many objects are there?'—the method of 'counting', or the notion of what constitutes an 'object'—depends on our choice . . . but the **answer** does not thereby become a matter of convention. If I choose Carnap's language, I must say there are three objects because **that is how many there are**. If I choose the Polish logician's language, I must say there are seven objects, **because that is how many objects** (in the Polish logician's sense of 'object') **there are**. There are 'external facts', and we can **say what they are**. What we **cannot** say—because it makes no sense—is what the facts are **independent of all conceptual choices**. (1987, 32–33)

I could not ask for a more explicit formulation of the thesis that the realist conception of truth is the one to employ if one is a conceptual relativist.

It may be suggested that even if conceptual relativity is compatible

13. See 1978, 132; 1990, 41.

with the T-schema it cannot coexist with a more full-blooded realist conception of truth that is formulated in terms of a correspondence between propositions (statements, beliefs) and facts. In Putnam's canonical formulation of metaphysical realism in *Reason, Truth, and History*, the truth component reads: "Truth involves some sort of correspondence relation between words or thought-signs and external things and sets of things" (p. 49). Can we discern a tension between conceptual relativism and correspondence theory that we don't find between the former and the T-schema derived versions of a realist account of truth?

NO. There are, of course, difficulties in many forms of correspondence theory that have nothing to do with the issue between relativity and absolutism. Leave all that aside, and focus on the trouble free version of correspondence theory I presented in Chapter 1. *To say that a proposition corresponds with a fact is just to say that if the proposition is the proposition that p, then it is a fact that p.* Thus to say that the statement that water is wet corresponds with a fact (viz., the fact that water is wet, naturally!) is just to say that there is an actual fact with the same content as that proposition, namely, *water is wet.* On this sanitized version of correspondence, I can see no reason why, if Putnam's conceptual relativity is otherwise in order, the obtaining of a fact, and so the correspondence of a proposition with this fact, could not always be relative to a certain conceptual scheme, rather than something that holds absolutely.

Putnam, of course, does not agree with me that conceptual relativity is compatible with a realist conception of truth. In his canonical presentation of the contrast between metaphysical realism and the "internalist perspective" (1981) he conjoins *"what objects does the world consist of? is a question that it only makes sense to ask within a theory or description"* (conceptual relativity) with an epistemic conception of truth: " 'Truth', in an internalist view, is some sort of (idealized) rational acceptability" (49), as if it were obvious that they go together.[14] And in his contribution to an 1982 Eastern Division American Philosophical Association symposium on *Reason, Truth, and History* (Field and Harman, 1982; Putnam's response is in Putnam 1990) he maintains with respect to the three theses of "metaphysical realism" (1981, 49), which include the contraries of both ontological relativity and an epistemic conception of truth,

14. If we ask how Putnam can maintain both that conceptual relativity requires an epistemic theory, and apply the T-schema while espousing conceptual relativity, as we have just seen him do, the answer is that he takes an epistemic conception of truth to be compatible with the T-schema. In taking the T-schema to be definitive of a realist conception of truth, and incompatible with an epistemic conception, I have been assuming the opposite. There will be an extended argument for this in Chapter 7.

that "each leans on the others" (1990, 31). This is a constant feature of his writings of the last fifteen years—to take ontological relativity and an epistemic conception of (or at least an epistemic constraint on) truth to be tightly interconnected. Here is a more recent example. In *Representation and Reality*, after expounding conceptual relativity, he continues:

> The suggestion I am making, in short, is that *a statement is true of a situation just in case it would be correct to use the words of which the statement consists in that way in describing the situation.* . . . [W]e can explain what "correct to use the words of which the statement consists in that way" means by saying that it means nothing more nor less than that a sufficiently well placed speaker who used the words in that way would be fully warranted in *counting* the statement as true of that situation. (1989, 115)

In other words, in setting out conceptual relativity what Putnam was "suggesting" was an epistemic conception of truth.

But it is difficult to determine what Putnam's reasons are for supposing there to be this tight connection. The closest thing I have found for an argument occurs in Chapter 3 of *Reason, Truth, and History* in which he is discussing Kant. There he suggests that Kant's view that the constitution of the physical world is dependent on our conceptually structuring our cognitions in a certain way (the physical world is "transcendentally ideal" though "empirically real"), commits him to an epistemic conception of truth, though Kant himself did not realize this.

> On Kant's view, any judgment about external or internal objects (physical things or mental entities) says that the noumenal world as a whole is such that this is the description that a rational being (one with our rational nature) given the information available to a being with our sense organs (a being with our sensible nature) would construct. . . . What then is a true judgment? . . . [T]he only answer that one can extract from Kant's writing is this: a piece of knowledge (i.e., a 'true statement' [*sic*]) is a statement that a rational being would accept on sufficient experience of the kind that it is actually possible for beings with our nature to have. 'Truth' in any other sense is inaccessible to us and inconceivable by us. *Truth is ultimate goodness of fit.* (1981, 63–64)

Here Putnam is saying, in a backhanded way, that once we recognize that any reality we can cognize is partly what it is by virtue of our conceptual activity, there is nothing left for truth to be except idealized rational acceptability. Having given up the supposition that we can be in effective

cognitive touch with a world that is what it is independently of our conceptual-cognitive doings, and so having given up the notion of correspondence to such an independent reality, there is nothing left but an
epistemic conception of truth. Putnam repeatedly presents us with this
stark alternative.

> 'Truth', in an internalist view, is . . . some sort of ideal coherence of
> our beliefs with each other and with our experiences *as those experiences
> are themselves represented in our belief system*—and not correspondence
> with mind-independent or discourse-independent 'states of affairs'.
> (1981, 49–50)

> If objects are, at least when you get small enough, or large enough, or
> theoretical enough, theory-dependent, then the whole idea of truth's
> being defined or explained in terms of "correspondence" between
> items in a language and items in a fixed theory-independent reality
> has to be given up. The picture I propose instead is . . . that truth
> comes to no more than idealized rational acceptability. (1990, 41)

If we can't hold that truth is correspondence *with theory-independent reality*, as we can't on the conceptual-relativity view, then the only alternative
is an epistemic conception of truth. But, as I fancy myself to have shown
above, those are not the only alternatives. We can, in the spirit of alethic
realism, continue to take truth to be a matter of what we are talking
about being as we say it is, but recognize that what we are talking about
is not theory independent.

Why doesn't Putnam see this? I'm not sure of the answer, but it may
throw light on the matter to distinguish two readings of conceptual relativism, for both of which there is some support in the corpus, though, I
suggest, not equal support. The construal I have been assuming is what
we may call "relativized Kantianism without noumena". Putnam frequently cites Kant with approval, while dissociating himself from noumena, including a transcendental self, and while pluralizing Kant's
unique conceptual scheme. On this interpretation there is objective reality (or rather there are objective realities) that are what they are independent of our wishes, fancies, or preferences. We can't just up and
decide what the facts are. We have seen various passages to this effect.
So in that respect this is realism. It differs from "metaphysical realism"
in that no reality is totally independent of our conceptual-cognitive activity. We are always dealing with the world as structured in some conceptual scheme to which there are acceptable alternatives. But within any
such scheme, Putnam argues, things are one way rather than another

independently of our choices or beliefs: "I shall advance a view in which the mind does not simply 'copy' a world which admits of description by One True Theory. But my view is not a view in which the mind *makes up* the world either. . . . If one must use metaphorical language, then let the metaphor be this: the mind and the world jointly make up the mind and the world" (1981, xi). On this construal internal realism has the familiar features of realism, with the important qualification that we have realism in each of many different ways of conceptualizing the world, instead of having realism "all at once" for a unique reality. *Within* a given scheme, and as long we don't remind ourselves of the possibility of alternative schemes, it is just as if we were "metaphysical realists". Hence, on this construal, it is clear that we can use a realist conception of truth inside each scheme, though we can't raise the question as to which scheme is the true one, in the realist sense of 'true' or in any other.

This "relativized Kantianism without noumena" construal is supported by Putnam's repeated insistence that we don't create the world *ex nihilo* by our cognitive-conceptual activity, but that *within* a conceptual scheme facts are there to be discovered, not made. "We can and should insist that some facts are there to be discovered and not legislated by us" (1989, 114). Putnam strikes a similar note in *The Many Faces of Realism*, where he espouses "commonsense realism".

> *[O]f course* there are tables and chairs, and any philosophy that tell us that there really aren't—that there are really only sense data, or only "texts", or whatever, is more than slightly crazy. (1987, 4)

> Internal realism is, at bottom, just the insistence that realism is *not* incompatible with conceptual relativity. Realism (with a small 'r') has already been introduced; as was said, it is a view that takes our familiar commonsense scheme, as well as our scientific and artistic and other schemes, at face value, without helping itself to the notion of the thing 'in itself'. (1987, 17)

This says as plainly as one could wish that internal realism is simply standard realism except for the claim that what is really there is always relative to one or another conceptual scheme. Again:

> Internalism is not a facile relativism that says 'Anything goes'. Denying that it makes sense to ask whether our concepts 'match' something totally uncontaminated by conceptualization is one thing; but to hold that every conceptual system is therefore just as good as every other would be something else. If anyone really believed that, and if they

were foolish enough to pick a conceptual system that told them they could fly and to act upon it by jumping out of a window, they would, if they were lucky enough to survive, see the weakness of the latter view at once. (1981, 54)

If this construal is relativized Kantianism, the alternative could be thought of as relativized Hegelianism. On this reading "internalism" takes everything to be internal in the strictest sense to our thought and discourse. There is nothing in any sense "outside" it. For Hegel and his absolute idealist followers "reality" is just thought fully realizing itself. Hence what we are aiming at in thought is not a correspondence, match, or fit with some reality that is other than thought. We are simply aiming at the perfect completion of thought—usually construed as a fully comprehensive and coherent system.[15] On the "relativized Hegelianism" interpretation Putnam is saying something similar about each alternative conceptual scheme.

This version of conceptual relativity really does support, indeed *implies*, some kind of epistemic conception of truth. If the aim of thought is to satisfy its own internal standards, rather than conform itself to the character of something other than thought it is about, then we can't suppose that what determines whether our beliefs are true or false is the character of what they are about. Reference goes down the drain along with realistically conceived truth. There is nothing left to determine truth other than the extent to which our thought realizes its own "internal" standards—coherence, completeness, or whatever. This construal is supported by Putnam's repeated claim that internal realism requires an epistemic conception of truth. It is also supported by Putnam's claim that only "metaphysical realism" is faced with the problems about indeterminacy of reference, whereas they pose no difficulty for "internal realism".[16] Finally, it is supported by the statements we have already noted that "the objects *and* the signs are alike *internal* to the scheme of description" (1981, 52).

Clearly there are tensions in Putnam's thought, or at least in the whole spread of his writings, on this matter. To put it bluntly, if internal realism requires an epistemic conception of truth it can't be relativized Kantianism, whereas if it is relativized Kantianism, it is hospitable to a realist conception of truth. I suggested above that Putnam's works do

15. See the quotations from Bradley and Blanshard in Chapter 7, section ii. It must be admitted that the position I here call "Hegelianism" is more unambiguously propounded by Anglo-American absolute idealists than by Hegel himself.

16. See Chapter 5, section v.

not equally support the two interpretations, and it does seem clear to me that the texts point most strongly in the direction of the Kantian alternative. Except for the allegation that internal realism requires an epistemic conception of truth, the suggestions of the Hegelian reading are at best ambiguous; they can be taken as simply emphasizing the conceptual relativity side of the relativized Kantianism; whereas the pointers to the Kantian reading are much stronger and more clear cut. The insistence that from the standpoint of a particular conceptual scheme, facts are what they are independent of our modes of thought is clearly incompatible with the "nothing outside of thought" construal, as is the reassurance that internalism is still committed to commonsense realism about familiar objects, but without the "thing in itself". Moreover, the temporal development of Putnam's thought is in that direction.[17] The Kantian motifs grow stronger, and the Hegelian weaker, as we move from "Realism and Reason" to *Representation and Reality*. I cannot reconcile the allegation that internal realism requires an epistemic conception of truth (or even an epistemic constraint on truth) with an espousal of the Kantian version. Obviously I cannot, since I have been arguing that that version is fully compatible with a realist conception of truth. I have to put this view of Putnam's down as a mistake, possibly encouraged by some ambiguity on his part as between the readings of internal realism I have distinguished.

The upshot of this chapter is that even if we embrace Putnam's conceptual relativity without reservation (and I am certainly not inclined to go that far), the realist conception of truth would be left standing. Qualifications would have to made to a full-blooded metaphysical realism. But, as I have argued in Chapter 2, alethic realism is almost completely neutral on metaphysical issues, and, as I have just been arguing, it does not require what Putnam calls "metaphysical realism". Conceptual relativity and internal realism, on my preferred Kantian reading, leaves alethic realism unscarred.

17. Note Putnam's statement in "Reply to Ebbs", in 1992, 353, that "the connotations of the word 'internal' have proved to be unfortunate".

Epistemic Conceptions of Truth

i The Realist Conception of Truth and Its Alternatives

I have been considering the most serious arguments known to me against the viability of a realist conception of truth. To cast the net as widely as possible and to minimize the risk of missing anything significant, I have included some arguments that may not properly fit that rubric. So be it. Philosophy is not so tidily divided into compartments that we can prevent discussions from spilling across such barriers as we erect. In any event, the main point is that I have not found any arguments that, in my judgment, shake the strong intuitive plausibility of the realist conception. Prima facie, it seems overwhelmingly obvious that the realist conception is the one we express with 'true', when that predicate is applied to propositions, statements, and beliefs. And nothing has turned up to disturb, or even qualify that obviousness. The realist conception remains in possession of the field.

But a complete defense of alethic realism will also include a critical assessment of the alternative conceptions of truth that have been put forward. To that task I now turn.

ii Varieties of Epistemic Conceptions of Truth

I have already pointed out that the only serious alternatives are epistemic conceptions, conceptions that identify truth with some favorable epistemic status of the truth-bearer.[1] But I haven't as yet done much to

---

1. Remember that I am restricting the field of alternatives to views that set out to explain *what truth is*, what that property is, at least to the extent of identifying and delineating the concept of truth. In Chapter 1, section xi, I explained why I reject deflationist accounts of truth that hold that sentences containing 'true' are to be understood otherwise than as attributions of a property to something.

display the lineaments of this category or to explore the variations to which it is subject. I begin by glancing at some important formulations.

The eminent British idealist of the turn of the century, F. H. Bradley, provides a convenient starting point. Bradley tells us that truth is "that which satisfies the intellect"[2], "an ideal expression of the Universe, at once coherent and comprehensive"[3]. In like vein Brand Blanshard holds that a proposition is true if it coheres with an all comprehensive and fully articulated whole.[4] From the pragmatist's side C. S. Peirce's well-known view is that "the opinion which is fated to be ultimately agreed to by all who investigate, is what we mean by the truth",[5] while William James writes that "true ideas are those that we can assimilate, validate, corroborate, and verify".[6] John Dewey holds true ideas to be those that are instrumental to "an active reorganization of the given environment, a removal of some specific trouble or perplexity".[7] More recently Hilary Putnam objects to "the most important consequence" of what he calls "metaphysical realism", namely, "that *truth* is supposed to be *radically non-epistemic* . . . and so the theory that is 'ideal' from the point of view of operational utility, inner beauty and elegance, 'plausibility', 'simplicity', 'conservatism', etc. *might be false*".[8] Putnam's alternative to this is not to identify truth with rational acceptability tout court, but to hold that "truth is an *idealization* of rational acceptability. We speak as if there were such things as epistemically ideal conditions, and we call a statement 'true' if it would be justified under such conditions".[9] Again, " 'Truth', in an internalist view [Putnam's term for his alternative to "metaphysical realism"], is some sort of (idealized) rational acceptability—some sort of ideal coherence of our beliefs with each other and with our experiences *as those experiences are themselves represented in our belief system*—and not correspondence with mind-independent or discourse-independent 'states of affairs'."[10]

Through all these variations there runs a single intuitive idea. The truth of a truth bearer consists not in its relation to some "transcendent" state of affairs, but in the epistemic virtues the former displays *within* our thought, experience, and discourse. Truth value is a matter

---

2. Bradley 1914, 1.
3. *Ibid.*, 223.
4. Blanshard 1939, 2: 264.
5. "How To Make Our Ideas Clear," in Peirce 1934, 268.
6. James 1975, 97.
7. Dewey 1920, 156.
8. Putnam 1978, 125.
9. Putnam 1981, 55.
10. *Ibid.*, 49–50.

of whether, or the extent to which, a belief is *justified, warranted, rational, well grounded,* or the like. To cut corners I will use the term JUSTIFIED to range over any positive epistemic status that is taken by some thinker to constitute truth. There are, of course, many theories of epistemic justification current in epistemology, carrying with them different *standards* or *criteria* of justification, and there are many *concepts* of epistemic justification as well. When we add other terms of positive epistemic appraisal, such as 'warrant' and 'rationality', the scene is even more chaotic. If I were to go into all that, I would turn this book into an epistemological treatise. To avoid that I will aim at maximum neutrality, endeavoring to limit my judgments about justification to what would be acceptable, on (almost) any theory or concept of justification.

One thing we need to consider is what reasons epistemic theorists have for preferring their account of truth to a realist view. Actually, apart from some bald statements that it is implausible to think of truth as conceptually independent of rational acceptability and the like, those reasons are confined to reasons for rejecting a realist conception, along with a tacit assumption that epistemic accounts are the only alternative. In the last four chapters I have explored at length arguments against the realist account of truth, and in section xi of this chapter I will return to that topic.

There are various differences between the ways in which the philosophers just cited develop their common intuitive idea. One difference concerns the choice of truth-value bearer. Our authors variously speak of truth as attaching to propositions, beliefs, opinions, ideas, statements, and theories. Taking a true theory to be made up of true statements, 'opinion' and 'belief' to be sufficiently near synonymy for present purposes, and 'idea' to be a loose designation for belief, this boils down to the triad on which the discussion in Chapter 1 was focused—statements, beliefs, and propositions. Now presumably the primary bearer of epistemic justification is belief. A statement could derivatively be said to be justified or unjustified in terms of the epistemic status of the belief expressed by the statement. But what of propositions? The proposition that life is not confined to the earth would seem to have no epistemic status in itself. It may be that I am justified in believing this, while you are not. However, we must remember the point made in Chapter 1 that when we speak of beliefs or statements (assertions) as true or false, we are referring not to the psychological state of belief or the act of stating, but to the contents of those states or acts—*what is believed* or *what is stated.* And this content, this "what" is a proposition. Hence, truth-value bearers are propositions all the way down. A true belief is a true proposition considered as believed, and a true statement is a true proposition considered as asserted. Hence if the epistemic status of a proposition is situation relative, exactly the same is true of the epistemic status of *beliefs* and *statements*, in the senses of those terms in which they range over truth-value bearers. Hence I will swing freely in the ensuing discussion between speaking of beliefs, statements, and propositions as bearers of truth value and of epistemic status. The situation relativity of the justification of beliefs (statements, propositions) is something an epistemic conception of truth has to deal with. I will discuss that shortly.

Another difference is this. One would expect the details of an epistemic conception of truth to be dependent on the epistemology of the thinker forging the conception, so that philosophers with different epistemologies will differ correspondingly in their versions of an epistemic conception of truth. Thus we find Bradley and Blanshard construing truth in terms of ideal conformity to the standards of a coherentist epistemology, while James's and Dewey's conceptions of the epistemic status that is to be identified with truth reflect a more pragmatist, empiricist epistemology. But some of these views are less specific. Putnam says, and Peirce says in effect, that a true belief or statement is one that satisfies ideal epistemic standards, or satisfies epistemic standards in an ideal or final fashion, without making any attempt to spell out what those standards are, or what is required to satisfy them fully. There are obvious advantages to refraining from tying an epistemic conception of truth to a particular epistemology. For one thing, it maximizes opportunities for acquiring converts from differing epistemological orientations. The version on which I shall eventually fasten, that of Putnam, will be on the unspecific side of this contrast.

On the other hand, there are disadvantages to unspecific versions. By sidestepping the task of spelling out in detail just what positive epistemic status of a belief constitutes truth, the epistemic theorist ties his hands when it comes to arguing for the view and defending it against objections. It makes a great deal of difference whether we construe an ideal epistemic situation in *externalist* or *internalist* terms, for example, whether we think of it as one in which a belief was formed in a maximally reliable way or as one in which the subject has conclusive evidence for the belief. (See Chapter 8 for a discussion of externalism and internalism in epistemology.) Again, foundationalist and coherence epistemologies have different stories as to what would constitute an ideal epistemic situation. In the ensuing discussion I will have to go considerably beyond Putnam in fleshing out the concept of an ideal epistemic situation, so as to have something definite enough to be worth discussing. But the enrichment will still fall short of what is ideally desirable.

iii Ideal Epistemic Conditions (1)

Rather than undertake the tedious task of examining each of a number of epistemic conceptions of truth, I will focus on the strongest form of the view. If I can succeed in disposing of this version, I can claim to have put the quietus on the enterprise generally. I shall work up to this by first examining simpler forms and considering why they don't work.

When we think about identifying the truth of a belief with something in the area of justification, the first thing to notice is the impossibility of supposing that a belief's being justified, as we ordinarily think of this, is sufficient for, much less identical with, its being true. There is more than one reason for this. (1) Whether a particular belief is justified for a particular person depends on that person's epistemic situation. The belief that gold is malleable (i.e., not someone's state of believing this at a certain time but *what is believed* when someone believes that) may be justified for one person, A, at t_1 and unjustified for A or another person, B, at t_2. This will be the case if A at t_1 has relevant evidence or experience lacking to her or to B at t_2. The epistemic status of a belief varies over different epistemic situations. But truth value does not vary in this way. A belief (i. e., a belief content) is true or false once for all; it does not alter its truth value through time or across the population.[11] If it is true that gold is malleable, it is true for everyone and at every time. How then can something immutable, truth, be identified with something situation relative, epistemic status? These considerations subvert any simple identification of truth and justification.

(2) If we try to identify *being true* with *being justified for someone at some time*, we run into the fact that there are many true propositions (actual or possible belief contents) that are never believed by any human being. Consider the set of propositions of this form: "It was raining on this spot at time *t* (where *t* is more than 5,000 years ago)." Most such propositions are never even entertained by anyone, and many of them are true. Thus if an epistemic conception of truth is to have any chance of complete coverage, it will have to range over possible as well as actual beliefs.

11. It is interesting that Putnam, whom I take as my paradigm epistemic theorist of truth, insists on this point.

(3) The last difficulty revealed that someone's actually being justified in believing that p is not necessary for p's being true. Here is a consideration that shows it not to be sufficient either. There are innumerable cases of false propositions that were justified for certain people in certain situations. One can be justified in believing that Sam killed Benny, even though that belief is false, since Joe was the murderer. There have been many cases in which the evidence possessed by the police strongly points to a certain person as the murderer, even though he is innocent. Newton was justified in believing his theory of gravitation, though we now realize that it is not strictly true. Many people in the sixteenth century were justified in believing that Columbus was the first European to sail to the western hemisphere, though now we know this to be incorrect. And so on.

In order to work toward an epistemic conception of truth that cannot be refuted in these ways, let's reflect on why the previous versions were so vulnerable. We have already indicated that the second difficulty can be evaded by ranging over belief contents that are not believed by anyone as well as those that are. As for the other two difficulties, we will best see our way to a solution by concentrating on the last objection—that some justified beliefs are false. How can that be? Isn't it because a belief can be justified by ordinary standards even though the epistemic situation of the believer is incomplete or otherwise defective? An epistemic situation is defective when it doesn't include all the relevant evidence. If we were proceeding on the basis of all relevant facts, we wouldn't mistakenly suppose, justifiably, that Sam killed Benny. If Newton knew what Einstein knew, he would not be justified in supposing his theory of gravitation to be correct. To take a quite different example, suppose that I am justified in believing a lamp to be in front of me because my visual experience is just as it would be if I were being visually presented with a lamp. But, unbeknownst to me, my visual experience is generated by a laser image. If I am in no way at fault in my ignorance of this fact, I am amply justified in the false belief that there is a lamp before me. But if I knew all the relevant facts, I would not longer be justified in believing this.

This suggests that if we were to consider what beliefs would be justified in situations that are ideal in the respects in which the ones we have been considering fall short, it would no longer be possible for justified beliefs to be false, and there would be no basis for prying truth and justification apart; that is, the suggestion is that a belief is true if and only if it would be justified in ideal epistemic circumstances, where those are circumstances in which all relevant evidence is available.

One might think that there should also be conditions on an ideal epistemic situation from the side of the subject. Shouldn't we require that the subject be in full possession of normal human cognitive powers, that she not be too distracted, biased, etc.? Certainly all this is required if the subject is to function cognitively in an ideal fashion, if she is to take full advantage of her opportunities. But remember that we are concerned here with a *situation* of the subject, rather than with the the characteristics or the behavior of the subject in that situation. The truth of a proposition, *p*, (a possible belief that *p*) is thought of here in terms of whether it would be *justifiable* (not actually *justified*) in the situation. And for that it is enough that the situation contains everything that is needed for complete justification of a belief that *p*, so that anyone who believed that *p* in that situation *could* believe that *p* with full justification simply by appropriating what is there for the taking. Thus we don't need to build into our specifications for the ideal situation any specification of the state of the subject. The belief is *justifiable* in the situation, whether a given subject takes advantage of this or not.

For ease of future reference, let's put this view in a canonical formulation.

> Ideal Justifiability Conception (IJC). To say of a belief that it is true is to say that it would be justifiable in a situation in which all relevant evidence (reasons, considerations) is readily available.

We can also see that the IJC is not vulnerable to the first difficulty. The variation in epistemic status of a belief across subjects and times came from variations in epistemic situations. But if all the subjects in question were in an ideal epistemic situation, there would be no room for such variation.

Looking back at the examples of epistemic accounts of truth I presented at the beginning of the chapter, we find some of them to be of the overly simple sort just criticized. When Dewey says that true ideas are those that are instrumental to "an active reorganization of the given environment, a removal of some specific trouble or perplexity", he is plausibly taken as asserting that any "idea" that has this function in any situation is thereby true. For the above reasons it would be more charitable to suppose that Dewey misspoke himself and had really intended not to tell us what truth is, but rather to present us with a function of "ideas" that we should concentrate on, rather than on their truth. As for James's statement that "true ideas are those that we can assimilate, validate, corroborate, and verify", the interpretation depends on how to read the "can". "Can" in what kinds of conditions? If he is thinking of idealized conditions, the view is of the sort we will be going on to consider. But a more natural reading, given the context of the remark, is that any "idea" that can be corroborated, verified, etc., at any time and under any circumstances thereby counts as true. And that view falls under the above strictures.

But all the other thinkers quoted above can be understood as advocating some version of the idealized view. Putnam uses just that terminology.[12] Peirce, in speaking of what would "be ultimately agreed to by all who investigate" is naturally taken as supposing that the limit of the process of inquiry would be an ideal epistemic situation in which all relevant facts are in. As for Bradley and Blanshard, their language makes clear that they are thinking of what coheres with what under highly idealized circumstances. Thus Bradley speaks of "*an ideal expression of the Universe*, at once coherent and comprehensive", and Blanshard of a proposition's cohering with an *all comprehensive and fully articulated whole.* Since I will be focusing on the "justifiability in ideal epistemic conditions" version of an epistemic conception of truth, and on one that is unspecific about epistemic criteria, and since Putnam is a particularly prominent recent advocate of such a version, I will be thinking of him as my main opponent. But to do so, I cannot be thinking of the most recent Putnam. As I will bring out in section vi, Putnam has more recently disavowed any attempt to *define* truth in epistemic terms. Hence the Putnam I will be criticizing is the one represented in the above quotations from works of the late seventies and early eighties.

Before concluding that Putnam's IJC is the strongest version of an epistemic conception of truth available, I need to say something about why I prefer it to the kind of coherence version represented by Bradley and Blanshard. I take their view to be one that identifies truth with being justified by the standards of a pure coherence theory, one which epistemically evaluates beliefs (propositions, statements) solely in terms of their coherence with a maximally coherent, maximally comprehensive system. The most obvious difficulty with this is that it is dubious at best that there is a unique maximally coherent and comprehensive system? It would seem that for any system of beliefs whatever we can construct an indefinitely large number of other systems that are equally coherent and comprehensive on any reasonable understanding of coherence. To

---

12. The reader may wonder why, given that the Putnam passages were already on the table, we took such a roundabout route to the "epistemically ideal situation" version. The answer is that one can best appreciate the virtues of a philosophical position if one sees it against the background of inferior alternatives.

argue this would require a long excursus, but here is a brief sketch. The details of the argument depend on the details of our concept of coherence. Suppose we take coherence to involve consistency, plus a rich matrix of inferential, probability conferring, explanatory, and unifying relationships. Consider a system of propositions so constituted. It seems clear that we could modify the observation reports, general principles, predictions, etc. to any given degree and still maintain coherence by making compensatory modifications elsewhere. Modifications in the observational base could be compensated for by suitable modifications in general laws and principles. Modifications in the conditions of accurate observations could be compensated for by modifications in propositions concerning the conditions under which observations taken to be veridical had been carried out. And so on. In the absence of additional constraints on what can go into the system, any coherent system will have innumerable equally coherent alternatives. And if this is the case, we can't possibly identify truth with the satisfaction of coherence demands. For if, as follows from the above, for any proposition both it and its contradictory finds a place in a maximally coherent and comprehensive system, we would be faced with the unpalatable consequence that for any proposition both it and its contradictory are true.

iv Ideal Epistemic Conditions (2)

To construct a serious version of the IJC I need to say more than I have so far as to what constitutes an "ideal epistemic situation". A full treatment of the problem would involve deciding all the major issues of epistemology, and I can't undertake that here. Nevertheless, I must make the conception more definite in certain respects.

(1) When we speak of a condition where all relevant "evidence" is available, we must understand 'evidence' in a wide sense. If we were to restrict evidence for p to other things known, or justifiably believed, that provide reasons of a propositional sort for or against a belief that p, that would freeze out direct, immediate justification by experience, self-evidence, and the like. We must include under 'evidence' anything that has a bearing on the epistemic status of the belief, including "reasons" (facts known or justifiably believed), experience, or intrinsic features of the proposition believed such as self-evidence.

(2) Some restrictions must be put on 'relevant evidence', if the conception is not to be doomed to triviality. If the belief in question is p, then one highly relevant bit of evidence (if p and q are both true) would

be p and q. But if we are to allow "evidence" like this, then every true proposition would automatically be ideally justifiable; for every true proposition is deducible from some other true proposition. This would make things much too easy for the epistemic theorist. What is needed is some way of singling out evidence of which one could be in possession while one is still trying to decide whether it is true that p. I don't know how to do this in some general, comprehensive way. I will just assume that my opponent can take care of this. If he can't, then so much the better for my criticism.[13]

(3) Though one may aim at maximal neutrality between opposing epistemic perspectives, it is impossible to escape the more radical divergencies. For example, most current discussion of the matter in English-speaking philosophy proceeds on the basis of a, broadly speaking, naturalistic orientation, in which the only considerations relevant to the epistemic assessment of belief are drawn from our acquaintance with, and what we have learned about, the natural world. One who, like myself, holds that (at least some) human beings have experiential access to God will see this as intolerably restrictive.[14] Again, if one thinks that we have intuitive awareness of (some) necessary truths and/or of moral facts, this will make a difference to what would be available in an "ideal" epistemic situation. The point is that one can hardly expect to work out the details of such a situation without getting into highly controverted issues.

(4) The Peircean formulation seems to envisage a single epistemic situation that would be ideal for any belief (statement) whatever. But there are troubles with that. For one thing, what beliefs is this situation supposed to cover? Any belief that any human being could hold or envisage? That is an enormous, perhaps nonfinite, class, and the possession of all the information relevant to the epistemic assessment of every such belief is not a real possibility for the likes of us. Putnam explicitly disavows any such aspiration and opts for tailoring ideal situations to the particular proposition in question.[15] Instead of thinking in terms of a single ideal epistemic situation he supposes there to be such a situation for any given belief. That is a somewhat more manageable idea, and I will be thinking in those terms.

13. I am indebted to Doris Olin for this point.
14. See Alston 1991.
15. To say that a statement is true of a certain situation "means nothing more nor less than that a sufficiently well placed speaker who used the words in that way would be fully warranted in *counting* the statement as true of that situation. What is 'a sufficiently well placed speaker'? That depends on the statement one is dealing with" (1989, 115).

(5) We can no longer suppose that there is a unique, context-free answer to the question of what is relevant evidence for settling a given question. It is recognized on all hands that this is relative to certain background assumptions. Given the theory of general relativity, what is relevant to determining the age of the universe is radically different from what is relevant to that issue, given Newtonian physics. From a psychoanalytic perspective what is relevant for deciding on the etiology of Jim's obsession is quite different from what is relevant from a behavioristic perspective. Thus there is no unique set of relevant considerations for a given statement. It all depends on the assumptions with which we are working. And how are those assumptions to be chosen for "ideal epistemic conditions"? They would have to be the assumptions that we are most justified in accepting. But most justified relative to what further background assumptions? An infinite regress looms. You might suppose this Gordian knot could be cut by stipulating that in epistemically ideal conditions all facts would be available to us. We wouldn't have to worry about which facts are relevant to deciding what issues. But this move retreats to thinking in terms of a single condition that is ideal for the epistemic assessment of all possible beliefs. And we have already seen reason not to work with such a global notion as that.

So what can we do to rescue the notion of an ideal epistemic situation from this fatal relativity to background assumptions? Since we have just seen that the attempt to neutralize the relativity by choosing the best justified background assumptions in each case gives rise to a viciously infinite regress, I see no alternative to an appeal to coherence. Instead of trying to pick a unique set of background assumptions case by case, we consider what total set of assumptions would yield the most coherent system.

It is crucial, however, that we appeal to coherence only as an auxiliary device, rather than depending on it to do the whole job, as we would if we were to define an ideal epistemic situation as one in which our system of beliefs is maximally coherent (and comprehensive?), à la Bradley and Blanshard. For, as we have just seen, that move is subject to the fatal objection that there is no unique maximally coherent and comprehensive system. Hence a pure coherence theory will not provide us with a unique set of background assumptions. But provided there are enough other constraints on the situation, coherence can play a significant supporting role. To wit, let's take observational, memory, and introspective beliefs, as well as the intuitively self-evident, to be at least prima facie justified apart from high-level background assumptions, to be justifiable by the experiences that give rise to them, though defeasible, in principle, by various considerations. This will give us a base of prima facie justified beliefs as an anchor for whatever larger system is constructed. We can then envisage that larger system as the one the members of which best cohere with each other and with the base just specified, or with as much of the base as survives defeaters. One can reasonably hope that a unique system is thereby determined from which the approved background beliefs can be drawn for assessing the justificatory status of any particular belief.

It is obvious that the above does not constitute anything like a proof that a unique system of belief, yielding a unique set of background assumptions, can be constructed along these lines. In addition to the fact that I have provided no more than hints at the lineaments of the view, I have done little or nothing to support the idea that anything close to uniqueness can be attained. If I were making use of the notion of an ideal epistemic situation for the development of my own views, this would be a serious liability. But in fact I am critical of the notion. My main contention will be that we cannot define truth in terms of justifiability in an ideal epistemic situation. And one part of my case for that is that there are serious difficulties in working out a satisfactory concept of such a situation. Hence if the approach I am suggesting for solving the "relativity to background assumptions" problem doesn't work, then again, so much the better for my side of the argument. I only maintain that the approach I have briefly adumbrated is the most promising one for surmounting this particular obstacle. Whether in the end it would be successful I do not know. That being the case, I will concede to the epistemic theorist that this problem can be solved, whether in this way or some other, and pass on to what I consider to be three serious difficulties for the IJC. I will put them in order of apparent conclusiveness. It is the third that I consider to be most obviously fatal. But the other two, especially the second, also point to weaknesses in the program.

v Are There Counterexamples to the Ideal Justifiability Conception?

If there are propositions (beliefs, statements) that are true but not ideally justifiable, or ideally justifiable but not true, there are counterexamples to the IJC, which claims these classes to be coextensive. I will concentrate here on considering whether there are true propositions that are not ideally justifiable. To be sure, there are various difficulties in exhibiting specific counterexamples. For one thing, we are all so far from an ideal epistemic situation, and the specifications for such a situation are so schematic, that it is difficult to be sure what beliefs would or would not be justified under ideal conditions, unless we just assume that true propositions would and false propositions would not, which would amount to conceding the issue to my opponent, at least on an extensional level. Moreover, even if I were in an ideal situation I could hardly suppose that a belief is true unless I supposed that I was justified in believing it. Hence I must proceed more indirectly. I must consider how plausible it is to suppose that there are true propositions that would not be justifiable in an ideal epistemic situation.

The most extreme candidates would be propositions such that nothing that tells for or against their truth is cognitively accessible to human beings, even in principle. Even in an epistemically ideal situation we would have no basis, however weak, for asserting one of these propositions rather than its negation. To make a case for this I need not restrict myself to propositions we are able to envisage. I might have considerable difficulty in rendering it plausible, with respect to any proposition I can formulate, that we are incapable in principle of uncovering any considerations that tell for or against its truth, but that is not the only possibility. Might there not be states of affairs, or even entire realms or aspects of reality, that are totally inaccessible to human cognition? If so, propositions to the effect that such states of affairs obtain will be true, even though no beliefs or statements bearing those propositions as their content would be justifiable in an epistemically ideal situation.

To this one might reply that even if there are such propositions, it doesn't follow that they would not be *justifiable* for human beings in ideal situations. From the fact that we can't envisage the proposition it doesn't follow that we could not acquire evidence or reasons that bear on its truth and that we could use to support belief in it if, per impossible, we should come to entertain it. I agree that this doesn't follow. And yet the situation envisaged by the objection seems thoroughly outlandish. Any body of evidence that would tend to show one of these propositions to be true would have, at least in part, some conceptual connection with it—inhabit the same conceptual field. But then if the proposition is closed to our discernment, confirmatory and disconfirmatory evidence would have the same status. Turning it around, if we were capable of cognitively possessing the evidence in question, why should it be impossible for us to entertain the proposition for which this is evidence? To go into this a bit more finely, it might be that some observational evidence open to us could count as evidence for or against the obtaining of some unenvisageable state of affairs. But what is not possible is that we should entertain the "bridging principles" that connect this evi-

dence with the proposition in question because to entertain such principles we would have to use the concepts involved in the proposition. Thus
I judge it to be at least extremely plausible that for any state of affairs
that is in principle closed to our consideration, we would likewise be
barred from acquiring anything that provides decisive *complete* evidence
for or against that state of affairs' obtaining.

But how plausible is it that there *are* realms or aspects of reality that
are in principle inaccessible to human cognition? There are general
considerations that render it quite plausible. Think of the limitations of
our cognitive powers—limitations on our storage and retrieval capacity,
on the amount of data we can process simultaneously, on the considerations we can hold together in our minds at one moment, on the complexity of propositions we are capable of grasping. Isn't it highly likely
that there are facts that will forever lie beyond us just because of these
limitations? And it is not just our finitude; there is also what we might
call our "particularity". The cognitive design of human beings represents only one out of a large multitude of possible designs for cognitive
subjects, even for embodied cognitive subjects as finite as we, leaving out
of account angels and God. It seems clear that there could be corporeal
cognitive subjects with forms of sensory receptivity different from ours—
sensitivity to different forms of physical energy. There could be subjects
with different innate cognitive tendencies, propensities, and hardwired
beliefs and concepts. There could be subjects who reason in patterns
different from those we employ. These sorts may or may not be instantiated elsewhere in the universe. Given all this, shouldn't we take seriously
the possibility that, even if there is something wrong with the idea of
facts that are in principle inaccessible to any cognitive subjects whatever
(and I don't see any fatal flaw in this idea), it could still be that there
are many facts accessible to cognizers with radically different hardware
and software but totally inaccessible to us. Those who airily endorse
some version of the "man is the measure of all things" doctrine should
take considerations like this much more seriously than they do.

If I am correct about this, there is a considerable case against the
thesis that truth can be defined as justifiability for human beings in the
most ideal situation possible for us. There will be innumerable true
propositions that do not satisfy that condition. One possible response to
this would be to make the thesis under discussion range over cognitive
subjects generally. Truth would then be identified with justifiability for
some cognitive subjects or others in situations that are the most ideal
for those subjects. And if there are still true propositions unenvisageable
by any actual subjects, we could make the conception range over possi-

ble subjects as well. The above reasoning does nothing to show that there are true propositions that would not be ideally justifiable for some possible cognitive subject. Note that in considering whether the IJC could be construed in this more extended way, we are raising a further question as to how an ideal epistemic situation should be construed. Should we think, anthropocentrically, of a situation that is maximally favorable for human beings finding out the truth, or should we think of it less specifically as a situation that is ideal in this way for whatever kind of cognitive subject we are considering? Since Putnam is the focus of my discussion, it is worth noting that Putnam makes it abundantly clear that he chooses the former alternative. "[A] true statement is a statement that a rational being would accept on sufficient experience of the kind that is actually possible for beings *with our nature* to have (1981, 64, my emphasis). " 'Truth', in an internalist view is some sort of idealized rational acceptability—some sort of ideal coherence of our beliefs with each other and with our experiences as those experiences are themselves represented in our belief system" (1981, 50).

But whatever is the case with Putnam, one could try out the less anthropocentric version. This would certainly take the sting out of the above objection. But it would also take much of the sting out of the IJC. If we survey the reasons that have been given for an epistemic definition of truth, we will see that they depend heavily on anthropocentrism. Dummet's arguments for a verificationist conception of truth, for example, depend on considering what sorts of truth conditions are such that we could learn to attach them to sentences. James and Dewey are preoccupied with the way in which *we* judge beliefs to be true or false and with the functions beliefs we call true play for *us* in *our* lives. And, in any event, we would have to restrict consideration to finite cognitive subjects. If an omniscient deity were brought into the picture, the position would lack the antirealist bite it is designed to have.[16] Realism should have no hesitation in recognizing that a necessary condition of the truth of a proposition is that it would be known (accepted, believed . . .) by an omniscient cognitive subject. And with the restriction to finite subjects in place we still have to take seriously the idea that there are aspects of reality that are inaccessible in principle to *any* such subjects—actual or possible. The essence of God has been a popular theological candidate.

Moreover, if there are serious problems, as I have urged, for working out in a satisfactory way a conception of an epistemic situation that is

16. See Plantinga 1982.

ideal for human beings, we would get those problems in spades if we tried to specify what would be a maximally ideal epistemic situation for possible cognitive subjects of which we have had no experience at all. This move, to say the least, does not look promising.

We should also consider less extreme counterexamples that involve propositions we can envisage and for which evidence is in principle accessible to us, but which are such that even in the most ideal possible epistemic situation there would be no basis for preferring such a proposition to its negation. We can think of this as an extrapolation from the claim that scientific theories are underdetermined by empirical evidence. It is often pointed out that for any theory that is supported by a good deal of empirical evidence, there will be an indefinitely large number of alternative theories that are equally well supported by that evidence. Those who make such claims often go on to say that it is reasonable to choose between the alternatives on grounds of simplicity, coherence with background knowledge, naturalness (given our cognitive predilections), intuitive plausibility, and the like. But isn't it possible that even in ideal circumstances there will sometimes be alternatives that score equally well on all those dimensions? Assuming that some of the alternatives are true, they would be true propositions such that even in an epistemically ideal situation there would be no rational basis for believing them.

Let me elaborate this last suggestion a bit. We are thinking of an ideal epistemic situation, vis-à-vis a given proposition, as one in which all relevant considerations are available. It follows right away that no true observational beliefs, or true beliefs rendered sufficiently probable by observations, and/or by propositions that satisfy this last condition, would fail to pass the ideal justifiability test. For in a situation in which everything relevant is readily available there would be experiences, evidence, or reasons that would justify any such belief. A counterexample of the present sort would have to be a true proposition that is so sheltered from evidence and experience that no augmentation of our present epistemic situation would provide any rational basis for preferring it to one or more contraries. The strongest candidates for this would be highly theoretical propositions the links of which to observational data (and what is more effectively supported by them) are extremely weak, tortuous, or dependent on equally recondite background assumptions.

But though I think that I have exhibited considerable plausibility for the supposition that there are true propositions that are not ideally justifiable, I do not wish to rest much weight on this extensional argument. For I do not know how to prove that there are such propositions. Hence

I would ask the reader to evaluate my criticism primarily on the basis of the other two arguments, and especially the third one.

vi The Concept of an Ideal Epistemic Situation Presupposes the Concept of Truth

The second main criticism is this. If the notion of an epistemically ideal condition cannot be defined without using the notion of truth (unless it is rendered defective in other ways), then the definition cannot go in the other direction. Is the IJC entangled in this circularity? I believe that there are several points at which we find ourselves driven to use the notion of truth in explaining the notion of an epistemically ideal situation. Recall the formulation of the IJC.

> Ideal Justifiability Conception (IJC). To say of a belief that it is true is to say that it would be justifiable in a situation in which all relevant evidence (reasons, considerations) is readily available.

First, there is the question of how to explain the notion of justifiability involved. Here I must refer you to the discussion in Chapter 8, sections iv–viii, where I distinguish between conceptions of epistemic justification that do and do not involve the notion of truth. I argue that the former are superior to the latter in three respects. (1) They specify a basic aim of cognition by reference to which the epistemic point of view can be defined and epistemic justification distinguished from other kinds. (2) They bring out why justification is desirable in the pursuit of knowledge. (3) They provide criteria for evaluating candidates for conditions of justification. This discussion is designed to show that a conceptual connection with truth is required for an adequate construal of epistemic justification. The allied point that is of special interest here is that if it is to be at all plausible that justifiability in ideal conditions is identical with truth, then the justification involved must be "truth conducive", that is, such that it is part of the concept of justification that one is justified in believing that p only if one's situation is such that it renders one's belief likely to be true. Thinking of justifiability in terms of adequate grounds for the belief, as I have been doing in spelling out the IJC, satisfies this condition. And where this condition is satisfied, the concept of truth enters into the concept of justification, since the latter involves, inter alia, a guarantee of the likelihood of truth for the belief to which it applies. To see that a conceptual tie of justification with truth conducivity is necessary as well as sufficient for any plausibility of the IJC, consider a way of thinking of justification that does not exhibit truth conducivity. The most prominent example is a "deontological" conception, according to which a belief's being justified amounts to one's satisfying, or not violating, one's intellectual obligations in holding the belief. It seems clear that one could be maximally justified, in this sense, in believing that p without its being true that p. Suppose one is deficient, psychologically or culturally, so that even if one does everything, cognitively, that could reasonably be required of one, one still often winds up in a poor position to get the truth, and so often forms false beliefs. In that case, one would often be fully, amply justified in a false belief. To obviate this possibility, or at least to minimize it, we would have to build truth conducivity into the concept of epistemic justification. And this would give rise to a circularity in trying to analyze truth in terms of the IJC.

Second, there is the notion of the "availability" of all evidence relevant to a given belief. Can we explain this notion without covertly making use of the concept of truth? Now to say that the evidence is "available," in the sense intended here, is to say that one could come into possession of it readily or easily. So the crucial notion here is *possession* of the evidence. The evidence will presumably consist of facts. What is it for the subject to *possess* those facts so as to make use of them in justifying a belief. The most obvious answer is that he or she comes to *know* them. But the notion of knowledge involves the notion of *truth*. (Knowledge is *true* belief that satisfies certain further conditions.) To avoid this we would have to construe the possession in terms of belief, without mentioning knowledge. But then we will have to require the beliefs to be *true*. Otherwise S is not in possession of genuine evidence, but only mistakenly supposes himself to be so. At this point the hard-pressed epistemic theorist might suggest that the possession of evidence consists in having *justified* beliefs. But this involves a different circle. The justification involved here obviously can't be justification by everyday standards. For, as we saw earlier, by those standards a belief can be justified in one situation and not in another, which means that there is no unique answer to what the relevant evidence is for a given target belief. Hence, if we are going to take possession of the relevant evidence to consist of justified beliefs, it will have to be beliefs that would be justified in *ideal epistemic circumstances*. But then we are in an even smaller circle. We define 'ideal justifiability' in terms of an ideal epistemic situation; but then we have to define such a situation in terms of what beliefs would be ideally justified in such a situation!

Third, there is the notion of "relevance". The epistemic situation that is ideal vis-à-vis a given belief involves the availability of all evidence that is *relevant* to the epistemic assessment of that belief. And what makes a bit of evidence relevant? Presumably it is that the evidence will increase or decrease the probability of the belief (in some appropriate sense of probability). That is, it has a bearing on the probability of the belief's being *true*. Once more truth enters in. This could be avoided only by using a truth-free notion of relevance. If we were to construe relevance in terms of a priori principles of evidential support that are not subject to a truth-conducivity constraint (are not deemed unacceptable if strong evidential support does not guarantee probability of truth), then once more the plausibility of identifying truth with ideal justification would evaporate.

These problems arise only for the way of construing an ideal epistemic situation that I developed out of Putnam's remarks. I think it is by far the most attractive way, but one might try other alternatives. Indeed, there are as many ways of specifying what makes an epistemic situation ideal as there are conceptions of justification, warrant, rational accept-ability, or other positive epistemic status the idealization of which consti-tutes the type of situation in question. I couldn't possibly survey all the possibilities here, but I will look at a few in order to give an idea of how I take the land to lie, still focusing on the term 'justified' as my representative of positive epistemic statuses.

The construal I have been working with is based on the idea that a belief is justified if and only if it is based on adequate grounds, reasons, or evidence. Idealizing that gives us the notion of a situation in which *all relevant* grounds, reasons, or evidence are available. If we start with a different understanding of justification, we get a different construal of epistemic ideality. Consider a "deontological" notion of justification, according to which one is justified in believing that *p* if and only if one's believing that *p* does not violate any intellectual obligations (or in a less voluntaristic version, if and only if one's belief that *p* does not stem from any violations of intellectual obligations). The notion of an epistemically ideal situation this engenders would be something like *a spotless record in fulfilling intellectual obligations* (at least those that are relevant to believing or abstaining from believing the proposition in question). But, as I pointed out above, being ideally justified in this deontological sense is obviously not identical with truth. For if one suffers from disabilities of one or another sort, one might have a perfect record in doing every-thing that could be expected of one in the conduct of one's cognitive affairs and still believe falsely.

If, on the other hand, we think in terms of other "truth-conducivity" conceptions of justification, we will run into the same circularity, at least with respect to the notion of justification involved. On a reliabilist conception of justification one is justified in believing that p if and only if that belief was acquired and/or sustained by a sufficiently reliable belief-forming (-preserving) mechanism. An idealization of this would involve a perfectly reliable mechanism. But 'reliable' means fitted to produce *true* beliefs. Again the notion of truth rears its head. As a final example, take Alvin Plantinga's recent proposal, in *Warrant and Proper Function* (1993), that what he calls "warrant" (that enough of which turns true belief into knowledge) is to be understood in terms of the "proper functioning" of one's cognitive faculties. The rough idea is that a belief is warranted if it is formed by such functioning. An idealization of this would presumably involve as "proper" (i.e., as efficient) a use of the faculties involved as possible. But in the course of refining his account Plantinga finds it necessary to add the qualification that the proper functioning be a carrying out of that part of one's "design plan" that is aimed at truth, rather than, for example, comfort. Thus once more the notion of truth makes an appearance in an attempt to say what epistemic ideality amounts to.

Coherence theory would seem to extricate us from this circularity. If we construe the ideal situation as one in which we have an ideally coherent system of beliefs, we need not invoke any conception of truth in delineating the ideal. A particular belief would then possess the kind of (ideal) justifiability needed for truth provided it was a member of a perfectly coherent system of belief. But this returns us to the pure coherence theory of Bradley and Blanshard, which we saw to be subject to the fatal flaw of being unable to provide sufficient constraints to determine a unique maximally coherent system.

Interestingly enough, the more contemporary Putnam acknowledges the circularity we have been considering.

> In *Reason, Truth, and History* I explained the idea thus: "truth is idealized rational acceptability". This formulation was taken by many as meaning that "rational acceptability" (and the notion of "better and worse epistemic situation", which I also employed) is supposed (by me) to be more basic than "truth"; that I was offering a reduction of truth to epistemic notions. Nothing was farther from my intention. The suggestion is simply that truth and rational acceptability are interdependent notions. Unfortunately, in *Reason, Truth and History* I gave examples of only one side of the interdependence: examples of the

way truth depends on rational acceptability. But it seems clear to me that the dependence goes both ways: whether an epistemic situation is any good or not typically depends on whether many different statements are true. (1988, 115; see also Putnam 1992b, 357–58, 365)

So Putnam now agrees that we cannot spell out what makes an epistemic situation ideal without employing the notion of truth to do so. But, as he notes, this still leaves the possibility of some conceptual dependence of truth on "rational acceptability", as well as vice versa. Unfortunately, Putnam does not spell out, here or elsewhere to the best of my knowledge, just what kind of conceptual interdependence he has in mind. Perhaps his thought is that *possessing* the concept of epistemic justification is a prerequisite for *possessing* the concept of truth and vice versa, and in such a way that the correct application of neither concept is a sufficient or necessary condition for the correct application of the other.[17] If that is the way the wind blows, the current Putnam drops out as a target for my arguments in this chapter. For here I am only opposing the view that some kind of epistemic status is a conceptually necessary and sufficient condition for truth.

vii An Intensional Argument against the Claim

What I am calling an "intensional argument" against the IJC is one that adduces reasons for denying that ideal justifiability makes up any part of the meaning of 'true' (the concept of truth). Such an argument is to be contrasted both with the extensional argument of section v that there are cases of truth that are not cases of ideal justifiability, and the circularity argument of section vi.

The most direct attack on the intensional front would be an intuitive claim that by carefully reflecting on what we mean when we say of a proposition, statement, or belief that it is true, we find nothing about justifiability, ideal or otherwise, in that meaning. I am strongly inclined to make this claim. I do think that, just by virtue of being a fluent speaker of English and by being sufficiently reflective, I can ascertain that it is no part of what I mean by saying 'It is true that gold is malleable' that a belief that gold is malleable would be justifiable under some conditions or other, however ideal. But in the face of widespread contemporary philosophical skepticism about meaning, and about reflec-

---

17. Putnam has informed me that he does not now regard justifiability in an ideal situation as a necessary condition of truth.

tive judgments as to what a term or utterance does or doesn't mean, it would be desirable to have an argument that does not depend on intuitive semantic judgments. Such an argument is not difficult to find.

The basic point is this. On a realist conception of truth the fact that sugar is sweet is both necessary and sufficient for its being true that sugar is sweet. It is true that p if and only if p. Moreover, any such biconditional is necessarily, conceptually true; it is rendered true by the concept of truth. Since the fact that p is (necessarily) both necessary and sufficient for its being true that p, that leaves no room for an epistemic necessary or sufficient condition for truth. Nothing more is required for its being true that p than just the fact that p; and nothing less will suffice. How then can some epistemic status of the proposition (belief, statement) that p be necessary and sufficient for the truth of p? It seems clear that the imposition of an epistemic necessary and sufficient condition for truth runs into conflict with the T-schema.

Note that this conflict arises with respect to the minimalist version of the realist conception. As just pointed out, the T-schema itself, or its generalization, XIII—the heart of the minimalist version—is sufficient to imply that the fact that p is necessary and sufficient for its being true that p. And that is what is incompatible with the imposition of any epistemic condition for truth. We do not have to get into further developments that involve the delineation of some sort of *correspondence* between propositions and facts in order to generate the incompatibility.

The idea that epistemic conceptions of truth are incompatible with the T-schema runs into contradiction with the widely held view that this schema and its near relations are neutral as between various theories of truth—including epistemic theories. Here is a sample of statements to this effect.

We could . . . *keep* formal semantics (including 'Tarski-type' truth-definitions); even keep classical logic; and yet *shift* our notion of 'truth' over to something approximating 'warranted assertibility'.[18]

I have argued that the formal logic of *true* and *refers* is captured by Tarskian semantics, but the concepts of truth and reference are *undetermined* by their formal logic . . . it is only by examining our theory of the world, and specifically by examining the connections between truth and various kinds of provability or warranted assertibility as they are drawn *within* that theory itself, that one can determine whether the notions of truth and reference we employ are realist or idealist, 'classical' or 'intuitionist'.[19]

18. Putnam 1978, 29.
19. *Ibid.*, 46.

It is not now very controversial that the neutral core of Tarski's work leaves us with reference, satisfaction, and truth in a tight little circle, nor that it would be acceptable to philosophers of any bent: realist, anti-realist, correspondence, coherence, dismissive neutralist, or whatever.[20]

However, the result, that truth and warranted assertibility, while normatively coincident, are potentially extensionally divergent, is of course equally implicit in any conception of truth which is prepared to endorse the DS [the "Disquotational Schema: 'P' is true if and only if P] as incorporating something conceptually correct about the nature of truth. . . . Since anything that aspires to be a competitive account of truth will presumably respect the DS, our finding has a claim to generality.[21]

To be sure, many of these thinkers are talking about Tarski's "Convention T", which, as noted earlier, differs from my T-schema both in taking sentences as truth-value bearers and in being (or rather yielding) only extensional biconditionals, whereas the T-schema yields conceptually, hence necessarily, true biconditionals. An extensional biconditional says only that the two sides of the "if and only if" have, in fact, the same truth value. This is not claimed to be necessarily the case. Hence it could be *extensionally* true that 'Snow is white' is true if and only if snow is white, even though some kind of epistemic justifiability is a necessary and/or sufficient condition for the truth of the left hand side. 'I live in New York State' is extensionally equivalent to 'I am a philosopher' (they are both true), even though there are various necessary conditions for the truth of each of these propositions that are quite different from what appears in this biconditional. For example, a necessary condition of my living in New York State is my living in the United States. So the claim of neutrality for Tarski's Convention T is thoroughly innocuous. But some of the above authors regard a necessarily true T-schema as also being compatible with various more substantive theories of truth, including epistemic theories. For example, Wright goes on to make similar claims for "the analogue of the DS for propositional contents, the 'Equivalence Schema': 'It is true that P if and only if P' ".[22] And that is by no means innocuous. More generally, I find a widespread acceptance of the view that any version of the T-schema—whether extensional or intensional, whether concerned with sentences, propositions, state-

20. Blackburn 1984, 273. See also Davidson 1990, pt. 1.
21. Wright 1992, 22–23.
22. Wright 1992, 24ff.

ments, or beliefs as truth bearers—is equally compatible with any serious contender for an account of the nature of truth.

I suspect that the popularity of this view is explained in part by the fact that those who hold it have simply not thought through the implications of combining the T-schema with an epistemic conception of truth, in particular the issues that have been and will be raised in this discussion. But another part of the explanation is, no doubt, that if an epistemic account has to reject the T-schema, that is a serious, even fatal, flaw. Surely the T-schema makes explicit something that is as fundamental to our concept of propositional truth as anything can be. Any account of truth that contradicts it is thereby unacceptable. Hence the anxiety of epistemic theorists to insist that their views are compatible with that schema.

viii Replies to the Intensional Argument

So far I have presented only a prima facie case for the incompatibility of the T-schema with an epistemic conception of truth. And there are ways in which the epistemic theorist might try to rebut this case. For one thing, she might claim that even though sugar's being sweet is necessary and sufficient for the truth of the statement that sugar is sweet, some epistemic condition is also necessary and sufficient just because it is necessary and sufficient for sugar's being sweet, the realist condition. That is, it could be claimed that though only the realist condition is proximately or directly necessary and sufficient for truth, some epistemic condition is indirectly or derivatively necessary and sufficient for truth through being necessary and sufficient for the more fundamental realist condition.[23] As for the necessary-condition claim, we would have a situation similar to that in which it is both necessary and sufficient for X's being Y's biological father that X impregnated the egg that developed into Y. Nevertheless it is also necessary for X's being Y's father that X had sperm at the appropriate time, for that itself was necessary for X's impregnating the egg in question. As for a sufficient condition claim, though X's heart's ceasing (permanently) to beat is sufficient for X's death, Y's shooting X in the way Y did was also sufficient for X's death, since it was sufficient for X's heart's ceasing (permanently) to beat.

What are the chances that the ideal justifiability of the belief that sugar is sweet is a necessary and sufficient condition of sugar's being

---

23. This move was suggested to me by Andrew Cortens.

sweet? First we may note that if sugar is sweet, we would expect this fact to be discovered by any normal human being with his wits about him who consumes sugar sufficiently often. This might encourage someone to suppose that *normal eaters of sugar's being justified in believing that sugar is sweet* is a necessary condition of *sugar's being sweet.* But we can't claim that it is a strictly necessary condition. It is (not merely logically) possible that a sugar eater not be justified in believing that sugar is sweet even if it is sweet. The person may through inattention, faulty memory, or whatever, fail to register, store, and process the information available from consuming sugar, with the result that he or she is not justified in believing sugar to be sweet. Thus, even though it would be extremely unusual for a normal person who has eaten a lot of sugar to fail to be justified in believing sugar to be sweet even though it is, it is not impossible. And hence this epistemic condition is not strictly necessary for sugar's being sweet and hence not indirectly necessary for the truth of the belief that sugar is sweet.

But these considerations are not strictly relevant to the matter at hand. According to the epistemic conception of truth, what is necessary (and sufficient) for the truth of *p*, along epistemic lines, is not that normal people are justified in believing that *p* in situations of the sort in which we typically find ourselves, but rather that the belief is *justifiable* in *epistemically ideal circumstances.* So what we have to consider is whether that sort of justifiability of the belief that sugar is sweet is necessary and sufficient for sugar's being sweet.

What should we say about that? Well, it does seem clear that as I have developed the notion of an epistemically ideal situation, the belief that sugar is sweet would be justifiable in such a situation. There are readily available facts that tell strongly for it, and nothing of any significance that tells against it. But, for two reasons, it would be premature to award the palm to the epistemic theorist.

(1) The case at hand involves a fact that can be verified by ordinary observation. But the epistemic theorist needs a universal generalization over all propositions. He needs it to be the case that for any proposition, *p*, it is the case that *p* only if a belief that *p* would be justifiable in epistemically ideal conditions. And what are the prospects of that? Here the extensional part of my criticism becomes relevant, thus indicating that the extensional and intensional parts are not so independent of each other as I may have made it appear. In section v I suggested that there are true propositions that would not be justifiable even in the most ideal epistemic circumstances. I suggested that this would be the case for two classes of propositions—those that are not envisageable by human be-

ings (or by any finite subjects), and those that are such that even in an ideal epistemic situation the available evidence would not suffice for choosing between the proposition in question and various incompatible alternatives. For such propositions the claim that ideal justifiability is necessary for its being the case that p (and for its being true that p) is obviously unacceptable, for in such cases the fact that p obtains without a belief that p's being ideally justifiable.

I do not wish to put the main weight of my argument on this consideration, however, because, as I pointed out when presenting it, I don't see how to prove that there are such true propositions. At most I claimed to exhibit a certain plausibility for the assumption. Hence I wish to concentrate on my second reason.

(2) That second reason runs as follows. Even if every true proposition were, in fact, ideally justifiable, and vice versa, that would not suffice to bail out the epistemic theorist. His position concerns the *concept* of truth (the *meaning* of 'true'). Therefore he must maintain that it is *conceptually* (semantically) necessary that it is the case that p (and hence that it is true that p) if and only if a belief that p would be ideally justifiable. Anything less than that would not reconcile his position with the T-schema. Even if it were non-conceptually, non-analytically true that, for any p it is the case that p, if and only if a belief that p would be justifiable in epistemically ideal circumstances, the *concept* of truth would not be specified by that biconditional. Thus the present line of defense against my objection that is based on the T-schema would have to be that it is *conceptually necessary* that it is the case that p if and only if a belief that p is ideally justifiable, and hence, from that and the T schema, that it is *conceptually necessary* that it is true that p if and only if a belief that p is ideally justifiable. And the mere truth of the biconditional—it is the case that p if and only if it is ideally justifiable that p—does not suffice for that conceptual linkage. Convincing ourselves that, in fact, sugar wouldn't be sweet without an idealized inquirer being justified in supposing it to be—or, for that matter, convincing ourselves that something parallel holds for all propositions—is not convincing ourselves that it is *by virtue of the concept of truth* that it is true that p only if it is ideally justifiable that p. In fact, wood would not burn unless there were oxygen in the immediate vicinity, but that does not show that having oxygen available is part of the (ordinary) concept of burning, or that part of what we are saying when we say that the log is burning is that oxygen is in the vicinity. A surface wouldn't look red, in "normal" circumstances, unless it were reflecting light with a frequency that falls within such-and-such a range (let's assume that something in this general ball park is true); but that

doesn't show that when we say that the sweater looks red we are saying something about the frequency of light waves reflected from the sweater.

Let me spell this out a bit more. Since a nonconceptual equivalence of the fact that p and the ideal justifiability of a belief that p would not, in conjunction with the T-schema, show that there is anything epistemic about the *concept* of truth or that we are *saying* anything about idealized justifiability when we say that a proposition is true, an alethic realist could cheerfully accept this result, however surprising it might be. He could say, in good logical and epistemological conscience, that what this shows is that truth is more accessible to human beings (at least idealized human beings) than one might have thought. But it doesn't show anything at all about the concept of truth. It shows that it is possible to develop a conception of epistemically ideal circumstances, relative to a given proposition, such that a human being in such circumstances would have available to her everything needed to justifiably accept that proposition if and only if it is true. This would tell us something about human cognitive powers, and about parameters of epistemic assessment. But why suppose that it would tell us anything about truth?

So the viability of this way of reconciling an epistemic conception of truth with the T-schema hangs on the assumption that it is conceptually true for any proposition p that it is the case that p if and only if a belief that p would be ideally justifiable. And what should we say about that? So far as I can see, it is totally lacking in plausibility. Here we have nothing like the case we have for taking the generalization of the T-schema, '(p) it is true that p if and only if p' to be conceptually necessary. There we are able to see what it is in the concept of truth that makes this necessarily true. But we found nothing analogous in our development of the concept of ideal justifiability. It does not violate that concept to suppose that in some cases a belief that p is ideally justifiable without its being the case that p or vice versa. We did see that the most plausible notion of ideal justifiability involves truth conducivity, so that a belief that p enjoys this status only if it is *likely* that p. But that falls far short of conceptually guaranteeing that no such belief is false. Hence I think we can legitimately ignore this way of reconciling the ideal justifiability account of truth with the T-schema.

ix An Epistemic Reinterpretation of Content

What recourse, then, is left to the epistemic theorist, other than rejecting the T-schema? I can see only one other option—a reinterpretation of the content of our statements. The T-schema takes the content of a statement to lay down what it takes for the statement to be true. Hence the reason why there are not conditions of an epistemic sort for most of our statements is that most of them don't assert that anything epistemic is the case. Of course, we can and do make epistemic statements; we say that Jim is justified in believing that Sam is out to get him. On the realist conception of truth, what it takes to make *that* statement true is that Jim's belief in question is justified. But usually we are not asserting anything of an epistemic sort. Rather we are saying something about sugar and salt, about ships and sealing wax, and about many other things. Or so it seems. But an epistemic theorist of truth may seek to save her position by maintaining, in the face of appearances to the contrary, that all of our statements are to the effect that some epistemic state of affairs holds. If that is what is asserted by saying "Sugar is sweet", then, by the T-schema, the truth of that statement would depend, after all, on some epistemic condition. What are the prospects for such a massive reinterpretation?

First, the thesis seems obviously false. Surely it is as evident as anything can be that most of our statements do not attribute epistemic statuses to anything, but make claims of quite different sorts. We say that it is raining, that Buffalo won the AFC championship, or that salt contains sodium. My opponent may claim that I am begging the question here by assuming a realist interpretation of our statements and beliefs. But what is the alternative? How can the view that all statements are epistemic statements be made remotely plausible?

The only way I can see of doing that is to buy into some version of the absolute-idealist view that there is no fundamental distinction between thought (discourse) and the reality it is about. The reality with which our statements and beliefs are concerned is nothing but thought and discourse that has attained its ultimate goal—to constitute an all embracing maximally coherent system. So when I believe that salt contains sodium I believe something about an aspect of a comprehensive and fully coherent system of thought. If that is an epistemic state of affairs, something epistemic is what it takes to make my belief true. If embracing *this* view is what it takes to save an epistemic conception of truth, few will be willing to pay the price. In any event, I can't undertake to go into the pros and cons of absolute idealism in this book. Hence I will pass on to what I take to be a decisive difficulty with this attempt at reinterpretation, regardless of the merits or demerits of absolute idealism.

The fatal flaw is this. The supposition that I am always making epistemic claims about beliefs (statements) does not get so far as to be false.

It cannot even be coherently thought. Consider the view that when I believe that sugar is sweet what I believe is that a certain belief is ideally justifiable, coheres with an all-comprehensive and fully articulated whole, or has some other epistemic status, E. Well, what belief is it that I believe to have E? It can't be the belief that sugar is sweet. If it were, the belief (i.e., proposition believed) that sugar is sweet would turn out to be a proper part of itself. The proposition that *sugar is sweet* is the proposition that *the proposition that sugar is sweet has E*. That way lies madness. It must be some other proposition that we are believing to have E. But whatever candidate we suggest, it too will have to be construed as a proposition to the effect that some proposition has E. And what proposition is *that*? The propositional content of the original belief keeps expanding. Each time we try to say what proposition is believed to have E, it turns out to be the proposition that some *other* proposition has E. The upshot is that we never succeed in saying what the propositional content of the original belief is. This is a mug's game or, to speak more philosophically, an infinite regress—not the kind that sends us on a never-ending chase up ever-ascending levels, but the kind that is more analogous to a broken record. We keep coming back to the same point without ever getting beyond it, without ever assigning a definite content to the belief in question.

The general point is clear. If we try to maintain that *every* belief is a belief to the effect that some belief has a certain epistemic status, we have left ourselves without any resources for specifying what belief it is we are asserting, on a given occasion, to have a certain epistemic status. I don't wish, of course, to deny that we can assert that a particular statement, proposition, or belief has a certain epistemic status. The trouble comes with the claim that *all* statements have this form. That is what gives rise to the infinite regress. This second way of trying to show an epistemic conception of truth to be compatible with the T-schema—the reinterpretation of propositional content—works no better than the first.

I want to make it explicit that I am not rejecting everything that might be called "epistemic" interpretations of propositional content. In particular, the above argument is not intended to be directed at a verificationist construal of propositional content, as put forward by Michael Dummett, for example. At least, it is not intended to be a criticism of that view on the construal that I take to be the most plausible one. So construed, Dummett's claim is that every statement is to be understood as asserting the "verification conditions" of that assertion. Thus if the verification condition of 'The orchestra played the Beethoven 7th Symphony' is that the sounds produced by the orchestra (at least roughly) instantiated a certain score, then what that statement says is that the sounds produced instantiated that score. This proposal does not run afoul of the above argument just because it does not construe a statement as attributing an epistemic status to that statement (or to any other statement), but rather equates it with a certain statement on the same level. That is a different ball game. I do not accept verificationist semantics, but that is another story.

Looking back at these two unsuccessful defensive maneuvers, we can see that epistemic accounts of truth are impaled on the horns of a trilemma. They can accept the T-schema only at the price of either maintaining a palpably false conceptual thesis, or giving an interpretation of propositional content that is not coherently thinkable. If, on the other hand, they reject the T-schema, they are thereby rejecting what, as Putnam acknowledges, is a mere truism about truth. In that case they reveal themselves as not talking about truth at all, and their doctrine is condemned to irrelevance. Palpable falsity, incoherence or irrelevance. Not an attractive array of alternatives.

It will not have escaped the reader's notice that my third objection to an epistemic conception of truth—incompatibility with the T-schema— is also, in effect, an argument for the central claim of this book that acceptance of the conceptual truth of each instance of the T-schema (which is what I mean by accepting the T-schema) amounts to accepting a distinctively realist conception of truth. For if I am right in claiming that epistemic accounts of the concept of truth are the only serious alternatives to a realist account, and if they are incompatible with an acceptance of the T-schema, the latter constitutes a distinctively realist way of construing the concept of truth, one that excludes important and widely held alternatives. Thus the argument of this section tells against the almost universally accepted supposition that the T-schema is completely neutral between different theories of truth, and constitutes a vindication of my claim that the T-schema is the core of a distinctively realist account of truth.

Perhaps one reason the T-schema argument, which forms the heart of my "intensional critique", has not been noticed by epistemic theorists is that they are attracted to an epistemic reading of principles like the T-schema itself, in which case an epistemic account of truth seems to go better with such principles. A good example of this is found in Crispin Wright's recent book, *Truth and Objectivity* (1992). In chapter 1 he argues that if one holds, as "redundancy theorists" typically do, that the "Disquotational Schema" ('P' is true if and only if P) (DS) "is (all but) a complete explanation of the truth predicate, then one is committed to denying what redundancy theorists notoriously assert—that 'true' expresses no real property but is merely a device of disquotation" (14–15). He argues that where we have sentences with "assertoric content", "there will be a distinction between cases where their assertion is justified and cases where it is not", and so "it follows that a norm, or complex of norms, of warranted assertibility will hold sway, both prescriptively and descriptively, over sincere and literal use of the sentences to which the T-predicate applies" (17). He then argues that 'true' and 'warrantedly assertible' "coincide in (positive) normative force" (18), even though they can still "diverge in extension" (19). What I am concerned with here is not these conclusions themselves, nor even the full content of Wright's argument for them, but with only one link in that argument. The argument gets under way with the following assertion.

[G]iven the explanatory biconditional link effected by the Disquotational Schema between the claim that a sentence is T [Wright's term for a maximally neutral truth predicate] and its proper assertoric use, it follows that "T" is likewise, both prescriptively and . . . descriptively, a predicate which is normative of assertoric practice. "T" is prescriptively normative, because any reason to think that a sentence is T may be transferred, across the biconditional, into reason to make or allow the assertoric move which it expresses. (1992, 17)

That is enough for my current purpose. What I want to point out is that Wright takes the right-hand side of the DS to say something about "proper assertoric use", that is, "warranted assertibility". It is by reading it in that way that he considers himself entitled to argue that 'true' is normative of "assertoric practice", and moreover normative in such a way that its normative force coincides with that of 'warrantedly assertible'. But this is a gross misreading. The right hand parts of the DS and the Equivalence Schema (ES) ("It is true that P if and only if P") say nothing about "proper assertoric use" or "warranted assertibility" or anything else of a metalinguistic character. Take a particular instantiation of the schema: 'It is true that sugar is sweet if and only if sugar is sweet.' The proposition on the right hand of the equivalence is about sugar; it attributes sweetness to sugar. It says nothing whatever about warranted assertibility; it says nothing of any kind about assertion or about the conditions under which an assertion is proper, correct, or in order. It asserts a fact about a substance, a foodstuff. There is no excuse for supposing that either of these schemata "effects a link" between truth and some positive epistemic status of assertions.

Why am I castigating Wright at this point for an argument that may seem totally irrelevant to my present concerns? Because the very misreading that Wright seeks to exploit for his purposes can easily encourage one to suppose that an epistemic conception of truth is compatible with these schemata. If what ES says to be equivalent to the truth of p is some positive epistemic status of an assertion that p, then, of course, the schema is compatible with the supposition that to say of a sentence (proposition) that it is true is to attribute some positive epistemic status to it. Indeed, the schema so interpreted implies that. But such a reading is a misreading in the service of alethic nonrealism. It substitutes for the truism that *the truth of the proposition that p is conceptually equivalent to the fact that p* (its being the case that p) a reading tailor-made for an epistemic constraint on truth, a reading in which the schema asserts a (presumably conceptual) equivalence between the truth of p and some positive epistemic status for the proposition that p. Since the epistemic constraint has been sneaked in at the outset, it is not difficult to find it there later.

x Back to Dummett

I should emphasize the limited scope of this criticism of epistemic concepts of truth. It applies only to accounts that identify the *concept* of truth with the *concept* of a positive epistemic status and understand this identification in the strictest way, so that in saying of a truth bearer that it is true we are saying of that truth bearer that *it* enjoys the positive epistemic status in question. It should be clear that my arguments against the view trade both on the fact that it makes a conceptual identification and on the fact that it retains the same subject (the truth-value bearer) for both the analysandum and the analysans. When presenting arguments from this chapter to audiences I often get reactions that reflect a supposition that the arguments are also directed against reductive accounts of propositional content that might also be considered to be epistemic in character, particularly verificationist reductions. But I do not suppose for a moment that these arguments tell against such views. Suppose that someone maintains, as empiricists from Schlick to Dummett have done, that every proposition is to be understood as a set of verification conditions, conditions under which, as we would naturally say, the proposition would be verified. One might think that my argument against the epistemic theorist's second way of avoiding the "conflict with the T-schema "objection would tell against this view. And, indeed, if the view were put by identifying the proposition that *U.S. mail boxes are blue* with the proposition that *the proposition that U.S. mail boxes are blue is verifiable by the fact that U.S. mail boxes look a certain way to a normal observer under normal conditions* (or something of the sort), that argument would apply. In that case a reference to the proposition that *p* would be a part of what we are saying the proposition that *p* to be, and we would again be involved in an infinite regress in attempting to say what the proposition that *p* is. But there is an easy way for the verificationist to avoid this difficulty. She can simply identify the proposition that *p* with a statement of the conditions that are such that if they were ascertained to obtain the proposition would thereby be verified, but without putting into the analysis the claim that ascertaining those conditions to obtain would verify the proposition, thereby forcing herself to refer to that very proposition in specifying its content. Thus the view could be that the proposition that *U.S. mail boxes are blue* is the proposition that *U.S. mail boxes look a certain way to a normal observer under normal conditions.* Here there is no reference to the proposition being analyzed as part of the analysis, and so the infinite regress is avoided. And, more generally, my arguments against the epistemic conception of truth do not apply to a verificationist reduction of propositional content just because the latter is not an account of truth at all.

These points have important application to Dummett's views that I discussed in chapter 4. To begin with, sometimes Dummett puts his verificationist semantics in such a way that it does seem to be vulnerable to my infinite regress argument. "According to a theory of meaning in terms of verification, the content of an assertion is that the statement asserted has been, or is capable of being, verified" (1976, 117). This suggests that the truth-value bearer is referred to in the specification of the content of that very bearer, thereby giving rise to the infinite regress. But elsewhere Dummett's formulations could be developed in a way that is not so vulnerable. For example:

> [T]he sense of a sentence is thought of as being fixed by determining, not the conditions under which it is to be true, as Frege thought, but the conditions under which we are able to recognize it as true. (1973, 586)

> For him [the anti-realist] the meaning of a statement is intrinsically connected with that which we count as evidence for or against the statement[.] (1978, 162)

I say that these statements "could be developed so as not to be vulnerable to the infinite regress argument", for Dummett notoriously restricts himself to more or less indeterminate indications of how the meaning of a sentence (statement) would be spelled out, rather than giving a precise recipe. But I take it that Dummett's verificationist reductionism of propositional content can be construed in the form in which it is not subject to the infinite regress argument, that form in which the specification of the content consists simply in listing the relevant verification conditions without also specifying that they suffice to verify the proposition in question.

But Dummett's verificationist account of truth is another story. Here it looks as if some of the arguments of this chapter do tell against the view.

> On a verificationist account . . . our notions of truth and falsity . . . consist merely in the conception of a situation's occurring which would thus conclusively determine its truth-value. (1973, 514)

> The truth of such a sentence can consist only in the occurrence of the sort of situation in which we have learned to recognize it as true, and its falsity in the occurrence of the sort of situation in which we have learned to recognize it as false. (1973, 468)

In other words, to say that a statement is true is to say that conditions exist that we could use to verify it. The concept of truth is the concept of verifiability. This view would seem to be a suitable target for some of the arguments of this chapter. Let's see whether some of them do tell against it.

First consider the two forms of the counterexample argument. The first involved the suggestion that there are true propositions that no human being can grasp. Whether such propositions constitute counterexamples to the identification of truth and verifiability depends on what restrictions are put on the notion of verifying conditions. If they include only conditions we are capable of ascertaining, then there would be no verifying conditions for such propositions, for the same reason that they would not be ideally justifiable (by us). If, on the other hand, no such restriction is put on verifying conditions, it may be that there can be verifying conditions for such propositions, even though we would never be able to discover what they are.

On the exegetical question it is clear that Dummett does understand verifying conditions as subject to such a restriction. This is clear from the way in which he insists that truth values have be construed in such a way that we can determine what truth value a given statement has. And his arguments for his position turn on the conditions under which we could learn the meaning of a sentence. Both these points are amply documented in chapter 4. Hence, it seems clear that this part of the counterexample argument applies as fully to Dummett as to Putnam.

The second part of the argument would seem to apply as well. This involved the suggestion that there are true propositions that are such that even in the most ideal epistemic situation there would not be enough evidence to decide between a given such proposition and one or more incompatible alternatives. It follows from this that there would be no verifying conditions for such a proposition. Hence if there are true propositions of this sort, they constitute counterexamples to Dummett's account of truth.

To be sure, we must recognize that it follows from Dummet's verificationist semantics that there could be no such propositions (no such sentence meanings) as the counterexample arguments posit. But in holding that these arguments tell against Dummett's view of truth, I am not saddling the arguer with Dummett's verificationist semantics. On the contrary, my suggestion is that these arguments reveal difficulties in the whole Dummettian package, though the specific point of application is the alethic component of the package.

Turning to the circularity argument, it clearly does not apply in the anti-Putnam form, for in that form it turns on the claim that the concept of truth is needed to explain the concept of ideal justifiability, and Dummett makes no use of the latter concept. But an exactly parallel argument can be wielded against Dummett. Indeed, it seems much more obvious that verifiability has to be explained in terms of truth, as I pointed out in chapter 4. For what does it mean to verify a statement, other than showing it to be true? Similarly, what it means to confirm a statement (where this is construed as something less decisive than verification) is that considerations have been adduced that show the statement likely to be true, or that constitute significant reasons for taking the statement to be true.

With respect to the final argument—incompatibility with the T-schema—there will be the same prima facie case against Dummett. If it is a conceptual necessity that grass's being green is both necessary and sufficient for its being true that grass is green, then what room is there for the existence of verifying conditions to be conceptually necessary and sufficient for the truth of grass's being green? Looking at the two ways we imagined the Putnamian seeking to rebut this prima facie case, we can easily see that the first way is no more available to Dummett than to Putnam. It seems no more plausible to take the existence of verifying conditions for the statement that grass is green to be conceptually necessary for grass's being green, than to take the ideal justifiability of that statement to be conceptually necessary for that state of affairs. In particular, there is nothing in the concept of verifying conditions that guarantees that there are such conditions for every state of affairs. Again, a verificationist semantics may imply the contrary, but so much the worse for that semantics.

But for reasons given above, the second attempt to escape conflict with the T-schema—namely, reinterpretation of propositional content—would seem to be viable for Dummett. For, as we have just seen, Dummett's account of propositional content in terms of verifying conditions can be in terms of a simple listing of such conditions for each statement, instead of a form in which the statement is referred to as what the conditions suffice to verify. This would enable him to avoid the infinite regress generated by the latter form. Thus, although his theory of truth comes into prima facie conflict with the T-schema, he can, unlike Putnam, avoid this by giving his verificationist interpretation of content a form that does not involve putting the content bearer in the analysandum.

And so, though not all the arguments of this chapter against Putnam tell against Dummett's account of truth, enough do to pose real problems for him. In addition there are difficulties with the verificationist theory of content he could use to escape the last objection, one of which I sketchily presented in Chapter 4, section iii.

If it is my view that some of the objections to Putnam in this chapter, or analogues thereof, tell against Dummett's verificationist account of the concept of truth, why didn't I use them against that account in chapter 4? To be sure, they weren't developed at that point of the book; but, obviously, I could have introduced them there. The significant reason is that in chapter 4 I argued that Dummett's verificationist account of truth was not at all required by his verificationism. Given his verificationist theory of meaning (propositional content), which is absolutely fundamental to his position in any case, the requirements of verificationism are fully satisfied by using that theory in conjunction with a realist conception of truth. For if all propositional content is made up of verification conditions, then the truth of any proposition, on a realist conception of truth, will depend on the obtaining of verification conditions anyway. There is no need to introduce verificationist restrictions twice, once for content and once for truth. Since in saying that salt contains sodium I am saying that certain verification conditions obtain, on a realist account of truth the truth value of what I say will depend on whether relevant verification conditions are satisfied. This is just a straight application of the realist idea that the conditions of truth are given by what is asserted. Since, on these grounds, I concluded that the verificationist account of truth was totally lacking in motivation, I did not feel that it was worthwhile making an argument against it part of my criticism of Dummett.

xi Realist and Antirealist Prospects for Determining Truth Value

Now I turn to a consideration of reasons epistemic theorists of truth give for their position. As I pointed out earlier, in a sense I have already done this. Since epistemic conceptions of truth constitute the only serious alternative to a realist conception, in criticizing various arguments against the realist conception in Chapters 3–6 I have been, in effect, criticizing arguments for an epistemic conception. However, when we think of antirealist arguments as pro-epistemic-conception arguments, there is still one piece of unfinished business. In Chapter 3 I discussed the antirealist argument that on a realist conception of truth it is impossible to determine whether a proposition is true. I believe that I succeeded in drawing the fangs of the argument by exposing the shallowness of the reasons given for that supposed incapacity. But implicit in that argument was the contention that we are in a better position to determine truth values on some nonrealist construal of truth. Since that issue could not be usefully addressed prior to the delineation of such a construal, I postponed its consideration until this chapter. Because Putnam's version of an epistemic conception of truth seems to me the strongest one, I will devote most of this section to asking what our prospects are of determining truth value on that conception, and whether those prospects are better than they are when we think of truth along realist lines.

Before getting into the nitty-gritty let me lay out the nonrealist's basic idea here and the reason for its intuitive appeal. While the realist makes truth value depend on states of affairs that go far beyond us—far beyond our experience, thought, and discourse—the epistemic theorist seems to "bring truth back home", lodge it in matters that are "within" our thought and experience—the epistemic status of our beliefs and statements.[24] The ensuing discussion will reveal whether this intuition holds up under critical scrutiny.

To forestall any impression that my conclusions hang on idiosyncratic features of Putnam's version, I will first say a few words about the accessibility of truth on a coherentist theory of truth. Near the beginning of this chapter I quoted Bradley as referring to truth as "that which satisfies the intellect"[25], "an ideal expression of the Universe, at once coherent and comprehensive".[26] And I noted that Blanshard holds that a proposition is true if it coheres with an all comprehensive and fully articulated whole.[27] I will understand 'coherence' in the way spelled out at the end of section iv. A system of propositions, statements, or beliefs is coherent to the extent that it is both consistent and tightly unified by logical, probabilistic, and explanatory relations. The components of the system "fit together" closely through mutual implication, explanatory ties, and other modes of reciprocal support.

In thinking about the extent to which we could tell whether a given belief is true in Bradley's or Blanshard's sense, we must remember that not any old coherent system is truth generative for its constituents. It must be a "comprehensive", "all-inclusive" system. This stipulation raises a serious question as to what "all inclusive" can mean on a coherence theory. It is not as if we can presuppose an independent realm of fact by reference to which the completeness of a system can be judged. If we could do that, we could say that a system is absolutely comprehensive if and only if for every existing entity and every property, it included either the proposition that that entity has that property or the proposition that it does not. But on the account of truth under consideration the constitution of reality is determined by the contents of the most coherent comprehensive system. So we have to have already identified a comprehensive system in order to examine a system for comprehensiveness. But let that pass and assume that there is some suitable way for the coherentist to assess degrees of inclusiveness. Presumably it would only be an enormously large system that would qualify—a system far in excess of anything we have on our hands at present or anything we have any real prospect of attaining. That being the case, let's consider the outlook for determining with respect to a given proposition whether it would find a place in an "all comprehensive and fully articulated whole" that would exhibit maximum coherence. It is clear that we would have little

24. This intuition is one that is at home in internalist, but not in externalist epistemologies.
25. 1914, 1.
26. 1914, 223.
27. 1939, 2: 264.

to go on. We are envisaging an ideal extension of our present and past efforts to develop unified systems of knowledge, an extension to the point at which all our knowledge becomes perfectly unified in a single all-comprehensive system. We have little idea of what shape this would take—much less what its detailed contents would be. It is true that programmes for "unified science" have been aired in the past. But they have been very programmatic indeed. Moreover, the actual development of science and other domains of knowledge have not followed the paths these pretentious programmes have marked out. Witness the fate of the unified science movement of the Vienna Circle in the first half of this century. So far is the second half of the century from following these directives that science is much less unified now than it was a hundred years ago. Thus the classical coherence theory of truth can hardly lay claim to making the determination of what propositions are true more feasible than a realist conception.

Now for Putnam's version, which is in terms of an ideal epistemic situation. We will first have to recapitulate the outcome of our lengthy and tortuous struggle to work out a respectable conception of such a situation. The salient points are these. (1) It will involve the cognitive availability of all relevant evidence. (2) In order to make sense of this we have to use the notion of truth. (3) In order to determine what facts are relevant we have to have some way of choosing among alternative sets of background assumptions, and the only way we saw to do this was to make heavy, though not exclusive, appeal to the coherence of a total system of belief. The background assumptions of choice would be those that are yielded by such a system.

In considering whether this conception of truth gives us a more cognitively accessible target than a realist conception, it is tempting to make short work of the whole question by focusing on (2), the point that the realist conception of truth is presupposed by the notion of an ideal epistemic situation. Hence to determine what is or isn't justifiable in such a situation we have to be able to determine what propositions are true in a realist sense, for that is necessary for determining the components of the ideal epistemic situation by reference to which ideal justifiability, and hence epistemically constrained truth, is determined. But this argument depends on assuming that it is truth in a realist sense that the notion of an ideal epistemic situation presupposes. That is clear to me, for I take realist truth to be truth. Hence if a certain concept presupposes truth, realist truth is what it presupposes. But to use this conviction in an argument against Putnam would be question begging. Hence I will base the assessment on the other features of an ideal epistemic situation, (1) and (3).

As for (1), the question concerns our capacity to determine whether a given belief would be justified in the light of *all* relevant considerations. The clinker here is "all". To what extent are we, presently or in the foreseeable future, in a position to determine what would come out as justified on the basis of *all* relevant considerations? Can we make an informed judgment on what would go into that totality? And if not, how can we make a sufficiently informed judgment as to whether a given belief would be ideally justifiable? We are better placed to make these assessments for some propositions than for others. For what is observable we can, *pace* extreme theory-relativity-of-observation views, pretty well survey what is relevant to epistemic status—the character of the sensory experience, background beliefs that bear on the likelihood of what is putatively observed, relevant features of the condition and situation of the observer, the properties of the medium, and so on. With more theoretical matters, on the other hand, it would be rash indeed to suppose that we can specify everything that is relevant to justification. To take an extreme example, how about views as to the course of events in the first one-tenth of a second after the Big Bang? With a domain of theory in as much flux as this, we constantly encounter new relevant facts or hitherto unsuspected relevance of previously known facts. If you consider this example too recherché to be significant, consider the inability of physicists in the eighteenth and nineteenth centuries to realize the relevance for Newtonian physics of the considerations—empirical and theoretical—that led to the development of relativity theory and quantum mechanics.

I believe that this line of thought could be extended to throw cold water on the idea that we are generally in a good position to make judgments as to what would and would not be justifiable under ideal epistemic circumstances, at least when we get away from the empirical and rational bases of our knowledge. And for those bases we are in a good position to determine truth in a realist sense. Hence it would seem that, so far as feature (1) is concerned, an ideal justifiability conception of truth does not give us any edge over a realist conception in determining truth values.

When we turn to feature (3) things look even bleaker for the epistemic theorist. Here the reasons given above for denying that coherence theory renders truth more accessible come into play. For what (3) says is that one thing we have to do to determine what considerations are relevant to the ideal epistemic assessment of a belief is to determine what more or less theoretical propositions would figure in a total system the members of which are most coherent with each other and with empirical (observational) and rational (self-evident) bases. Ideally this would mean spelling out the full constitution of such a system, and that is obviously far beyond our powers. But even something more modest that would still provide a basis for a sound judgment as to which of alternative sets of propositions would be in the maximally coherent system would seem to be a pipe dream. How could we make an informed judgment on this without a more complete grasp of the nature of a maximally coherent system than we are able to attain? Thus feature (3) is such as to make it beyond doubt that we are in a much worse position to determine Putnamian truth than we are to determine realist truth. Even for observation reports, since they are inherently defeasible, we would need a considerable grasp of the (allegedly unique) maximally coherent system to determine whether it contains sufficient defeaters for a given prima facie justified observation report. Thus, ironically enough, the very thing that has made an epistemic account of truth seem attractive to many—its promise to remove truth from the status of something inaccessibly transcendent by making it internal to our cognitive operations and hence easily within our grasp—turns out to be one of its most serious liabilities. What has happened is that in order to develop an epistemic conception that is not desperately implausible as an account of *truth*, we are forced to introduce a conception of epistemically ideal circumstances that are so far removed from our actual epistemic situation as to make it impossible for us to make informed judgments as to what would or would not be justifiable in such circumstances. The best laid plans of mice and men!

xii A Nonconceptual Epistemic Theory of Truth

I have devoted this chapter to laying out and criticizing an epistemic theory of the *concept* of propositional truth, in other terms, an epistemic theory of the meaning of 'true' in which it is applied to propositions, beliefs, and statements. But even if these criticisms are decisive, an epistemic theorist might make a stand at another point. He might reformulate his position as a theory of the nature of the *property* of truth. To be sure, the property with which he would be dealing is the one picked out by our concept of propositional truth. Nevertheless, as I pointed out in chapter 1, there could be facts about the nature of the property that are no part of the content of our concept of that property. This is a familiar theme in recent philosophical literature.[28] The property of *being water* is the property of *having the chemical constitution H_2O*, even though the (ordinary) concept of water involves nothing about hydrogen or oxygen. The property of *being hot to a certain degree* is the property of *having a certain average kinetic energy of constituent molecules*, but our ordinary concept of heat involves no reference to kinetic energy of molecules. In parallel fashion, it might be that the property of being true is the property of being justifiable in ideal epistemic circumstances, even though the concept of truth contains nothing about justification.

What are the chances that this property-identification form of an epistemic theory of truth is correct? I want to consider this question in two parts. (1) Do the arguments in this chapter against an epistemic conception of truth have any force against this "nature of the property" view? (2) To what extent is this view at all plausible?

As for (1), my second main criticism—that the concept of ideal justifiability involves the concept of truth—has no application to the property version, just because that version is not concerned with a definition of the term 'true' or an analysis of the concept of truth. Hence definitional or analytical circularity is not a problem. The *property* of being true could be the *property* of being justifiable in ideal epistemic conditions, even if the *concept* of ideal epistemic conditions cannot be explained without using the *concept* of truth. This is analogous to the way in which the property of (a physical object's) being red could be the property of being disposed to produce sensations of redness, even if the concept of a sensation of redness could not be explained without using the concept of a physical object's being red.

Nor does the third criticism—that the epistemic theory conflicts with the T-schema—apply to the property version. For although the view that the property of truth is the property of being ideally justifiable does put forward something as necessary and sufficient for a belief that p's being true other than the fact that p, it doesn't claim ideal justifiability to be *conceptually* necessary and sufficient for truth. And, as I brought out in developing my criticism, it is this claim that brings the epistemic account into conflict with the T-schema. Where we can distinguish between what belongs to the concept of P and what belongs to the property of P, there may be necessary and sufficient conditions for the application of the property that are not embodied in the concept. Having a chemical composition of sodium chloride is necessary and sufficient for a substance's being salt, even though that is different from the conditions embedded

28. See especially Saul Kripke's "Naming and Necessity" in Davidson and Harman 1972.

in our (ordinary) concept of salt (looking and tasting a certain way). One who claims that the property of truth is ideal justifiability, and avoids claiming that the *concept* of truth is the *concept* of ideal justifiability, need run into no conflict with the view that the concept of truth is specified by the T-schema.

On the other hand, the first criticism—that there are counterexamples to the equation of truth and ideal justifiability—has equal force against the property version. An identification of the property of truth and the property of ideal justifiability is certainly incompatible with the existence of true propositions that would not be justifiable in ideal epistemic circumstances. But since this is the only one of the three that applies to the property version, and since I admitted it to be less than conclusive, I cannot claim that my criticisms of the concept version of an epistemic account of truth also dispose of the property version.

That being the case, we should go on to consider whether the property version possesses any plausibility, given that the concept version is untenable. Since the concept of truth is realist—uniquely identified by the T-schema—what reason could there be for the hypothesis that the property picked out by that concept is ideal justifiability? To be sure, if the concept does not make explicit everything necessarily involved in the property, as we are assuming, that leaves open the *possibility* that this something extra is ideal justifiability. But what reason could there be for this suggestion? What could so much as give anyone the idea that a proposition has the property of truth if and only if it is justifiable in an ideal epistemic situation? Once we have given up the idea that the concept of truth is to be analyzed in terms of ideal justifiability, I can see no rationale whatever for supposing that it is the property of ideal justifiability that fits the specifications laid down by the T-schema. The natural way of going from the T-schema to a further delineation of the property so marked out is the path of the correspondence theory. Since the concept of truth is such that a proposition is true if and only if there obtains a fact that realizes the content of the proposition, that naturally suggests that if we are to say something further about the property of truth, it would be in terms of what it is for a fact to have the same content as a proposition; that is, it would involve some account of the correspondence of proposition and fact, some way of spelling out what it is for them to have the same content. By contrast, I can see no plausible route from the T-schema to the idea that it is ideal justifiability that constitutes the property in question. Thus the property identification version of an epistemic account of truth fares no better than its conceptual cousin.

CHAPTER 8

Doing without Truth

i The Scope of This Chapter

At the beginning of Chapter 1 I formulated alethic realism as a conjunction of two theses.

(1) THE REALIST CONCEPTION OF TRUTH IS THE CORRECT ONE (for that use of 'true' in which statements, beliefs, and propositions are evaluated as true or false).

(2) TRUTH IS IMPORTANT. It is important, for a variety of purposes, that statements, beliefs, and propositions, be assessed for truth value.

Up to this point the book has been solely concerned with (1). I have been explicating the realist conception of truth (Chapter 1), exploring its relations to other positions thought of as forms of realism (Chapter 2), defending it against various criticisms (Chapters 4–6), and criticizing the main rival conception. (Chapter 7). The time has now come to address the second thesis. I will not give it equal billing. I don't see that it requires the kind of defense in depth I have accorded (1). Nevertheless, like any philosophical position, it is by no means universally accepted. Hence it will not be inappropriate to defend it against its detractors.

Do I take 'truth' in (2) to be restricted to realist truth? Does (2) say that it is important that propositions be assessed for truth in the realist sense? Since (2) is a component of alethic realism, it would be natural to read it that way. But there is also a good reason for giving it a more modest interpretation, according to which (2) in itself leaves open how propositional truth is to be explicated. The reason is that (2) is but one component of a complex view, the other component of which is (1), the thesis that the realist conception of truth is the conception expressed by 'true' when attributed to propositions. This implies that it would be unnecessary duplication to build a commitment to the realist conception into thesis (2) itself. In defending (2), I can simply bring out the importance of assessing propositions, statements, and beliefs for truth, without worrying about how 'true' is to be understood, leaving it to thesis (1) to deal with that. This is the procedure I will follow in this chapter. My opponents here will not be those who advocate some nonrealist account of propositional truth, but rather those who question or deny the importance of determining truth values. Against such views I will be pointing out some of the reasons it does matter a great deal whether our beliefs and statements are true or false. This result is then to be interpreted in the light of the argument of the rest of the book to the effect that the truth that is shown here to be important is realist truth.

I should also give advance notice that I will not be dealing in this chapter with one sort of view that might be thought to fall under the general description, "views that deny the importance of truth". These are the deflationary theories that deny that we are attributing any property to a proposition, statement or belief when we utter a sentence of the form 'X is true'. In a sense, such views imply that it is not important to determine what truth values propositions have. Since they deny that there are any such things as truth values for propositions to "have", they are committed to denying that it is important (or unimportant for that matter) to find out which truth value a given proposition has. Nevertheless, there are two reasons for not bringing them into this discussion. First, I take myself to have disposed of deflationary views in Chapter 1, section xi. Hence I feel free here to presuppose that there are genuine properties of propositional truth and falsity, however they are to be construed, and on that basis to consider whether, and if so why, it is important for central human concerns to ascribe these properties correctly. Second, and more importantly, it is not necessary to read deflationary accounts as opposed to the thesis of this chapter. Though they construe apparent truth-value attributions as not seriously involving the attribution of properties to alleged truth-value bearers, they by no means want to eliminate those putative attributions or minimize their importance. It is just that they construe such utterances as not seriously asserting *properties* of truth or falsity to anything. Since their position is not opposed to the importance of engaging in (apparent) truth-value attributions and determining which of them to accept, they cannot be reckoned as opponents of the position defended here.

ii Reasons for De-Emphasizing Truth

The most natural way to proceed in this chapter would be to first present my story of why it is important to assess propositions for truth value, and then consider various objections to that story. But I think that the smoothest entrée into this controversy is to begin with some reasons for denying the importance of truth and then, as a response to that denial, get into the story of why truth is indispensable. This is the order I will follow.

Perhaps the commonest route to pooh-poohing truth goes through epistemic theories of truth I have been criticizing. One impressed by Bradley, James, or Dewey may thereby favor the idea of construing truth in terms of some favorable epistemic status. But then he begins to have doubts as to whether this epistemic conception captures what people typically have in mind when they call a belief, statement, or proposition 'true'. But in spite of these doubts, it still seems to him that the epistemic status in question is what we are really after in our cognitive enterprises, rather than truth in the realist sense. It seems to him that the quest for realist truth is a wild-goose chase, while the quest for coherence, "being fruitfully led through our experience", or resolution of problematic situations is not only feasible, but of central importance for human life. These reflections might lead him to express his position not by proferring the epistemic status as a reinterpretation of truth, but rather by pushing for the *replacement* of truth with the favored epistemic status. It is like the difference between behaviorism as a view about the correct analysis of mental terms (concepts) ["analytical" or "logical" behaviorism], and behaviorism as a *proposal* to quit dealing in mentalistic terms or concepts altogether (however construed) and restrict our consideration of the psychology of human beings to their behavior and dispositions thereto [what is sometimes called "methodological" behaviorism].

In Chapter 7 I presented the great pragmatist figures—Peirce, James, and Dewey—as pursuing the former line, and I picked quotations that support that attribution. But we can find the other strain in their writings as well. Thus James not infrequently denigrates the aim at realist truth, under the guise of some such term as "copying", rather than claiming that truth is best construed in some other way, such as getting into satisfactory relations with other parts of our experience.

A priori, however, it is not self-evident that the sole business of our minds with realities should be to copy them. (1909, 50)

> If our symbols *fit* the world, in the sense of determining our expectations rightly, they may even be the better for not copying its terms. (1909, 51)

> Theoretic truth, truth of passive copying, sought in the sole interests of copying as such, not because copying is *good for something* . . . seems, if you look at it coldly, to be an almost preposterous ideal. Why should the universe, existing in itself, also exist in copies? (1909, 40)

In Richard Rorty's latter-day adherence to what he calls "pragmatism" we find this emphasis in a purer form.

> The pragmatist agrees that if one wants to preserve the notion of "correspondence with reality" then a physicalistic theory of reference is necessary—but he sees no point in preserving that notion. The pragmatist has no notion of truth which would enable him to make sense of the claim that if we achieved everything we ever hoped to achieve by making assertions we might still be making *false* assertions, failing to "correspond with something". (Rorty 1982, xxiv)

> When he [the pragmatist] asks himself about a given statement S, whether he "knows what has to be the case for it to be true" or merely knows "the conditions which we recognize as establishing the truth or falsity of statements of that class", he feels as helpless as when asked "Are you really in love, or merely inflamed by passion?" . . . He refuses to take a stand—to provide an "analysis" of "S is true", for example, or to either assert or deny bivalence. He refuses to make a move in *any* of the games in which he is invited to take part. (Rorty 1982, xxviii)

> What really needs debate between the pragmatist and the intuitive realist is *not* whether we have intuitions to the effect that "truth is more than assertibility". . . . Of course we have such intuitions. How could we escape having them? We have been educated within an intellectual tradition built around such claims . . . But it begs the question between pragmatist and realist to say that we must find a philosophical view which "captures" such intuitions. The pragmatist is urging that we do our best to *stop having* such intuitions, that we develop a *new* intellectual tradition. (Rorty 1982, xxix–xxx)[1]

Thus instead of advocating what we have seen in Chapter 7 to be desperately implausible equations of truth with one or another favorable epistemic status, the pragmatist, or other epistemic theorist of truth, may

---

1. In fairness to Rorty I should point out that he has since disavowed these comments. See Rorty, forthcoming.

urge instead that we give up concern for "truth" (naturally thought of in realist terms) and set our sights instead on the favored epistemic status(es) in question.

But though this may be the most common pathway to the abandonment of truth, it is by no means the only one. Philosophers innocent of any truck with epistemic theories of truth have been led, in one way or another, to question the apparent truism that the ultimate goal of cognition is to believe what is true and refrain from believing what is false and to propose alternative goals as more basic, central, or worthwhile. Thus the central aim might be identified as "predictive power" or "explanatory efficacy" or "maximal coherence in our belief system". When thinkers seek to dethrone truth in favor of claimants like these, without coming to this from disenchantment with an epistemic theory of truth, it is typically because of suppositions like those I sought to discredit in Chapter 3, to the effect that truth is unattainable or that we can never know whether we have attained it or not. It is then supposed that predictive or explanatory power, or coherence, is something that we can get at, something the presence or absence of which we can ascertain, and hence something it is reasonable and feasible to look for. In section viii I will look at a still different route to the denigration of truth.

iii Why Truth Is Important

Whatever the motivation of a thinker who rejects a concern for the truth values of our beliefs and assertions, the question she raises must be confronted. What reasons are there for supposing that truth plays a crucial, perhaps indispensable role in our intellectual and practical transactions with the world?

The most obvious answer to the question, "Why, if at all, is it important for us to consider whether our beliefs are true?" is: "Because it is important for us to determine what states of affairs obtain where that has a bearing on our practical or theoretical concerns". No one, I assume, will question the point that it often makes a big difference to how we should conduct ourselves, theoretically or practically, whether a certain state of affairs obtains. It is important to my thinking about causality whether causality amounts to counterfactual dependence, and it makes a crucial difference to what it is most advisable for me to do next whether a burglar is in the house. But then it follows from the T-schema that it is correspondingly important whether *it is true that* causality amounts to counterfactual dependence and whether *it is true that* a burglar is in the house. For the state of affairs that p obtains if and only if it is true that p. However I won't concentrate on these cases in which a truth value is attributed to a specified proposition. For in these cases it is very plausible to suppose that our ordinary concerns can be satisfied by attention to the proposition itself, rather than to what truth value the proposition bears. And hence a concern with truth would not seem to be ineliminable here. If I should be philosophical enough to express my concern in the second case by saying, "I've got to find out whether it's true that there's a burglar in the house", the likes of Ramsey could point out that I might just as well have said "I've got to find out whether there's a burglar in the house", thereby short circuiting any reference to truth.[2]

But the need for considering truth value is by no means limited to determining whether this or that particular proposition is true. There are also more general concerns that involve the concepts of truth and falsity. We often have occasion to make general statements involving 'true' and 'false', statements that generalize over propositions without predicating 'true' or 'false' of any particular proposition. For each of these areas a consideration of truth values is often of capital importance. I will illustrate this with a look at several such areas—logic, semantics, practical reasoning, and epistemology, the first three briefly and the last more fully.

As for deductive logic, the most obvious place for truth is in the characterization of such central logical relations as entailment and contradiction. One proposition entails another if and only if it is impossible for the former to be true and the latter false. Hence the use of truth tables to check the validity of arguments that turn on propositional connectives. One proposition contradicts another if and only if it is necessary that they have different truth values (assuming here only two truth values—true and false).[3] There are much more complex ways in which the concept of truth figures in one or another approach to logic, for example, model theory. But I will leave that exposition to others.

The role of truth in semantics has been highlighted in recent decades by Davidson's advocacy of a truth-conditions theory of meaning.[4] I my-

2. In diverting attention away from these attributions of truth to a specified proposition, I am not reneging on my rejection of redundancy theory in Chapter 1. The point here is not that 'It is true that p' "says the same thing" as 'p', a view I reject, but that our concerns can usually be as well served by considering whether that p as by considering whether it is true that p.

3. As pointed out in Chapter 4, section iv, even Dummett acknowledges that a realist conception of truth is needed to explicate the notion of logical validity.

4. See his "Truth and Meaning", reprinted in Davidson 1984, and the enormous literature spawned by this.

self do not agree with this as a general theory of linguistic meaning (Alston 1994), but a felicitous way of bringing out what it is for sentences that are usable to make assertions to have a certain meaning, is to make explicit the contribution such a sentence makes to the truth conditions of an assertion it is used to make.

A concern with truth bulks large in practical reasoning and, more generally, in the mental direction of our efforts to deal with the environment. The basic point can be stated very simply and seems overwhelmingly obvious. If our interactions with X are guided by true beliefs about X they are much more likely to be successful in attaining the goals of that interaction, ceteris paribus, than if they are guided by false beliefs. In trying to accomplish something it is of the utmost importance to act on true beliefs about matters relevant to that enterprise. If I set out to repair an air conditioner I am well advised to have true rather than false beliefs about the structure and operation of that device. If I am trying to influence someone to adopt a certain course of action it is crucial for me to have true beliefs about the present beliefs, attitudes, and prejudices of that person. And so on. What could be more obvious? Nevertheless, as Cicero wrote, there is nothing so obvious that it has not been denied in the books of the philosophers. One book in which this obvious truism is denied is Stich's *The Fragmentation of Reason* (1990). In section viii of this chapter I will examine Stich's position. Pending that, I will be taking it that the above truism is, indeed, true.

At this point I must take account of a likely reaction to the illustrations I give of the importance of generalizations concerning truth values. This reaction extends to generalizations the same judgment I made on attributions of truth to particular propositions. It might be expressed as follows. "You tell us that it is important in logic to construe the entailment of q by p as the impossibility of p's being true and q's being false. But why couldn't that same point be made without mentioning truth and falsity simply by saying that for any p and q, p entails q if and only if it is not possible that p and not-q? The same response can be made to your point that if a certain belief plays an essential role in guiding my attempts to reach goal G, then I am more likely to reach G if that belief is true than if it is false. Why can't that same point be made without mentioning truth and falsity by saying that for any G and p, if my attempts to reach G are guided by a belief that p, then I am more likely to reach G if p. And the first point to be made in this next section about the importance of truth for epistemology (my critic is endowed with foreknowledge!) is that a belief counts as knowledge only if it is true. But why can't we make that same point by saying: "For any p, a belief that p counts as knowledge that p only if p?" Thus it appears that the cases in which you claim an importance for considerations of truth values can be handled without saying anything about truth values."

This sounds as if it thoroughly deflates my claims in this chapter. To be sure, I have not yet exhibited all my cases, but they can all be responded to in the same vein. Before explaining why I think this reaction does not vitiate the thesis of this chapter, let me set aside a response some thinkers would favor. My critic, along with many deflationists, relies on substitutional quantification to carry out the 'true'-free replacements. If substitutional quantification were subject to crippling defects, that would secure an unassailable place for 'true' and 'false' in generalizations of the sort I consider in this chapter. It is often pointed out that truth-value attributions in generalizations enable us to avoid substitutional quantification.[5] But I have already made explicit that I take substitutional quantification to be unproblematically intelligible. Indeed, I have made use of it in my own formulations. Hence I will not take a reliance on it to vitiate the above response.

To come to the reply I will give, it is clear that this criticism trades on the form of deflationism we have in C. F. J. Williams's *What Is Truth?* (1976). It is the pattern of analysis featured there that the critic employs to blunt my claims for the importance of a consideration of truth values. To be sure, this does not mean that he is committed to the central deflationary thesis that apparent truth-value attributions are something quite different. Nevertheless my objections in Chapter 1 to that thesis can be used in another way to reveal the hollowness of the present objection. There I pointed out that the strongest forms of deflationism—those of Grover and Williams—could lay claim to providing alternative formulations for apparent truth attributions that are analyses in the strictest sense, synonymous sentences that put the content in different terms. I did express doubts that the prosentential analyses really did say what the originals do, but in any event our concern here is with analyses of the sort produced by Williams; and in those cases I did unqualifiedly endorse the synonymy thesis. 'For any p if p is asserted in the book, p' seems to say just exactly what 'Everything asserted in the book is true' does. But if that is how they are related, we haven't made any real change of substance, of content, by switching from one formulation to the other. We have merely changed to a different way of saying the same thing. We have not gotten rid of truth and falsity; we have only gotten rid of 'true' and 'false'. The concepts of truth and falsity are still there; it is just that

5. See, e.g., Horwich 1990, chap. 1, sec. 6.

they are not exhibited by the manifest verbal content of the sentence. There is much less in the substitution than meets the eye. Hence the critic's substitutivity thesis doesn't really imply that my thesis of the importance of considering truth value is false. For even when we eschew 'true' and 'false' in favor of substitutional quantification over propositions, we are still considering truth and falsity, but by another name. The rose still smells as sweet.[6]

Now we can see why truth attributions to specified propositions are to be treated differently, for the present purpose, from generalizations. Just because the Ramsey equivalence of 'p' and 'It is true that p' *cannot* lay claim to synonymy, the way is left clear for recognizing that they have different contents. And hence when we see that the former can serve the same purposes as the latter, we have seen that those purposes can be served without any consideration of truth value. But for the generalizations the Williams treatment leaves the content unaffected, and so the replacement leaves us still considering truth value, though what we are saying or thinking is expressed differently.

I would make essentially the same response to another claim that the points I make do not require bringing in truth values. "None of this shows that truth must be brought into epistemology, etc. The functions of the concept of truth could equally well be performed by other concepts such as *fact*, and *what is the case*. Thus instead of saying that a belief counts as knowledge only if it is true, we could just as well say that it counts as knowledge only if it is a belief *as to what is the case*. Instead of saying that a condition renders a belief justified only if it renders it likely to be true, we could just as well say, 'only if it renders it likely that the belief *corresponds to a fact*'. And so for my other claims for the indispensability of truth."

My response to this, again, is not to deny that we could just as well use the "fact" or the "is the case" lingo instead of "true" lingo, but rather to deny that this makes any significant difference. These notions, though not exactly the same, are tightly bound in a small package. As I pointed out in Chapter 1, the T-schema itself can be formulated in such

---

6. This response is, of course, related to the remarks I made at the beginning of the chapter about deflationary theories, but it is not just the same. There I was explaining why I was not discussing deflationary theories as opponents of the chapter's thesis. One of the reasons was that they were not denying the importance of considering (putative) truth-value attributions but rather giving a particular construal of them. The present response, by contrast, is directed at an argument for the thesis that truth-value attributions have no essential importance, an argument that employs tools developed by deflationists for purposes they, if I am right, do not share. The common feature of my two discussions, as well as the critique of deflationism in Chapter 1, is the idea that if analyses like those of Williams work, then they do not have some of the implications we might suppose they have, and that some thinkers have supposed they have.

a way as to make this explicit. Instead of saying "It is true that p if and only if p" I could make essentially the same point by saying "It is the case that p if and only if p" or "It is a fact that p if and only if p". These locutions are necessarily equivalent to each other. Hence they can be freely interchanged in larger contexts without running any risk of altering truth value. 'True' is the more natural adjective to use in attribution to propositions, beliefs, and statements, but the alternative epistemological dicta just exhibited, in terms of "is the case that" and "is a fact that", make basically the same point as the more familiar formulations in terms of 'true'. Thus the objection holds on a verbal level, but the verbal shifts make no difference to the substantive issues. One who decries reliance on the concept of truth would not be cheered by being told that instead of thinking of knowledge as requiring true belief, we can say instead that it requires belief in what is actually the case. "With a friend like that" he may say, "who needs an enemy?"

iv Truth and Epistemology: Knowledge and Justification

This brings me to epistemology for which I promised a more extended treatment. Here truth figures heavily in accounts of both knowledge and the justification of belief, two of the main concerns of epistemology. I will begin with knowledge.

It is admitted on almost all hands that the truth of p is a necessary condition of knowing that p. If it is false that you are an English nobleman, then it is impossible for me to know that you are an English nobleman, whatever else is the case. There is considerable controversy over what else is necessary for one's knowing that p. The dominant twentieth-century approach is to suppose that knowledge that p is a kind of belief that p, one that satisfies certain further conditions. The most popular line has been that what turns a true belief into knowledge is *justification*. To know that p is to have a true justified belief that p. Even after Gettier effectively exploded the idea that having a true justified belief is *sufficient* for knowledge, a majority of epistemologists continue to suppose that it is at least *necessary*, and that what is required for sufficiency is this plus one or more additional conditions. Others in the post-Gettier era turn their backs on justification and look for a quite different approach. But through all this there is general agreement that at least truth is required. And how could it be otherwise? What sense could we make of the suggestion that even though there is no life on Mars you or I know that there is life on Mars? There are, of course, derivative or ironical uses of 'know' that are compatible with falsity. "I just *knew* that he was going to be here. So where is he?" But it is clear, if anything is, that a fully serious attribution of knowledge that p requires the truth of p for its truth.

Before launching on what will turn out to be an extended discussion of epistemic justification, I must call attention to a way in which the discussion will be, by my lights, oversimplified. Since this is not a treatise on epistemology, and since I can make the points I am concerned to make most simply by talking as if there is some unique objective reality called 'epistemic justification' about the nature of which epistemologists have different and incompatible views, I proceed to talk that way. Actually I hold that there is no such reality, and that putative disagreements about the nature of epistemic justification are best viewed as emphases on one or another "epistemic desideratum", each of which is cognitively valuable in some way. Since my concern here is only to illustrate the ways in which the notion of truth appears in epistemology, those appearances would still be there if epistemology were conducted under the aegis of "epistemic desiderata" rather than in the context of an attempt to determine what epistemic justification is.

The relation of truth to justification is both more complex and more controversial than its relation to knowledge. On the one hand, it is generally agreed that it is conceptually possible for one to be justified (rational) in believing that p when it is false that p. That point was underlined in the last chapter, where I pointed out the impossibility of identifying truth with justification of the ordinary sort. On the other hand, it is generally thought that justification has some intimate relation with truth, though there is no agreement on just what this is. On a "truth conducivity" position, it is a fundamental constraint on conditions of justification that the satisfaction of those conditions guarantee that it is at least highly probable that the belief in question be true. Thus if I claim that one is justified in believing that p provided one has done everything one can to assure oneself that the belief is true, and if it can be shown that this does not guarantee a probability of truth for the belief, my claim must be rejected. Furthermore, it is held that this constraint stems from the *concept* of epistemic justification. It is part of what is meant by "being justified in believing that p" that one has satisfied conditions that guarantee a significant likelihood that the belief is true.

If entailment does not constitute the general connection between justification and truth, what weaker tie might? Consider a case. Judy and Jack are taking a train on a fall evening. His view is obscured and he asks what color the foliage is. She might say, "Green", to which he might reply, "Can it still be green this far north?" A natural answer would be, "I can see it clearly, and it certainly looks green". It is significant that this answer *both* responds to a challenge of the truth of her statement and expresses a justification for her believing it. Imagine, moreover, that Jack perversely rejoins: "I know your seeing it clearly and its looking green to you justifies your belief, but is that relevant to its *truth?*" What are we to make of this? . . . [H]is rejoinder seems unintelligible. I believe that it appears unintelligible precisely because of the conceptual connection between (epistemic) justification and truth: it seems to be at least partly constitutive of justification that, in *some* way, it *counts toward truth.* (Audi 1993, 300–301)

An improved alternative to the normative concepts of justification is the notion of justification as *an adequate indication, relative to one's total evidence, that a proposition is true.* Such an adequate indication is provided for one by something that makes a proposition, P, evidentially more probable for one, on one's total evidence, than not only −P but also P's probabilistic competitors. . . . On this notion, an epistemic justifier of a proposition is simply a certain sort of truth indicator, or evidential probability-maker for that proposition. (Moser 1989, 42–43)

S's believing that *h* on the basis of R is epistemically justified at *t iff:* S's believing that *h* on the basis of R is a reliable indication that *h* at *t*. (Swain 1981, 99)

From a different point of view Alvin Plantinga, after initially identifying a belief's being what he calls "warranted"[7] with its being "produced by my cognitive faculties functioning properly in a congenial environment", feels constrained to add the requirement that "the segment of the design plan governing the production of the belief in question must also be aimed at truth" (1993b, 17)

The claim that justification is essentially truth conducive is often supported by taking the basic aim of cognition to be the acquisition of true beliefs and the avoidance of false beliefs.

[Epistemic justification] has to do with a specifically *epistemic* dimension of evaluation. Beliefs can be evaluated in different ways. One may be more or less prudent, fortunate, or faithful in holding a certain

---

7. This is a stronger notion than 'justification', as usually conceived, for Plantinga characterizes warrant as "that, whatever precisely it is, which . . . makes the difference between knowledge and mere true belief" (1993a, 3). Most epistemologists of the post-Gettier era who use the term 'justification' do not hold that justification is enough by itself to make true belief into knowledge. I will ignore this difference in these remarks.

belief. Epistemic justification is different from all that. Epistemic evaluation is undertaken from what we might call "the epistemic point of
view". That point of view is defined by the aim at maximizing truth
and minimizing falsity in a large body of beliefs. . . . [A]ny concept of
epistemic justification is a concept of some condition that is desirable
or commendable from the standpoint of the aim at maximizing truth
and minimizing falsity[.] (Alston 1989, 83–84)

[E]pistemic justification is essentially related to the so-called cognitive
goal of truth, insofar as an individual belief is epistemically justified
only if it is appropriately directed toward the goal of truth. More specifically, on the present conception, one is epistemically justified in
believing a proposition only if one has good reason to believe it is true.
To accept a proposition in the absence of good reason is to neglect the
cognitive goal of truth. (Moser 1985, 4)

Why should we, as cognitive beings, care whether our beliefs are epistemically justified? Why is such justification something to be sought
and valued? . . . [T]he following answer seems obviously correct. . . .
What makes us cognitive beings at all is our capacity for belief, and
the goal of our distinctively cognitive endeavors is *truth*: we want our
beliefs to correctly and accurately depict the world. If truth were somehow immediately and unproblematically accessible . . . then the concept of justification would be of little significance. . . . But we have no
such immediate and unproblematic access to truth, and it is for this
reason that justification comes into the picture. The basic role of justification is that of a *means* to truth, a more directly attainable mediating
link between our subjective starting point and our objective goal. . . .
If our standards of epistemic justification are appropriately chosen, bringing
it about that our beliefs are epistemically justified will also tend to
bring it about . . . that they are true. If epistemic justification were not
conducive to truth in this way, if finding epistemically justified beliefs
did not substantially increase the likelihood of finding true ones, then
epistemic justification would be irrelevant to our main cognitive goal
and of dubious worth. (Bonjour 1985, 7–8)

Finally, Goldman (1986) surveys a number of criteria for the rightness
of "J-rules", rules that lay down conditions for a belief's being justified.
These criteria are based on one or another valuable consequence of
belief. Consequences Goldman considers as candidates for this slot include coherence, explanation, practical usefulness, and truth. The upshot of his discussion is that truth, the "verific consequence", is the only
one that survives critical scrutiny. This leads to the view that a set of
J-rules is acceptable only if following them would lead to a preponder-
ance of true over false beliefs (98–106).

Thus on this truth-conducivity view the concept of truth plays a crucial role in the concept of justification. Because of this we can't provide the most basic defense of a thesis as to what conditions are sufficient for the justification without considering whether the satisfaction of those conditions would make it likely that the belief in question is *true*.[8]

But by no means all theorists of epistemic justification embrace truth conducivity. Its rejection typically stems from an "internalist" orientation, according to which being justified in believing that p is a matter of how things seem from the subject's own perspective—where that perspective is usually identified with what one can ascertain just on reflection—rather than a matter of the objective likelihood of the belief's being true.

> [T]he concept of epistemic justification is . . . *internal* and *immediate* . . . in that one can find out directly, by *reflection*, what one is justified in believing at any time. (Chisholm 1989, 7)

> The usual approach to the traditional questions of theory of knowledge is properly called "internal" or "internalistic". The internalist assumes that, merely by reflecting upon his own conscious state, he can formulate a set of epistemic principles that will enable him to find out, with respect to any possible belief he has, whether he is *justified* in having that belief. The epistemic principles that he formulates are principles that one may come upon and apply merely by sitting in one's armchair, so to speak, and without calling for any outside assistance. In a word, one need consider only one's own state of mind. (Chisholm 1989, 76)

> Every one of every set of facts about S's position that minimally suffices to make S, at a given time, justified in being confident that p must be *directly recognizable* to S at that time. By 'directly recognizable' I mean this: if a certain fact obtains, then it is directly recognizable to S at a given time if and only if, provided that S at that time has the concept of that sort of fact, S needs at that time only to reflect clear-headedly on the question of whether or not that fact obtains in order to know that it does. (Ginet 1975, 34)

---

8. On the contemporary scene this truth-conducivity perspective on justification is specially connected with a "reliabilist" approach to justification, the view that to be justified in believing that p is for the belief that p to be generated, or sustained, by a *reliable* process, mechanism, or disposition, where a process is reliable provided it would, in a wide range of suitably varied cases, produce a large proportion of true beliefs. But a truth-conducivity account of justification is by no means restricted to reliabilism and other forms of "externalism", where externalism is the view that what makes for justification need not be accessible to the subject just on reflection. Among the authors we have cited, Goldman and Swain are reliabilists, but Bonjour and Moser, so far from being reliabilists, are not even externalists. Plantinga is only partially a reliabilist, while Alston and Audi represent different ways of combining internalism and externalism.

Internalism . . . treats justifiedness as a purely internal matter: if p is justified for S, then S must be aware (or at least be immediately capable of being aware) of what makes it justified and why. (Bach 1985, 32)

There is a tension between internalism and truth conducivity just because the fact that a condition bestows an objective likelihood of truth on a belief is not something that one can ascertain just on reflection. Hence internalists typically reject truth conducivity.[9]

According to this traditional conception of "internal" epistemic justification, there is no *logical* connection between epistemic justification and truth. (Chisholm 1989, 76)

Epistemic rationality is distinguished from other kinds of rationality by its truth-directed goal. The goal is for one now to believe those propositions that are true and now not to believe those propositions that are false.

However, to say that the goal that helps distinguish epistemic rationality from other kinds of rationality is a truth-directed goal is not to say that truth is a prerequisite of epistemic rationality. In particular, it is not to say that it impossible for what is epistemically rational to be false, and likewise it is not even to say that it is impossible for most of what is epistemically rational to be false. (Foley 1987, 155; see the whole chapter, "Epistemic Rationality and Truth")

There are many versions of just how justification is a function of the subject's "perspective". One idea is that it is a matter of whether the subject is satisfying intellectual obligations, or not violating intellectual obligations, in believing that *p*. I will call such a conception of justification (one in terms of some version of the "required-forbidden-permitted" triad) a DEONTOLOGICAL conception.

One is *justified* in being confident that *p* if and only if it is not the case that one ought not to be confident that *p*; one could not be justly reproached for being confident that *p*. (Ginet 1975, 28)

The rational belief is the belief which does not violate our noetic obligations. The rational belief is the belief which, by reference to our noetic obligations, is permitted. . . . Rationality consists in not violating *those* duties concerning one's believings. (Wolterstorff 1983, 144)

---

9. But not invariably. Recall the earlier quotations from Bonjour and Moser, who are both internalists in the present sense and who take justification to be essentially truth conducive.

Another idea is that a belief is justified if the subject has sufficient (adequate) reasons, grounds, or evidence for the belief: "Doxastic attitude D toward proposition p is epistemically justified for S at t if and only if having D toward p fits the evidence S has at t" (Feldman and Conee, "Evidentialism", in Moser and Vander Nat, 1987, 334). We have already seen formulations of this sort in the two passages from Moser quoted above, but Moser combined this idea with a truth-conducivity conception of justification, whereas Feldman and Conee disavow any such connection.

It is clear that accounts of justification in terms either of nonviolation of obligations or of evidence will be compatible with internalism only if whatever is deemed sufficient for justification is so construed that it is cognitively accessible on reflection. For the deontological accounts, that means that we will have to understand nonviolation of an obligation in terms of how it seems to the subject or what the subject is justified in supposing, rather than in terms of objective facts that the subject might or might not be capable of ascertaining. Thus if the obligation, objectively formulated, is to believe a proposition only if it is true, justification will depend not on whether one satisfies that objective condition but on whether one believes what one *supposes* to be the truth or what one is *justified* in supposing to be the truth, where the latter alternative is so construed that whether one's belief is justified is always something reflectively accessible, as Chisholm maintains above. As for the account in terms of "fitting the evidence", we will have to understand "evidence", "reasons", or "grounds" in such a way that they are, to use Ginet's terminology, always "directly recognizable" by the subject. Moreover we will have to construe the requirement that the grounds are "adequate" or "sufficient" so that this too can be determined by the subject just by considering the question. This means that the "adequacy" of the grounds cannot be construed in terms of their conferring an objective probability of truth on the belief they ground, or in terms of constituting an adequate indication of the truth of the belief. The "adequacy" will have to construed more subjectively—as a matter of satisfying an intuitively endorsed epistemic principle (Chisholm) or as being such that the subject would, on sufficient reflection, deem the grounds to be an adequate indication of the truth of the belief (Foley).

I go through these internalist accounts of justification in order to point out that here too truth plays an essential role in the understanding of justification, though a different role from the one it plays in truth-conducive conceptions of justification. In the latter there was a straightforward conceptual connection between justification of the belief and the likelihood of its truth. Here the connection is more indirect. I have already hinted at it, but let me spell it out more explicitly.

On the deontological version of internalism, truth comes in by virtue of the fact that a prominent place, among intellectual obligations, is typically given to the obligation to believe what is true and to avoid believing what is false. (As already made explicit, such an obligation will have to construed more subjectively, for example, as an obligation to believe what in one's best judgment is true and to avoid believing what in one's best judgment is false.) This is spelled out in the following passage from Chisholm, in which he is explaining his notion of 'more reasonable than', in terms of which he defines terms for various degrees of justification. The variables 'p' and 'q' range over "doxastic attitudes" toward propositions—accepting, rejecting, and "withholding" (neither accepting nor rejecting).

> We may assume that every person is subject to a purely intellectual requirement—that of trying his best to bring it about that, for every proposition h that he considers, he accepts h if and only if h is true. One might say that this is the person's responsibility or duty *qua* intellectual being. . . . One way, then, of re-expressing the locution "p is more reasonable than q for S at t" is to say this: "S is so situated at t that his intellectual requirement, his responsibility as an intellectual being, is better fulfilled by p than by q". (Chisholm 1977, 14)

On this view we cannot think about whether S is justified in believing that p without employing the concept of truth. For S will be justified in her belief only if she is trying her best to believe what is true.

Truth comes into the second internalist account in either of two ways. According to the first, adequate evidence, reasons, or grounds for a belief are those that satisfy the believer's intuitive sense of what is sufficient to establish the likelihood of the truth of the belief, whether it is an objectively adequate indication of truth or not. According to the second, given definitive expression by Foley (1987), one is justified in believing that p (Foley says "rational" rather than "justified") if and only if one would believe on sufficient reflection that one has adequate reasons or grounds for supposing it to be true that p.[10] On both versions truth enters into the conception of rationality (justification) but indirectly, as filtered, so to say, through the subject's conception of the situation, ei-

10. This is not exactly Foley's formulation (see 1987, chap. 1), but I don't believe that I am misrepresenting him.

ther her actual conception or the conception she would have if she reflected sufficiently.

Thus on all the accounts of justification I have been considering we cannot raise and answer questions of whether various beliefs are justified without employing, or presupposing, the notion of truth. My argument here would be much simpler if I could claim, in good conscience, that the same holds for all the prominent, not obviously misguided ways of thinking about epistemic justification, but, alas, such is not the case. I will point out some theories of justification that seek to get along without bringing in reference to truth in the next section when we consider what happens to epistemology if we turn our backs on truth.

v Justification without Truth

It may be claimed that the above points merely reflect the fact that epistemologists are working within a tradition in which truth plays a major role. And it might be suggested, as Rorty said in one of the above passages, that we should break free of that tradition and strike out in new ways. Rorty would not be impressed with my survey of the standard ways of construing knowledge and epistemic justification. He would take this as reinforcing his contention that traditional epistemology has reached a dead end and constitutes a useless foot shuffling that holds no promise of advancing our understanding. In the face of challenges like that it behooves me to go beyond what I have just done and confront the question of whether anything valuable or essential would be lost if we were to turn our backs on truth.

Here too we can usefully divide the discussion into two parts, one on knowledge and one on justification. As for the former, it seems clear that we cannot preserve anything like the standard conception of knowledge if we cannot distinguish knowledge from (mere) belief by the fact that knowledge entails truth. 'Know' is the preeminent "success term" in epistemology; and the most basic kind of success it involves consists in truth. I really know that the document is in that safe when I am in a position to pick out the true answer as to where the document is. That is not, of course, to say that knowledge is merely true belief. A belief could be true by accident. I might have a completely irrational conviction that the document is in that safe and, by luck, get it right. That isn't knowledge. But, on the other hand, if the document isn't there, it is impossible that I should know that it is. No power on earth, or in heaven, could enable me to know what isn't so, since no power can override conceptual necessities.[11]

Again, justification presents a more complex picture. Matters are quite straightforward with truth-conducivity views. They will obviously go by the board if we jettison truth. For on such a view a crucial necessary condition for something's being a justifying condition for a belief of a certain type is that it renders the belief likely to be true. If truth is abandoned, that constraint goes down the drain and with it this whole way of thinking about the matter. There are, of course, also non-truth-conducivity conceptions of justification. But, as we saw, at least some of these depend on the notion of truth, though in a more indirect way. These accounts of justification too would fall by the wayside if the concept of truth were abandoned. So what is left? At this point we must turn to the hitherto unexplored internalist views of justification that keep it free of any sort of conceptual entanglement with truth. I will look briefly at two.

Earlier I quoted Ginet (1975) as characterizing justified belief as belief that is *permitted* by the relevant intellectual norms or standards. It is belief for which one "could not be justly reproached". In developing this idea Ginet, unlike Chisholm, does not say anything about a master obligation to try one's best to believe what is true and avoid believing what is false. No supreme intellectual standard of any sort is identified. Instead Ginet identifies particular conditions of permitted belief when discussing various modes of justification—inferential, perceptual, memorial. There is no suggestion that these are derivable from a fundamental aim at truth and the avoidance of falsity. The specific principles are represented as standing on their own feet.

To be sure, Ginet avoids identifying epistemic justification with the mere permissibility of belief, for he recognizes that it can be permissible for one to believe that p (one can "have a justification" for believing that p) for other than epistemically relevant reasons. He mentions a case in which "S's strong desire that R should be his trustworthy friend, and S's reasons for having that desire . . . may *justify* S, in a perfectly good sense, in maintaining his confidence that R would not do such a thing [lift cash from the till]" (1975, 29). This is the sort of consideration that leads epistemologists to distinguish epistemic justification of belief from moral or prudential justification.[12] The usual way of making that

11. One may suggest that what distinguishes knowledge from mere belief is that the former involves *conclusive* justification. But in order for justification to be conclusive enough to convert mere belief into knowledge, it has to be strong enough to guarantee the *truth* of the belief. And so the concept of truth still comes into the picture.

12. See, e.g., Alston 1989, 83; Bonjour 1985, 6–7; Moser 1985, 4–5.

distinction is in terms of truth as the basic goal by reference to which beliefs are to be assessed as *epistemically* justified or not.[13] Ginet, however, does not mention truth in this connection. Instead he lays it down that epistemic justification is *disinterested* justification, which he explains as justification "that does not involve wanting it to be the case that p" (29). I don't think that this succeeds in separating epistemic justification of belief from all others, for the moral justification of a belief that *p* may well not involve *wanting* the proposition that *p* to be true. If I am justified in believing Smith innocent of a crime because I have promised to trust him, it may or may not be that I want Smith to be innocent. But leave that aside. The point is that Ginet lays out a concept of epistemic justification that makes no reference to truth. If this conception is viable, something I will be considering shortly, it enables us to develop a theory of epistemic justification without any reliance on truth.

Pollock (1974) puts forward the view that the content of our most basic concepts are given by "justification conditions".

> To learn the meaning of a concept is certainly not to learn its "definition". It is to learn how to use it, which is to learn how to make justifiable assertions involving it. Thus it seems to me inescapable that the meaning of a concept is determined by its justification conditions. (12)
>
> Just what is necessary before we can truly say of a person that he has learned the concept of a certain kind of thing, such as "red thing" or "bird"? . . . [I]f in fact the child did not *know how* to ascribe the concept and its complement justifiably (i.e., he did not know how to justifiably determine whether something was a bird), this would show that he had not learned how to identify birds and so does not have the concept.
>
> Conversely, when the child has learned to judge justifiably whether a thing is a bird (i.e., he has learned to ascribe the concept and its complement to things justifiably), we are satisfied that he knows how to identify birds and so has got the concept right—he knows what a bird is. (13–15)

In other words, to possess the concept of a bird, or of any other kind of thing or property that is perceivable (let's follow Pollock in calling these "perceptual properties"), is to have the ability to make justified attributions of it; it is to have a working knowledge of the "justification conditions" of the concept. But if that is what it is to have the concept, then

---

13. See the passages cited in n. 12.

what the concept is can be specified by laying out those justification conditions. Those conditions constitute the content of the concept.

> It was assumed that having once spelled out the justification conditions for a statement, we would have to go on to prove that those are the justification conditions by deriving them from the meaning of the statement (which was identified with the truth conditions). To prove that the purported justification conditions are the justification conditions would be to derive them from something deeper. But in fact there is generally nothing deeper. The justification conditions are themselves constitutive of the meaning of the statement. We can no more *prove* that the justification conditions of "That is red" are the justification conditions than we can prove on the basis of something deeper about the meaning of "bachelor" that all bachelors are unmarried. Being unmarried constitutes part of the meaning of "bachelor" and as such cannot be derived from anything deeper about the meaning of "bachelor"; and analogously the justification conditions of "That is red" or "He is in pain" are constitutive of the meanings of those statements and hence cannot be derived from any deeper features of their meanings. There are no deeper features. (1974, 21)

To say that a belief that X is a bird is justified by a perceptual presentation of such-and-such a kind is simply to spell out what is involved in the concept of a bird. What justifies a certain concept attribution is determined by the constitution of that concept and requires no further basis. Justification stands on its own feet, without any support from considerations of truth.

Unfortunately, Pollock, unlike Ginet, neglects in his 1974 account to tell us what he means by 'justified' in the epistemic sense. Without some account of the sense of 'justification' in which, he avers, (many) concepts are made up of "justification" conditions, one doesn't know what to make of the position. Nor, with respect to our present concern, do we have any basis for judging whether the concept of justification is free of entanglements with the concept of truth. However, in a later book (1986) Pollock has more to say about the concept. Like Ginet he identifies it with "epistemic permissibility". "A justified belief is one that it is 'epistemically permissible' to hold. Epistemic justification is a normative notion. It pertains to what you *should* or *should not* believe. But it is a uniquely epistemic normative notion. Epistemic permissibility must be distinguished from both moral and prudential permissibility" (7; See also 124–25). But Pollock does not distinguish the epistemic permissibility of belief from other kinds in terms of the interested–disinterested distinction, as Ginet does. Indeed, he does not make it very explicit how he is drawing the distinction. He speaks of the epistemic point of view. "Thus I will think of epistemic justification as being concerned with questions of the form, 'When is it permissible (from an epistemological point of view) to believe P?' " (124). But he fails to spell out just what he takes this point of view to consist in. What I gather from the discussion as a whole is that he supposes what makes permissibility of belief *epistemic* is that it stems from a certain kind of source, namely, the norms we have internalized that govern "right reasoning". "Epistemic norms are supposed to guide us in reasoning and thereby in forming beliefs. The concept of epistemic justification can be explained by explaining the nature and origin of the epistemic norms that govern our reasoning.[14] I have called this 'the reason-guiding concept of epistemic justification' " (p. 125). In supposing that this gives a sufficient answer to the question, "What distinguishes epistemic permissibility from prudential or moral permissibility?", Pollock is assuming that we have not also internalized moral or prudential norms that govern reasoning. In any event, it is clear that he does not mark out epistemic justification in terms of an aim at truth or in any other way that involves the concept of truth.[15]

vi Troubles with Deontological Conceptions of Justification

It is not without significance that both of the attempts to explain justification without bringing in truth construe justification as a kind of permissibility of belief. Perhaps truth-free accounts of justification must be like this. As we saw earlier, one can also have a deontological conception of justification that brings truth into the account by taking the master epistemic obligation to be the obligation to believe what is true and to refrain from believing what is false, or some more subjective version of this.[16] Nevertheless, it is also possible to take intellectual obligations or norms for belief to stand on their own and not owe their authority to their relation to truth, as both Ginet and Pollock do.

In fairness to these authors, I should point out that they do not ignore

14. Pollock makes it explicit that he is using 'reasoning' in a broad sense in which it includes basing beliefs on experience. In other words 'reasoning' is used to cover any sort of belief formation.

15. He explicitly rejects the thesis that a belief is epistemically permissible if and only if what is believed is sufficiently probable (1986, 135).

16. Among the epistemologists I have cited, Bonjour, Moser (1985), and Goldman are good examples of deontologists who bring truth into the account. Indeed, they all hold a truth-conducivity view of epistemic justification.

truth in epistemology altogether. They go along with the customary truth condition for knowledge, and Ginet makes use of the notion of truth in explaining his fourth condition for knowledge (over and above having a true justified belief), the requirement of what he calls "external conclusiveness". But they do eschew any reference to truth in the theory of epistemic justification, and it is this that we are presently examining.

If it is true that only deontological conceptions of epistemic justification can be laid out without using the concept of truth, that in itself, in my opinion, lands them in a peck of trouble. For, as I have argued at length elsewhere[17], no such concept is viable. If the relevant requirements (proscriptions, permissions . . .) are applied directly to doxastic attitudes themselves (believing, rejecting, withholding), then we are committed to an untenable assumption of the effective voluntary control of doxastic attitudes. If, on the other hand, the justification of a doxastic attitude depends on the causal antecedents of that attitude—antecedents that don't contain any (or too much) of what is epistemically forbidden—then justification becomes too easy; it doesn't have the cutting edge for the sake of which it is thought to be epistemically valuable. I will not repeat my arguments for these claims but will instead pass on to three difficulties with the "justification without truth" position that can be more succinctly set out in full.

vii Problems with Any Truth-Free Justification

First there is the question of how to distinguish epistemic justification of belief from other sorts of justification. As we have seen, a reference to the "epistemic point of view", defined by a concern for believing what is true and avoiding believing what is false, is an obvious way to do this. What distinguishes epistemic justification is that it is valuable for the pursuit of those goals. If we eschew that way of making the distinction, how can we do it? We have seen that Ginet's interested–disinterested distinction doesn't suffice. Pollock, as we saw, thinks that the distinction can be made by identifying epistemic justification with what is permitted by internalized norms for reasoning. But why should we suppose that we possess only epistemic norms for reasoning? Why shouldn't there be moral or prudential norms for what Pollock calls "reasoning", that is, belief formation. How else could there be moral

17. "The Deontological Conception of Epistemic Justification", in Alston 1989.

or prudential *permissibility* of belief, except by way of conformity with appropriate moral or prudential norms? If that is right, Pollock's way of marking off *epistemic* permissibility works no better than Ginet's.

Another suggestion for distinguishing epistemic justification from other kinds without bringing in truth would be to think of it as conducivity to some other master goal of cognition. I will take as my guide Goldman's discussion in chapter 5 of *Epistemology and Cognition* (1986). Goldman distinguishes five candidates for "justificationally valuable consequences":

(1) *verific* consequences: believing truths, not believing falsehoods
(2) *coherence* consequences: achieving coherence in one's belief (or creedal probability) corpus
(3) *explanatory* consequences: believing propositions that explain other believed propositions
(4) *pragmatic* consequences: realizing one's practical, nonintellectual goals
(5) *biological* consequences: surviving, reproducing, propagating one's genes. (Goldman 1986, 98)[18]

For each of these we can consider whether we can bring out what is distinctive of epistemic justification in terms of its conducivity to that kind of consequence.

Consequences (4) and (5) can be eliminated right away as insufficiently discriminative. It obviously won't distinguish epistemic from prudential justification to claim that only the former is valuable for the attainment of "practical", "nonintellectual" or basic biological goals! As for (2), though it is a distinctively intellectual desideratum, we have already seen that there are decisive reasons for denying that pure coherence suffices for epistemic justification, the main reason being that there is a potential infinity of incompatible but equally coherent systems of belief. That leaves (1) and (3). Consequence (1) explicitly involves the notion of truth, and it does not take much probing of (3) to find

18. I don't mean to suggest that Goldman is concerned here with my current problem of distinguishing epistemic from other kinds of justification. He is rather engaged in finding a criterion for right rules of justification. However, I find his list of "justificationally valuable consequences" useful for my purpose.

Note too that although one might well think that *justification of belief* is a central goal of cognition, one could hardly bring in that goal to explain what differentiates epistemic from other justification. For if the goal is to have the necessary relevance it will have to be *epistemic* justification of which we are speaking. And saying that what is distinctive of epistemic justification is that it is valuable in attaining the goal of epistemic justification could scarcely be thought to throw light on what epistemic justification is!

that notion under the surface. What is it to explain something? That is a difficult question and one for which, in my opinion, no illuminating, generally applicable answer has been given. But I don't need to get into that to make the present point. In whatever way we spell out what is involved in rendering something 'explained', it will remain the case that an adequate, successful explanation involves citing something true as providing the explanation. In whatever way a set of false statements is explanatorily related to the explanandum, they will not constitute the explanation of it. If the target of my explanation is the fact that I am getting no sound from my loudspeakers, it is obvious that their not being hooked up to a source of signals is related to this explanandum in the right sort of way to be an explanans. If that is true, it will explain it. But *only* if. We haven't lit on what really explains the defect until we have specified some *true* proposition(s) that is (are) related to the explanandum in the right sort of way.

Thus this survey of candidates for the basic goal of cognition, by reference to which epistemic justification could be distinguished from other types, provides no hope of any satisfactory choice that does not involve the concept of truth. Doing without truth leaves us without any way of framing an adequate concept of epistemic justification.

The second difficulty has to do with criteria for the assessment of principles that lay down conditions of justification. How do we tell which principles to adopt? So long as we are working with a truth-conducivity conception of justification we have something to go on. If a necessary condition for C's justifying belief B is that C renders B significantly likely to be true, we have a lodestar that will guide us in distinguishing between genuine justifiers and impostors. At least we do if, as seems to be the case, we can often tell when conditions do render a belief probably true. If a certain type of perceptual presentation is a strong indication that there is maple tree in front of me, then such a presentation passes at least that requirement for being a justifier of that belief. And if that is all it takes to be a justifier (perhaps together with the requirement, obviously satisfied here, of being cognitively accessible to the subject), we can without more ado judge that being perceptually appeared to in that way justifies the belief that one is face to face with a maple tree. If a great deal of a certain kind of noise emanating from a certain house is a reliable sign that a party is going on therein, then by observing that noise we are thereby (truth-conducively) justified in supposing that a party is going on. And so on.

But how will we make a rational, principled choice between competing claims to justificatory efficacy if we abandon all reference to truth, likelihood of truth, probability of truth, reliable indication of truth, and the like? What will there be for us to go on in determining what justifies what? Let's see what our truth-value-free justification theorists have to say about this. Here is Ginet's answer.

> Insofar as positions directly recognizable to a person can be *objectively* ranked as to how strong a belief in a given proposition, *p*, they justify that person in having—that is, insofar as we have a concept and practice of objective justification of degrees of belief—the ultimate authority for this ranking must be the concurring judgments of reasonable, experienced people who have the notion of and an interest in the practice of rational, objective justification of degrees of belief and who give the positions in question their thoughtful consideration. If we say of two sorts of directly recognizable positions that one would clearly justify a stronger belief in *p* than the other . . . we are right if and only if this would be the overwhelming judgment of reasonable, experienced people who knew what they were considering (so that their judgment would not be changed by their attending better to the nature of the positions in question or their having more experience or more rational intelligence). (Ginet 1975, 37)

The chief difficulty with Ginet's view is that his ultimate appeal is to raw intuition. I call this appeal "ultimate" because there is no provision for any check on the accuracy or validity of those intuitions. They constitute the last word, from which there is no further court of appeal. If that is the best we can do, we can learn to live with it. But since a truth-conducivity conception of justification gives us something better, we are ill advised to rest content with bare, unexamined intuition in this sphere.

As for Pollock, his story as to how we tell whether we have the right principles of justification is that they are determined by the concepts involved in the beliefs in question. In section v I laid out this position as it is expounded in Pollock 1974. The account of the structure of concepts is more elaborate and more sophisticated in Pollock's later work (1986, 147–48), but the application to the basis of justification is the same. Since concepts are constituted, at least in part, by "justification conditions", it is conceptually true that the belief that a tree is in front of me is justified by what the concept of a tree (in conjunction with the other concepts involved) lays down as sufficient for justification of such a belief.

I believe that this position fares no better than Ginet's. For one thing, there are reasons to doubt that our concepts are constituted, even in part, by justification conditions. If our concept of a tree, for example, were so constituted, how could that concept be possessed by subjects that have no inkling, even in a practical, know-how sense of justification or conditions of justification? Moreover if, as Pollock acknowledges in the later book, a given concept contains more than a set of justification conditions, we are faced with the question of why we should suppose that the satisfaction of the justification conditions involved guarantees the justification of the application of the rest of the concept to something. Let's say that part of the concept of *tree* is *vegetable organism,* and that the concept also contains a specification of the kind of perceptual experience that would justify taking a perceived object to be a tree. That raises the question why we should suppose that this perceptual condition justifies the attribution of the rest of the concept—being a vegetable organism, for example? To be sure, by hypothesis, we find them stuck together in the same concept. But what guarantees, or even gives us reason to think, that they have been advisedly combined? Is this just another appeal to the status quo, along with Ginet's appeal to the judgment of "reasonable, experienced people"? Again, we would like a deeper, more impressive rationale than this.[19]

The demerit that attaches to truth-value-free justification by reason of its relatively uncritical character is intimately connected with the third defect—the fact that it fails to throw light on why we should be interested in justification. Remember Bonjour on this point.

> If epistemic justification were not conducive to truth in this way, if finding epistemically justified beliefs did not substantially increase the likelihood of finding true ones, then epistemic justification would be irrelevant to our main cognitive goal and of dubious worth. It is only if we have some reason for thinking that epistemic justification constitutes a path to truth that we as cognitive beings have any motive for preferring epistemically justified beliefs to epistemically unjustified ones. (1985, 8)

Ginet's and Pollock's construals of justification fall under this stricture. Ginet, to focus on him, says that we are epistemically justified in believing that *p* if we have a disinterested justification for *p*, where its being disinterested just amounts to its not depending on our wanting it to be the case that *p*. And that is to say that if we were to believe that *p* we would be doing what we are permitted to do, what we could not be

---

19. For a more extended discussion of difficulties in Pollock's position see Alston 1993, 39–45.

reproached for, again where this is not because of what we want to be the case. But why should it be so important to us whether we have a "disinterested" justification, or whether we are "disinterestedly" permitted to believe that *p*? Before we get terribly exercised about this, we need to know a good deal more about what it comes to than Ginet gives us. In particular, why should we suppose that justification, so construed, is of any value or importance in the quest for knowledge? Why should we suppose, as Ginet claims, that justification, as he has portrayed it, is necessary for knowledge? So long as no connection with truth or the probability thereof is built into the concept of justification, it is difficult to see why we should aim at our beliefs being justified rather than the reverse if we are seeking truth and knowledge.

These defects stem from the thinness of what our theorists have provided by way of a concept of epistemic justification. It is a matter of permissibility of belief, not by reason of what we *want* (Ginet), or it is based on the norms of belief formation that we have in fact internalized (Pollock). With no more than this to go on, it is small wonder that we are left wondering how to distinguish epistemic justification from other modes, how to assess principles of justification, and why we should regard justified belief as a pearl of great price. These are grave disabilities, indeed. If this is the result of shunning truth, we had better think twice before signing on to that enterprise.

I have been considering the effects of eliminating truth in the epistemology of knowledge and justification. As for knowledge we have seen that it would disembowel the concept to the point of unrecognizability. As for justification, it would strip us of any sufficiently contentful conception of epistemic justification, leave mysterious the reason we should find it valuable in the pursuit of knowledge, prevent us from giving an adequate account of what distinguishes epistemic from other species of justification of belief, and leave us without any effective means for making rational choices between competing claims as to what justifies what. Not an attractive prospect. The advantages of dispensing with truth would have to be enormous if they were to outweigh the cost.

viii   Stich on the Unimportance of Truth

The last bad-mouther of truth I will consider is Stephen Stich. In his recent book, *The Fragmentation of Reason* (1990) he undertakes the heroic task of arguing that it is of no importance whether our beliefs are true. The argument, in brief summary, goes as follows.

Beliefs are treated as brain-state tokens that have propositional content by virtue of being "mapped" onto propositions (or something playing the same role) by some "interpretation function". He thinks in terms of bits or aspects of these brain-state tokens as functioning like linguistic items in a "language of thought". "[T]he idea is that beliefs are complex psychological states which, like sentences, can be viewed as built up out of simpler components" (109). Stich opts for a "causal/ functional" understanding of the interpretation function. To simplify matters lets say that a belief gets content by virtue of a causal relation to "referents". But, Stich points out, there are a lot of causal relations out there, and not all of them will be relevant to determining the referent of a given mental "term". On one choice of causal relations 'water' refers to H_2O, while on another choice it refers to Putnam's notorious XYZ (stuff that looks and tastes just like H_2O but has a different chemical constitution), while on still another it refers to the sum of the two. But, of course, the truth conditions for a mental "sentence" are intimately dependent on the interpretation function that assigns referents to the sentence components. And Stich takes this to imply that we have different concepts of truth (or truth-like relations) for different interpretation functions: "So while the interpretation function based on the intuitively sanctioned notion of reference might specify that a certain belief token of mine is true if and only if there is no H_2O on the sun, an interpretation function based on REFERENCE*** would specify that the same belief token is true (or, better, TRUE***) if and only if there is no H_2O or XYZ on the sun" (117). Stich then proceeds to argue that we have no sufficient reason, either intellectual or practical, for preferring our beliefs to exhibit TRUTH rather than any of its innumerable alternatives, TRUTH*, TRUTH**, TRUTH***, and so on.

What are we to say of these astounding results? I could challenge Stich on the last point and argue that good, old-fashioned truth is preferable to its heterodox alternatives, but as I see it, the main trouble with the argument comes much earlier. Stich is, in fact, flying under false colors. He purports to be offering us a choice between different truth relations, whereas the alternatives he considers are really between different ways of assigning propositional content to bearers of such content—beliefs, sentences, assertions, or whatever. The apparently startling results simply amount to the familiar claim that there is, in principle, an indefinite number of ways of assigning referents (and, I would say more basically, meanings) to sentences or any sentence-like entities[20], together with the

20. I don't agree that beliefs can be taken in the way Stich does. A string of phonemes can,

equally banal point that the propositional content of the entity, and hence its truth conditions, will vary depending on those assignments. So the variation is a semantic one. Stich, as we have seen, takes this to show that there is an indefinitely large number of different truth-like concepts that can be applied to beliefs and in terms of which they can be assessed, our familiar concept of propositional truth being only one of them. But I see absolutely no justification for this further step. Let's agree that the propositional content of a belief depends on the "interpretation function". But for any such function there will be a (more or less precise) propositional content, and that will give us something whose truth value we can consider. *It is only after the proposition has been assigned that the question of truth value can be raised.* Stich has been led astray by the common practice, already decried more than once in this book, of treating sentences and the like as bearers of truth value. Indeed, he pushes this common fallacy one step further by taking *uninterpreted* sentences as bearers of truth value. It is only by making this move that he can suppose that different propositional interpretations of sentences (real or mental) determine different concepts of truth. As I said earlier, truth is a "post-semantic" concept. Questions of truth come up only *after* we have semantic content. Hence, even if we are as free as Stich supposes to choose an "interpretation function" for a belief, this would only imply a *semantic* indeterminacy. It would have no tendency to imply an indeterminacy of the truth concept. It would still remain true that whatever the propositional content with which we endow a particular belief or sentence, there is no alternative in sight to asking the old, familiar question about truth value.

Put this point in another way. Stich thinks that truth is a relation that directly connects bearers of meaning, reference, and propositional content, to truth values (or, perhaps, to what is responsible for the bearer being true or false). Thus whenever we have a different way of associating a belief, sentence, or whatever to a proposition—a different propositional function—we have a fundamentally different way of associating the belief or whatever to a truth value, and so a different concept of truth. But in fact the variability or indeterminacy, if any, applies only to the first step—the assignment of propositional content. *Once that is re-*

---

in principle, bear any one of indefinitely many different meanings, depending on what semantic rules hold sway in the language in which it is a word, phrase, or sentence. But beliefs are not, in my view, semantically neutral in their intrinsic character in this way. We can't first (correctly) identify something as a belief and then proceed to choose between many different "interpretations" for it. We can't recognize it as a belief except in terms of some particular propositional content or other. But I won't press this point here.

solved, there is no room for any further indeterminacy with respect to truth. Our familiar realist conception of truth goes into action on whatever proposition we wind up with. If the belief is the belief that p, then it is true if and only if p, and that uniquely identifies truth. There is no plethora of truth concepts between which a choice is called for. Thus there is no need to challenge Stich's argument that there are no sufficient reasons for preferring old-fashioned truth to its innumerable rivals, for there are no such rivals between which to choose.

In my delineation of his position, I have more than once hinted that I am not at all disposed to accept Stich's claims of indeterminacy even on the semantic level. I take propositional contents of beliefs to be "built in" by virtue of their functional role in the psyche, thereby forestalling any need for choice between "interpretation functions". Sentences in a language are, obviously, more semantically flexible in principle. Nevertheless, facts of how people use language in a community largely fix the available interpretations of phrases, words, and sentences, again leaving little room for anyone to come along with a kit of "interpretation functions". Of course, it is always possible to propose new meanings for linguistic units, but one may or may not be successful in moving the language in that direction. One cannot endow a semantic unit in an actual language with a new meaning just by a wave of the wand. However, it has not been necessary for my purposes here to challenge Stich on this point. Even if he is fully justified in his suppositions about semantic indeterminacy, he is not entitled, I have argued, to move from that to alethic indeterminacy.

Epilogue

This completes my exposition and defense of alethic realism. In Chapters 1 and 2 I have presented and discussed a variety of ways of formulating a realist conception of truth and have explored its connections with various forms of realism. Since I take this way of thinking of propositional truth to be overwhelmingly plausible on the face of it, my efforts in its defense have been directed to answering its critics, who have both claimed that it is untenable and put forward alternative construals. Chapters 2–6 are devoted, in large part, to defusing attacks on the realist conception, and Chapter 7 presents what I take to be fatal objections to its only serious rival—an epistemic conception. Finally, in Chapter 8 I defend the other component of alethic realism—that a concern with (realist) truth is important both theoretically and practically.

I can imagine someone accepting everything I have said in this book and still feeling dissatisfied with the outcome. For one thing, a reader might find cause for complaint in various things I haven't done. I will mention just two examples.

(1) I haven't explained how to determine whether a given statement is true. True. I haven't done so, because that is a completely different enterprise, one called "epistemology". I am very interested in epistemology and have published extensively in the field. But my concern here is with the concept of propositional truth, how to get straight as to what propositional truth *is*. To be sure, that has a bearing on what is relevant to determining truth value. We can scarcely undertake to determine whether x is P without understanding what it is for something to be P. But for any property, P, a grasp of what it is constitutes only the first step in figuring how to tell whether a particular kind of x is P. It is only that first step with which this book is concerned, and I assume that one who

has read this far will agree that I have found plenty to occupy me in taking that first step.

(2) I haven't defended a more robustly realist account of truth, according to which the facts that render a given statement true or false, or most of them, obtain and are what they are independent of our cognitive activity. True again. As you will remember, in Chapter 1 I explicitly abstained from making the realist conception I defend that robust. To do so would involve quite another range of considerations from those with which I have been concerned, and it would have required at least doubling the length of the book, which is still far below appending to it a complete epistemology in order to satisfy the first complaint. My rationale for undertaking the more restricted task is that a variety of fundamental issues arise with respect to alethic realism as I have construed it, and these issues deserve a full hearing on their own, unencumbered by entanglement with further questions like the one concerning the independence of truth makers from our cognitive activity. Hence I felt that it was important to isolate the fairly austere realist conception of truth I have been discussing and to go fully into its pros and cons, without tying the discussion to metaphysical questions concerning the relation of thought and reality.

One reader of the manuscript, Jonathan Bennett, made the following comment.

> I am convinced by most of what you say on the topic, but I'm not at all sure that I really know what is going on. This is a trouble that I have always had with this general realism issue. With limited realism debates—especially the one about morality—I can see what the argument is about and why there is an argument about it. I don't have that same sense, with realism versus nonrealism in general, that I can see why there are two sides. At some places in this book you seem to take the line that the position you are defending would be trivial if it weren't for the fact that able people deny it. I'm intensely dissatisfied with this. I want a better sense than I have of why they deny it. (Personal communication)

After reading this I pointed out to Bennett that I had spent a good part of the book detailing reasons given by people like Dummett and Putnam for denying it. But trotting out those arguments didn't give him what he was after. He said he still felt the lack of any specification of a basic intuitive sense that is behind such rejections.

I am not sure that I can satisfy Bennett on this. There may be no *single* gut intuition behind nonrealism about truth. That position would seem to stem from several sources—verificationism about meaning, anti-absolutism in metaphysics, objections to claims to immediate knowledge, to name a few that have surfaced in my discussion. (To be sure, I have argued that it is misguided to suppose that any of these positions do tell against a realist construal of truth.) If someone were to put a gun to my head and force me to formulate a single fundamental root of opposition to realism about truth, I suppose that I would say "intolerance of vulnerability". In supposing that what we believe and assert is rendered true or false by whether what a belief or assertion is about is as the belief or assertion would have it to be, we are acknowledging a liability to falsity that is, in a fundamental way, out of our control. We can, of course, take such precautions as are open to us to ensure that this condition for truth is satisfied. But in the final analysis whether what we say is true is determined not by anything we do or think, but by the way things are—the things we are talking about. This vulnerability to the outside world, this "subjection" to stubborn, unyielding facts beyond our thought, experience, and discourse, seems powerfully repugnant, even intolerable to many. As a Christian, I see in this reaction a special case of *the* original sin, insisting on human autonomy and control and refusing to be subservient to that on which our being and our fate depends, which for the Christian is God. But in this context I don't want to insist on a theological interpretation. The attitude of which I am speaking can be found among many philosophers who are, at least consciously, wholly innocent of any tendencies to rebel against God, a being not accorded a place in their pantheon. Assuming that there is something to this diagnosis, I will leave it to the reader to reflect on whether this "intolerance of vulnerability" is an attitude that commends itself on reflection.

I will comment on one more possible reaction to my argument, and here, as in the initial reactions I considered, I cannot quote a live reactor but will have to construct her as I go along. Still sticking with the creature of my fond imagination who agrees with everything I have said, let's now suppose this creature to ask the following. "Why does it make so much difference after all whether we have the right conception of truth? Why make such a fuss over it? Even if an epistemic conception is subject to fatal flaws, what harm does it do?"

The best answer to this question is the simplest one. "It is better to have things straight than to have them distorted or confused. It is better to have a correct understanding of concepts, especially fundamental ones, than to misunderstand them. And this is the case, apart from any further consequences there might be. After all, as philosophers we are dedicated to getting as accurate and perspicuous a view as possible of the basic concepts we use in our thought and discourse."

BIBLIOGRAPHY

Alston, William P. 1958. "Ontological Commitments". *Philosophical Studies* 9: 8–17.
———. 1989. *Epistemic Justification: Essays in the Theory of Knowledge*. Ithaca, N.Y.: Cornell University Press.
———. 1991. *Perceiving God: The Epistemology of Religious Experience*. Ithaca, N.Y.: Cornell University Press.
———. 1993a. *The Reliability of Sense Perception*. Ithaca, N.Y.: Cornell University Press.
———. 1993b. "Epistemic Desiderata". *Philosophy and Phenomenological Research* 53, 3.
———. 1994. "Illocutionary Acts and Linguistic Meaning". In *Foundations of Speech Act Theory*, ed. S. L. Tsohadtzidis. London: Routledge.
———. 1995. "Realism and the Christian Faith". *International Journal for Philosophy of Religion* 38, 3.
Audi, Robert. 1993. *The Structure of Justification*. Cambridge: Cambridge University Press.
Ayer, A. J. 1946. *Language, Truth, and Logic*. 2d. ed. London: Victor Gollancz Ltd.
———, ed. 1959. *Logical Positivism*. New York: The Free Press.
Bach, Kent. 1985 "A Rationale for Reliabilism". *The Monist* 68, no. 2.
Bennett, Jonathan. 1988. *Events and Their Names*. Indianapolis: Hackett.
Blackburn, Simon. 1984. *Spreading the Word*. Oxford: Clarendon Press.
Blanshard, Brand. 1939. *The Nature of Thought*. 2 vols. London: George Allen & Unwin.
Bonjour, Laurence. 1985. *The Structure of Empirical Knowledge*. Cambridge, Mass.: Harvard University Press.
Bouwsma, O. K. 1965. *Philosophical Essays*. Lincoln: University of Nebraska Press.
Bradley, F. H. 1914. *Essays on Truth and Reality*. Oxford: Clarendon Press.
Carnap, Rudolf. 1947. *Meaning and Necessity*. Chicago: University of Chicago Press.
Chisholm, Roderick. 1976. *Person and Object*. La Salle, Ill.: Open Court.
———. 1977. *Theory of Knowledge* 2d. ed. Englewood Cliffs, N.J.: Prentice-Hall.
———. 1981. *The First Person*. Minneapolis: University of Minnesota Press.
———. 1989. *Theory of Knowledge*. 3d. ed. Englewood Cliffs, N.J.: Prentice-Hall.
David, Marian. 1994. *Correspondence and Disquotation: An Essay on the Nature of Truth*. New York: Oxford University Press.
Davidson, Donald. 1984. *Inquiries Into Truth and Interpretation*. Oxford: Oxford University Press.

——. 1990. "The Structure and Content of Truth". *Journal of Philosophy* 87, no. 6, 279–328.

Davidson, Donald, and Gilbert Harman, eds. 1972. *Semantics of Natural Language*. Dordrecht: D. Reidel.

Devitt, Michael. 1984. *Realism and Truth*. Oxford: Basil Blackwell.

Dewey, John. 1920. *Reconstruction in Philosophy*. New York: Henry Holt.

Dretske, Fred. 1969. *Seeing and Knowing*. London: Routledge & Kegan Paul.

——. 1981. *Knowledge and the Flow of Information*. Cambridge, Mass.: MIT Press.

Dummett, Michael. 1973. *Frege: Philosophy of Language*. New York: Harper & Row.

——. 1975. "What is a Theory of Meaning? I". In *Mind and Language*, ed. Samuel Guttenplan. London: Oxford University Press.

——. 1976. "What is a Theory of Meaning? II". In *Truth and Meaning*, ed. Gareth Evans and John McDowell. London: Oxford University Press.

——. 1978. *Truth and Other Enigmas*. Cambridge, Mass.: Harvard University Press.

——. 1991. *The Logical Basis of Metaphysics*. Cambridge, Mass.: Harvard University Press.

Edwards, Paul. 1967. *The Encyclopedia of Philosophy*. New York: Macmillan and the Free Press.

Field, Hartry and Gilbert Harman. 1982. "Symposium on Putnam's *Reason, Truth and History*". *Journal of Philosophy* 79, 10.

Fodor, Jerry. 1975. *The Language of Thought*. New York: Thomas Y. Crowell.

Foley, Richard. 1987. *The Theory of Epistemic Rationality*. Cambridge, Mass.: Harvard University Press.

Ginet, Carl. 1975. *Knowledge, Perception, and Memory*. Dordrecht: D. Reidel.

Goldman, Alvin I. 1986. *Epistemology and Cognition*. Cambridge, Mass.: Harvard University Press.

Grover, Dorothy L. 1992. *A Prosentential Theory of Truth*. Princeton, N.J.: Princeton University Press.

Gunderson, Keith. 1975. *Language, Mind, and Knowledge: Minnesota Studies in the Philosophy of Science*, Vol. VII. Minneapolis: University of Minnesota Press.

Hahn, Lewis E., and Paul A. Schilpp, eds. 1986. *The Philosophy of W. V. Quine*. LaSalle, Ill.: Open Court.

Heller, Mark. 1988. "Putnam, Reference, and Realism". *Midwest Studies in Philosophy*, 12. *Realism and Antirealism*.

Hempel, Carl G. 1935. "On the Logical Positivists' Theory of Truth". *Analysis* 2, no. 4, 50–59.

Hesse, Mary B. 1966. *Models and Analogies in Science*. Notre Dame: University of Notre Dame Press.

Horwich, Paul. 1990. *Truth*. Oxford: Basil Blackwell.

James, William. 1909. *The Meaning of Truth*. Cambridge, Mass.: Harvard University Press.

——. 1975. *Pragmatism*. Cambridge, Mass.: Harvard University Press.

Katz, Jerrold J. 1981. *Language and Other Abstract Objects*. Totowa, N.J.: Rowman and Littlefield.

Kirkham, Richard L. 1992. *Theories of Truth: A Critical Introduction*. Cambridge, Mass.: MIT Press.

Lehrer, Keith. 1974. *Knowledge*. Oxford: Clarendon Press.

LePore, Ernest, ed. 1986. *Truth and Interpretation: Perspectives on the Philosophy of Donald Davidson*. New York: Blackwell.

Lewis, David. 1984. "Putnam's Paradox". *Australasian Journal of Philosophy* 62.

Macdonald, Margaret, ed. 1954. *Philosophy and Analysis.* Oxford: Basil Blackwell.

Mackie, J. L. 1973. *Truth, Probability, and Paradox: Studies in Philosophical Logic.* Oxford: Clarendon Press.

Moser, Paul K. 1985. *Empirical Justification.* Dordrecht: D. Reidel.

——. 1989. *Knowledge and Evidence.* Cambridge: Cambridge University Press.

Moser, Paul K., and Arnold Vander Nat. 1987. *Human Knowledge: Classical and Contemporary Approaches.* New York: Oxford University Press.

Peacocke, Christopher. 1983. *Sense and Content.* Oxford: Oxford University Press.

Peirce, Charles Sanders. 1934. "How To Make Our Ideas Clear." In *Collected Papers,* ed. C. Hartshorne and P. Weiss, vol. 5. Cambridge, Mass.: Harvard University Press.

Plantinga, Alvin. 1982. "How To Be an Anti-Realist". *Proceedings and Addresses of the American Philosophical Association.*

——. 1993. *Warrant and Proper Function.* New York: Oxford University Press.

Pollock, John. 1974. *Knowledge and Justification.* Princeton, N.J.: Princeton University Press.

——. 1986. *Contemporary Theories of Knowledge.* Totowa, N.J.: Rowman & Littlefield.

Price, Huw. 1988. *Facts and the Function of Truth.* Oxford: Basil Blackwell.

Prior, A. N. 1971. *Objects of Thought.* Oxford: Clarendon Press.

Putnam, Hilary. 1978. *Meaning and the Moral Sciences.* London: Routledge & Kegan Paul.

——. 1981. *Reason, Truth, and History.* Cambridge: Cambridge University Press.

——. 1983. *Realism and Reason: Philosophical Papers,* Vol. 3. Cambridge: Cambridge University Press.

——. 1987. *The Many Faces of Realism.* LaSalle, Ill.: Open Court.

——. 1989. *Representation and Reality.* Cambridge, Mass.: MIT Press.

——. 1990. *Realism With a Human Face.* Cambridge, Mass.: Harvard University Press.

——. 1992a. *Renewing Philosophy.* Cambridge, Mass.: Harvard University Press.

——. 1992b. "Replies". *Philosophical Topics,* 20, no. 1.

Quine, Willard van Orman. 1953. *From a Logical Point of View.* Cambridge, Mass.: Harvard University Press.

——. 1960. *Word and Object.* Cambridge, Mass.: MIT Press.

——. 1969. *Ontological Relativity and Other Essays.* New York: Columbia University Press.

Ramsey, F. P. 1978. *Foundations: Essays in Philosophy, Logic, Mathematics and Economics,* ed. D. H. Mellor. Atlantic Highlands, N.J.: Humanities Press.

Rorty, Richard. 1979. *Philosophy and the Mirror of Nature.* Princeton, N.J.: Princeton University Press.

——. 1982. *Consequences of Pragmatism.* Minneapolis: University of Minnesota Press.

——. Forthcoming. "Comments". In *Realism/Antirealism and Epistemology,* ed. Christopher Kulp. Totowa, N.J.: Rowman & Littlefield.

Russell, Bertrand. 1912. *The Problems of Philosophy.* New York: Henry Holt and Company.

——. 1919. *Introduction to Mathematical Philosophy.* London: George Allen & Unwin.

Schlick, Moritz. 1936. "Meaning and Verification". *Philosophical Review,* 45.

Searle, John. 1983. *Intentionality.* Cambridge: Cambridge University Press.

Stalnaker, Robert. 1984. *Inquiry.* Cambridge, Mass.: MIT Press.

Stevenson, Charles L. 1944. *Ethics and Language.* New Haven: Yale University Press.

Stich, Stephen. 1983. *From Folk Psychology to Cognitive Science: The Case Against Belief.* Cambridge, Mass.: MIT Press.

——. 1990. *The Fragmentation of Reason.* Cambridge, Mass.: MIT Press.

Strawson, Peter F. 1950a. "Truth". *Aristotelian Society Supplementary Volume* 24.

——. 1950b. "On Referring". *Mind,* 59, no. 235.

——. 1964. "A Problem About Truth—A Reply to Mr. Warnock". In *Truth,* ed. George Pitcher. Englewood Cliffs, N.J.: Prentice-Hall.

Swain, Marshall. 1981. *Reasons and Knowledge.* Ithaca, N.Y.: Cornell University Press.

Van Cleve, James. 1985. "Epistemic Supervenience and the Rule of Belief". *The Monist,* 68, no. 1.

Van Inwagen, Peter. 1988. "On Always Being Wrong". *Midwest Studies in Philosophy,* 12.

——. 1990. *Material Beings.* Ithaca, N.Y.: Cornell University Press.

Vendler, Zeno. 1967. *Linguistics in Philosophy.* Ithaca, N.Y.: Cornell University Press.

Vision, Gerald. 1988. *Modern Anti-Realism and Manufactured Truth.* London: Routledge.

Wiggins, David 1980. "What Would Be a Substantial Theory of Truth?" In *Philosophical Subjects: Essays Presented to P. F. Strawson,* ed. Zak Van Stratten. Oxford: Clarendon Press.

Williams, Bernard. 1973. *Problems of the Self.* Cambridge: Cambridge University Press.

Williams, C. J. F. 1976. *What is Truth?* Cambridge: Cambridge University Press.

Williams, Michael. 1977. *Groundless Belief.* New Haven: Yale University Press.

——. 1986. "Do We (Epistemologists) Need a Theory of Truth?" *Philosophical Topics* 14, no. 1.

Wittgenstein, Ludwig. 1922. *Tractatus Logico-Philosophicus.* London: Routledge & Kegan Paul.

Wolterstorff, Nicholas. 1983. "Can Belief in God Be Rational If It Has No Foundations?" In *Faith and Rationality: Reason and Belief in God,* ed. Alvin Plantinga & Nicholas Wolterstorff. Notre Dame: University of Notre Dame Press.

Wright, Crispin. 1992. *Truth and Objectivity.* Cambridge, Mass.: Harvard University Press.

INDEX